Praise for *All Hands On Deck*:

"Peter Boni has distilled his long experience and hard-won wisdom into a good read, a useful educational tool and a sensible framework for disciplined day-to-day execution. He breaks the big job of leading success-fully into bite-sized chunks that any conscientious leader can execute."

—Alfred R. Berkeley III, Chairman, Princeton Capital Management, President Emeritus, NASDAQ Stock Market, Inc.

"*All Hands on Deck* is an interesting, informative and real-life look at organizational situations going off course and the opportunities that are available for the intrepid entrepreneur/leader to move forward in spite of seemingly insurmountable odds Peter Boni captures the spirit of the risk-taker in unchartered waters. His own experiences and the stories he documents are instructive and inspiring for entrepreneurs/mangers/leaders dealing with inevitable change, adversity and yet, determined to find opportunity and move forward."

—J. Thomas York Jr. (AKA "Tucker"), Managing Director of The Goldman Sachs Group

"Listen up my hardy's, these ABC's may very well put your team in the most favorable winds. This is all about clear principles that work in both stable and trying times—skills welcomed by any organization's board. A good read."

—Ken Daly, President and CEO of The Association of Corporate Directors

"*All Hands on Deck* provides the reader with authentic and candid stories by inspirational leaders who have transformed businesses, non-profits and academic organizations. A must read for those who value an introspective appraisal by leaders on their journey in navigating adver-sity and crises, while being humble enough to share their flaws in deci-sion making and lessons learned."

—Lorraine Lavet, Senior Client Partner, Korn Ferry

ALL HANDS

ON

DECK

Navigating Your Team Through Crises,
Getting Your Organization Unstuck,
and Emerging Victorious

Peter J. Boni

CAREER
PRESS

ALL HANDS ON DECK
EDITED BY JODI BRANDON
TYPESET BY EILEEN MUNSON
Cover design by Jeff Piasky
Printed in the U.S.A.

To order this title, please call toll-free 1-800-CAREER-1 (NJ and Canada: 201-848-0310) to order using VISA or MasterCard, or for further information on books from Career Press.

CAREER
PRESS

The Career Press, Inc.
220 West Parkway, Unit 12
Pompton Plains, NJ 07444
www.careerpress.com

Library of Congress Cataloging-in-Publication Data

Boni, Peter J., 1945-
  All hands on deck : navigating your team through crises, getting your organization unstuck, and emerging victorious / by Peter J. Boni.
     pages cm
  Includes bibliographical references and index.
  ISBN 978-1-60163-372-9 -- ISBN 978-1-60163-380-4 (ebook) 1. Leadership. 2. Teams in the workplace--Management. 3. Organizational effectiveness. I. Title.
HD57.7.B646 2015
658.4'022--dc23
                                                                          2015008945

To all my teams who courageously

manned the decks

with me in stormy seas.

Contents

Section III:
Stories of the ABCs to Advance in Action

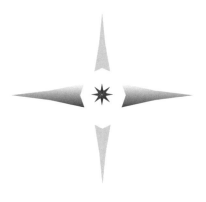

Introduction:
The Kedge Way

How do career opportunities, both at junior and senior levels, get created?

One factor is an organization's growth; that's when a need for new skills and talent emerges. Another is attrition due to promotions, moves, or perhaps a new boss installing a loyal team. But a third factor—when something (internally or externally) gets messed up—outnumbers all others in frequency by 10 to one. Opportunity knocks.

Disruption Offers Opportunities to Advance

When a ship runs aground, the captain has to get the ship moving to "kedge off"—a sailing term for getting it off the mud, sand, or rocks. Like ships, organizations run aground, too, and competition for the captain's role thins out.

Why? It takes both knowledge of how to kedge off and the guts to do it. Those with an Ivy League pedigree or an inside track might stick with less dramatic roles. Yet if you're up to the challenge, consider this "grounded" situation a chance to advance your organization—and your career. That's exactly the tack I took. With the knowledge and guts required, your story of career advancement can follow mine.

How? That's what I addressed in this book, *All Hands on Deck: Navigating Your Team Through Crises, Getting Your Organization Unstuck, and Emerging Victorious.* While explaining my success as a repositioning artist, it provides the strategies and tactics for you to kedge off *fast.* Its principles apply no matter your age, your level on the totem pole, or your field: business, education, government, military, medical, nonprofit, or athletics. Following these principles, you not only learn to anticipate and overcome obstacles, you'll avoid needlessly running aground altogether—both in work and in life.

From Stalled to Fast-Track by Kedging Off

I admit, I had an edge. A lifelong calculated risk-taker, I'd always had an entrepreneur's mentality. In college, I had taken a shine to studying group dynamics so I could combine the right ingredients and lead high-performance teams. Even more important, I had earned field credits for a Rice Paddy MBA in "leadership through adversity" on a full scholarship courtesy of Uncle Sam. (After slogging through Vietnamese and Cambodian jungles, I coined the term for my "Rice Paddy MBA.") After 15 months in combat as a U.S. Army Special Operations infantry officer, I took leadership lessons from my life-altering military experience into the corporate world. There, I advanced by taking on situations that had run aground. Doing so enabled me to realize my goal—to become the VP of a Fortune 500 firm—within a decade of returning from Southeast Asia.

It took me eight years to attain that coveted goal; it took another two to deem it a lousy job for me. Although I felt successful in the VP slot, I found myself confined to a box. I wanted to color outside the lines. I was impatient. I craved more. How was I going to make the jump to a high-technology CEO?

Fortunately, I got my first chance to kedge off as a CEO at age 36.

A 12-Step Process Refined

I drew on my earlier career success and found something on its last leg: a failed startup telecommunications company. It had sound technology, but its first application failed to gain market traction. Revenue was near zero. The company was stuck in the mud. It was up to me to find the way forward. To reposition it, I employed a 12-step "kedge off" process—later termed the ABCs to Advance (explained in Section II).

My first CEO assignment was deemed a success. Revenue grew and the company earned *Inc.* 500 recognition. It later achieved an IPO, continued its growth, and was acquired by Cisco Systems. That assignment led to my heading several technology companies (public, private, IPO) in various stages of growth, maturity, trouble, and renewal. These firms were recognized among the *Inc.* 500 five times, the Software 100 three times, and the Fast 50 and the *Fortune* 1000 twice. To that, I've added management consulting, board of director, and venture capital/private equity assignments.

Along the way, I suffered setbacks that humbled me and taxed my ability to rebound from momentary defeats. Yet each time I came up for air, I refined my 12-step process. The result? Over three decades, I consistently played an active role at creating nearly $5 billion of incremental value.

Kedging Off Transformed Safeguard Scientifics

In late 2005, I was recruited as CEO of Safeguard Scientifics, a six-decades-old NYSE holding company positioned as a high-flying Internet incubator during the heady days of the high-tech bubble. After the bubble burst, Safeguard nearly "lost the farm." It joined what the press labeled "the 90% club" by dropping more than 90 percent of its market value. It actually lost 99 percent and risked losing its public listing.

To avoid a shipwreck, I used my ability to lead high-performance teams, my Adversity MBA, and the ABCs to Advance to kedge off from this serious grounding. My team transformed this company. As a result, Safeguard has realized nearly $1 billion cash proceeds, three IPOs, and top-tier returns from the acquisition of companies within its portfolio by big guns like Oracle, McKesson, Eli Lilly, Shire, Beckton

Dickenson, Teva Pharmaceuticals, Parametric Technology Corp., and General Electric. Cash from these sales enabled Safeguard to repay its choking debt and reinvest in an exciting new portfolio of companies. Its stock hit a decade high and its trading volume increased six-fold. Analysts who covered the company grew from one to seven. Net cash achieved record levels, and its debt-to-equity ratio moved from 1:1 to 1:8. Its institutional shareholder base grew from 25 percent to 75 percent, and its stock far and away outperformed the Russell 2000 and S&P 500.

Let's call that a good run.

After retiring from Safeguard in May 2013, I formed Kedgeway (*www.kedgeway.com*) as a platform to write, consult, speak, teach, invest, direct my philanthropy, and sit on a board or two. Like this book, Kedgeway exists to help a whole new generation of gutsy organizational risk-takers advance.

SECTION
I

The Greatest Captain
of
Them All

1

Captain Josiah Nickerson Knowles and *Wild Wave*

The 21st century holds no exclusivity on leadership through adversity or surviving disruption to emerge victorious. A highly successful young sea captain put those principles to work in the mid 19th century. Meet Captain Josiah Nickerson Knowles from Cape Cod.

In 1858, Captain Knowles' clipper ship *Wild Wave* was on a commercial voyage in the Pacific some 3,800 miles from its port of departure, San Francisco, when, crushed by 30-foot breakers and stormy seas, it ran aground at night into a coral barrier reef. That's when the term "kedging off" took on a whole new scale. The stories of Captain Knowles and *Wild Wave*'s crew have become shipwreck survival folklore. Centuries later, psychologists and management researchers studying how high-performance teams deal with adversity still highlight Knowles' techniques to get to safety and the key lessons learned.

Image 1.1: Captain Josiah Nickerson Knowles. Photo by Michael Colbruno. Courtesy of Volveo Marketing Group

Captain Knowles was only 26 years old, a young rock star for his time. Mentored by two accomplished sea captains, his father and his grandfather, Knowles had a huge edge. They fostered both his education and his training, with young Josiah crewing on their ships learning seamanship, leadership, and survival. Among their teachings:

* Set high standards;

* Employ the best trained, most experienced, and highly motivated officers and crew; and

* Treat them with respect.

Over time, they taught young Knowles how to create an environment in which his crew of the best and brightest would function at a high level. They taught him to persist in training his stellar crew members so they'd continue to increase their competence.

They also taught him to spot and discharge less-competent sailors who might place the captain and crew in jeopardy. Surrounding himself with a top-notch crew gives any captain a better chance to survive when seas are harsh and adversity strikes.

Knowles' First Command

Captain Knowles took on his first command at age 21. He demanded high personal behavioral and performance standards from his crew. But when he encountered a discipline problem on board, he refused to practice the favored technique of his day, flogging. Instead, he assigned errant sailors the least-desirable work details—latrine duty, galley duty, and the like.

Captain Knowles sought to recruit top sailors and foster compatibility among his crew members, who enjoyed great camaraderie. Employing an open communications style uncommon in its day, he shared with his crew members the vision of every mission so they could feel a sense of ownership in a mutual goal. On the leading edge in his style and an early adopter in his methods, he constructed a profit-sharing plan for each of his commercial voyages, then only used by whaling ships. This would ensure the entire crew shared his goals and would reap rewards for their achievements. In short, he treated his crew members with respect.

Within a few years of being a ship's captain, word spread of Knowles' leadership prowess. The best and brightest lined up at his cabin door whenever he recruited for a new voyage. Several crew members returned for mission after mission; they knew he was a special captain. At 5' 11", Josiah Knowles was considered tall for the times, with intense brown eyes. His brown hair and beard, with a tinge of red apparent in the sunlight, were closely trimmed. Captain Knowles' attire was always neat and orderly, as were his cabin, his ship, and his command. A disarming smile came easily on the face of this intense man.

Then adversity hit.

Within five minutes of running aground in a huge storm, *Wild Wave*'s large-standing wooden masts were downed, smashed into kindling littered across the deck. The copper bottom of the hull pushed up through the deck. It looked like several large pots and pans lying in the sudsy water of the frothy, angry sea that quickly engulfed the ship.

Captain Knowles, his well-trained 29-man crew, and 10 passengers retreated into two undamaged lifeboats. *Wild Wave* hung to the rocks and coral, and broke apart from the battering-ram waves that drove it like a stake into the razor-sharp sea bottom. The reef was just 2 miles from Oeno Island, a spit of barrier land miles away from shipping lanes. Both being rescued and surviving this ordeal came with long odds. In addition, Captain Knowles calculated that the charts had erroneously marked Oeno 20 miles west of its actual location.

When *Wild Wave* ran aground in uncharted waters, its passengers and crew—drilled and trained by the young captain—sprang into action. Well-practiced for an unforeseen event like this abrupt, gale-driven grounding, they quickly threw provisions into the lifeboats and abandoned ship. No fatalities.

Once they landed on a scrubby beach 2 miles away, the castaways sheltered themselves for eight stormy, lightning-filled days and nights under a tattered canvas tent they'd salvaged from the shipwreck. Oeno was an uninhabited and hostile island. Although it housed abundant wildlife and limited quantities of water, it was overrun with aggressive rats. To make matters worse, the beach crawled with flesh-biting, territorial hermit crabs that attacked and pinched the castaways in their bedrolls day and night.

The passengers and crew, anxious about remaining undiscovered on this island for the remainder of their lives, turned to Captain Knowles for answers. The captain had hatched the rudiments of a plan, although he needed the others' buy-in and input to refine it. When they discussed it, he answered their questions with questions of his own. The collaboration-bred answers put forth a vision with a single purpose: survival and rescue.

By Knowles' calculation (and if the charts weren't totally inaccurate), the island of Pitcairn was about 100 miles due east. Pitcairn was reputed to be a provisioning point for whalers. Indeed, it was once the home of Captain Fletcher Christian and his crew from *Mutiny on the Bounty* fame.

The Plan

According to the plan, Captain Knowles, his trusted first mate, James Bartlett, and four handpicked crew members would take one of the lifeboats and attempt to secure rescue for the remaining passengers and crew. Second mate John Trehune would stay behind and be in charge. The ship's doctor and cook, several craftsmen, and other able-muscled men would also stay to guide their provisioning and survival.

To communicate they completed and survived the journey, Captain Knowles ordered the capture of several local birds and asked that his second mate make note of the nests' locations. Once on Pitcairn, he planned to write notes and secure them to the birds' legs. The birds would fly back to their nests and, in that way, transmit the rescue crew's progress, success, and plans.

With oars and a makeshift sail, Captain Knowles and his team made their way to Pitcairn while they again encountered the violent storms that commonly plague the Pacific in March. Within several days, they sighted Pitcairn land. Jagged rocks and column-like cliffs that would need to be scaled before they could stand on level ground met their entry. In fact, only 10 percent of the island had level ground.

Shipwrecked once again on Pitcairn with a rock-damaged lifeboat, they came upon a small island just a few miles square. The island had been abandoned years earlier because it was too small to provision its growing population. It wasn't too small, however, to house nasty wild boars that weren't happy at the sight of intruders.

This was clearly a dangerous place, and the captain knew he couldn't stay there to secure rescue. But he released the birds with a series of messages advising the remaining castaways on Oeno that the six-person rescue crew was safe (but alone) on an abandoned island. As the Oeno castaways received each message that added detail to their evolving plan, morale and hope for eventual rescue soared.

Captain Knowles and his small team had no tools—no saw, hammer, ax, or chisel—other than rusted discards found in the abandoned Pitcairn huts. All they could do was figure out how best to use any tools to repair their boat. They knew men in the Stone Age could craft tools from the land, and there was plenty of stone on Pitcairn. Perhaps they could, too. They had no nails, but the ramshackle huts and sheds left behind by descendants of *The Bounty* crew did. They set fire to most of those huts and shacks, rummaging through the ashes to gather nails.

With their improvised tools, they crafted lumber from various trees and supplemented that material with siding from old sheds they found. They then stone-hammered hull patches onto their damaged lifeboat and created a 30-foot sail craft equipped with a bare-bones cabin and oars. It was such a patched-together kluge that half the crew refused to board her for fear of sinking en route to the closest inhabited Pacific island. Captain Knowles reckoned that place to be the Sandwich Islands (today known as Hawaii), some 3,000 miles away.

Knowles left Pitcairn on his newly christened craft, *John Adams*, with his first mate, Mr. Bartlett, and one volunteer. Three crew members who refused to come were left to survive in the abandoned huts

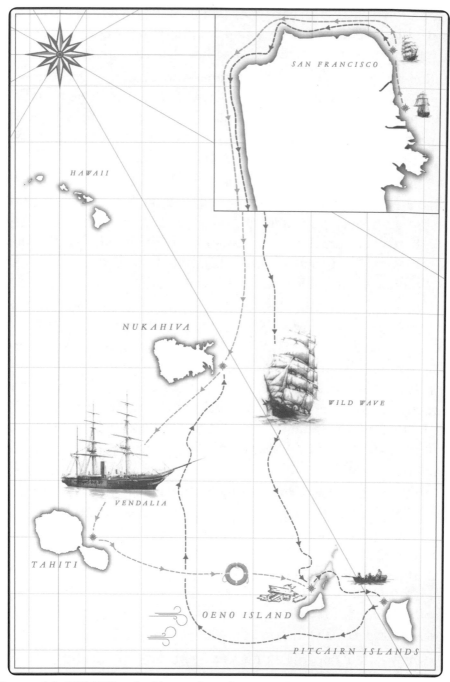

Image 1.2: Wild Wave's *shipwreck and rescue. Courtesy of Volveo Marketing Group.*

until help arrived. They could only hope. Mr. Bartlett had sufficiently provisioned the *John Adams* to enable his small crew to get to another uninhabited island en route: Nukahiva. According to the charts, he estimated they'd encounter that island inside of a month if they averaged a good 25 miles each day.

The Relief

That was a hard month, rowing and sailing with periodic storms and wind doldrums on the front and back ends of the storms. When they sighted Nukahiva, they encountered more rocks, reefs, cliffs, and danger. They circled the island in search of an inlet or beach to land safely. To their relief, they discovered not only a beautiful harbor around a blind bend but a sizable, fairly recent French settlement. At anchor in the harbor floated a single vessel, the 18-gun Corvette American sloop of war *Vendalia*. Flags blazed atop its huge masts like flashing welcome lights. *Vendalia* was the first ship they had set eyes on since leaving the San Francisco port some six months and 3,800 miles earlier!

Vendalia had arrived in Nukahiva a few days before the *John Adams*. That day, it was preparing to hoist its anchor and set sail toward Tahiti. Talk about luck! As the tattered and weary patch-job of a lifeboat approached *Vendalia*, its equally tattered and weary passengers bore huge beard-covered smiles and expressed relief. To increase his command presence, Captain Knowles made a hasty retreat into the boat's makeshift cabin to trim his hair and beard, and change into a fresh shirt. He greeted the *Vendalia* crew equipped with the same ear-to-ear smile and overwhelming sense of relief as his crew. Rescued!

Upon arriving in Tahiti on the *Vendalia,* Captain Knowles and one crew member disembarked. His first mate, Mr. Bartlett, signed onto the *Vendalia* crew and guided the ship on its new mission to rescue the castaways on Oeno and Pitcairn. The three crew members who had refused to board *John Adams* in Pitcairn were rescued. So were the remaining 29 crew and 10 passengers on Oeno, with only one having died of natural causes.

Finally Reached Home

By the end of 1858, Captain Knowles arrived home to Brewster on Cape Cod. There, concerned friends and family greeted him, including his wife and a baby daughter born during his absence.

Not surprisingly, it took a full year for Captain Knowles to regain his strength and recuperate from his adventure. In late 1859, the captain and first mate reunited in Boston, where Mr. Bartlett detailed the *Vendalia* rescue and the crew's adventures of the trip home. The press of the day latched on to their story of courage and survival, deeming Josiah Knowles the "greatest captain of them all."

At the time, the "Knowles Kedge" became pop culture vernacular for thinking outside the box and unselfishly doing what needed to be done in the face of adversity. Knowles humbly gave all the credit to his first and second mates and crew. He also applauded the shipwrecked passengers for their sensibility and courage in the face of long odds. Of course, praising others only increased his popularity and acclaim.

The storied reputation of Captain Knowles made him highly sought-after and handsomely compensated to skipper the larger and faster clipper ships of the day. Specifically, he was asked to captain a fleet of ships owned by entrepreneur and industrialist Joseph Hamblin Sears.

While commanding the flagship of the fleet, *Glory of the Seas,* Captain Knowles went on to break two clipper-ship world speed records that hold to this day. His first mate, Mr. Bartlett, and his second mate, Mr. Trehune, went on to become accomplished captains themselves. Many from *Wild Wave*'s crew were recruited as first and second mates, maritime instructors, and marine consultants; clearly people wanted the competence that Captain Knowles had fostered on board *Wild Wave,* and they were willing to pay for it. The crew's experience spoke to their strength of character and ability to stay focused on the critical success factors that enabled their rescue and survival. They continued to advance.

As for Captain Knowles, after retiring from the sea in 1884, he set up shop in San Francisco and advanced from a ship captain to a captain of industry. His merchant business featured products ranging from exotic Asian luxury goods to whale oil. The business grew and prospered until his death in 1896, as did his legend as "the greatest captain of them all."

Vulnerable to Loss and Disaster

Today, extraordinary opportunities exist to lead teams and organizations that aren't necessarily on the rocks in a storm-driven sea, but they *are* stuck and need help to kedge off. Without help, these stranded organizations are vulnerable to loss and disaster.

In the Pilgrims' time, and for the ensuing few centuries, ships didn't have the benefit of advanced weather forecasting or navigational instruments such as GPS, radar, accurate charts, and the like. As a result, it wasn't unusual to hear a passerby holler the alarm, "Ship ashore! All hands perishing!"

At that time, no Coast Guard existed to save the day for passengers and crew. Instead, help came from the townspeople who showed up on the beach to volunteer. With high winds and surf from punishing storms, most rescue attempts failed. Indeed, by the end of a storm, there might be no one left to rescue. And more often than not, for a few survivors, the cargo was "saved"—gathered and carted away as booty for the opportunistic. The misfortune of a shipwreck might mean a wealth of legitimate spoils that could be consumed or sold. These might include wine, tobacco, cotton, silk, exotic spices from faraway lands, tea, coffee, and even precious jewels, silver, and gold.

Running Aground for Organizations

Running aground is dangerous for commercial ships, sailboats, and organizations alike. A team, department, company, or organization that's stranded on the rocks stands to lose its precious cargo: its investors, supporters, customers, partners, money, and talent. Raiders will take advantage for their own gain. Survival skills will be tested. When the grounding is serious, an organizational shipwreck is imminent—*unless* leaders can engage those on board or find help to kedge off and right the ship. By using the right tools and training, that's where you come in.

Captain Knowles had put into practice principles that still work today: creating the right dynamics for a high-performance team, leading through adversity, and knowing how to kedge off. Read on to learn how to apply these principles when an organization runs aground and *you* are the best hope to get it moving safely and swiftly.

And like Captain Knowles and his crew, you, too, will experience rapid advancement as others recognize your achievements in a difficult situation.

SECTION
II

The ABCs to Advance

The ABCs to Advance:
The Origin

For four decades I've developed and refined a strategy to lead organizations through adversity. This strategy has proven successful over and over again. Used early enough, my approach has also kept organizations out of difficulty. After being honed in the volatile technology industry for more than 30 years, I applied it to Safeguard Scientifics' now-thriving venture capital business as well as some highly regarded nonprofit organizations. Those successes didn't happen overnight. The inevitable scars of experience have played a big part in their evolution.

I call my strategy **The ABCs to Advance.** If you have the passion, courage, and persistence to face challenges head on, this strategy will not only benefit your organization but will also earn recognition, financial rewards, and career advancement for you and your team.

The ABCs to Advance has three phases: 1) hatch the plan, 2) kick off the plan, and 3) execute the plan. There are four steps to each phase, each headlined with a starting letter A, B, C, and S—hence, the ABCs.

Captain Knowles practiced these principles, too, although they weren't categorized as neatly in the 19th century. I've also found that many who have successfully led a team through adversity practiced these same fundamental principles. Thus, six case studies (including my own at Safeguard) are featured in Section III to show these ABCs in action.

From Stalled to Fast-Tracker by Kedging Off

As a management trainee and then a sales rep in what was then Standard Oil—my first job out of college and the military—I was enormously impatient. Just after starting my career, I was hit with a three-year interruption and a Vietnam combat assignment, courtesy of Uncle Sam and the U.S. Army. I was fortunate to achieve some rank and wind my way into an elite force. It saved my life and, to a degree, shaped how I approached living after that. The experience also defined my sense of teamwork with highly competent people. We were kids, really, in tough situations, scared as hell, covering each other's backs to accomplish the mission at hand.

With real-life lessons picked up in combat and happy to be alive, I returned to my first job. I would pick up where I left off but with a huge goal in mind: to advance to a VP of a Fortune 500 company within 10 years.

My original management training classmates had a three-year head start over me, and I needed to catch up fast. Here's what threw me off: I was a working-class kid and the first in my family to get a college education. I had no notion of an old boys' network but saw first-hand that certain plum promotional assignments—better known as the "first big break"—were handed out *first* to those in the old boys' networks. Their networks stemmed from their educational pedigree and/or close family ties at the top echelon.

After my training, I was assigned a sales territory among the top performers in the district. Through my efforts, I kept my territory in the top spot. For me, there was no "first big break" in the near-term offing. Bummer! So what could I use as an edge to speed up the process of gaining my first big break?

Adjacent to my top-performing territory was one of the poorest-performing ones. After a bit of study, I learned its performance suffered due to neglect, so I asked to transfer to it. I convinced myself I could make a difference and be better able to springboard from that platform. Then I crafted a deal with my boss: I'd blow the doors off in the new territory, and he'd sponsor me for that first move up the ladder.

As I worked my tail off, I also clued in some of my customers and prospects about my ambitions, asking for their help. As long as I put out for *them,* they seemed willing to put out for *me.* I achieved stellar gains, got recognized, and earned my first big break—ahead of some of those with the right "connections." That worked out pretty well!

A formula for leapfrogging my career emerged. That is, I could "kedge off"—the sailing term for how a boat that's run aground can get off the mud, sand, or rocks.

Later, I was recruited by a multi-divisional Fortune 500 firm to serve first in market research and then as a product manager. We were to re-launch an underachieving product line that had initially sputtered. Competition for that job thinned out. Who wants a sputtering product line? I found I was skilled at doing due diligence to determine if I had a shot at kedging off successfully.

In Special Operations (Special Ops), we practiced an active form of situation assessment called the "OODA loop." OODA stands for orient, observe, decide, and act. I put OODA into practice in civilian life. Indications were that the product was sound, the market was sizable, and competitive differentiation was in place. But packaging, pricing, and distribution needed to change. That seemed doable. I took on the job and put into practice some of those ABCs before I'd ever given them a label.

Success followed. The product line turned profitable in the first year and became a market leader.

ABCs Put to Work

That success led to recognition and a meaningful promotion in another division. I was to organize and integrate a botched acquisition—an issue that was the source of a good deal of company anguish. Team-building skills and the unlabeled ABCs were put to work. Before long, this mission was accomplished and I was dubbed "a rising star." My reward? I got to work for a new boss. He was a lifelong company bureaucrat and micromanager focused on maintaining his status—and the status quo—until he retired in a few years.

I learned a good deal from the negative examples set by my worst boss ever. His formulas: *Never pass the credit. Take the bow. Never do the right thing. Do the right thing for him, and just make sure he looked good.* This wasn't the stage for achieving my 10-year goal.

The whole experience, however, gave me visibility and credentials. It qualified me and led to my being recruited to that coveted VP job at a Fortune 500 technology company. In this case, no insider held an edge, and many outsiders shied away from what was considered a tough assignment. My mission: to reformulate its failed thrust to penetrate the market with the low end of its product line. How? By using alternate channels of distribution—a skill picked up from my industrial products' days.

Inside of two years, we captured newsworthy market penetration, $100 million of revenue from scratch, and profitability for the division. This was achieved with the benefit of:

* Well-developed situation assessment skill,
* OODA loop (to reinforce successfully kedging off),
* A great team of people around me, and
* The evolving formula—the ABCs to Advance.

That previous negative example had come in handy. Don't take the bow; extend the credit. Stand tall! Position properly, do the right thing, and win hearts and minds. I realized the strong impact my military training and wartime experience had on my management style.

It also seemed that the burgeoning technology industry was more of a meritocracy and less hierarchical than the giants of industry. In those, the style, connections, pedigree, and politics played (in my view) too much of a role in advancement. It had taken me eight years to attain that longed-for Fortune 500 VP goal and another two years to realize it was a lousy job, at least for me—someone who wanted to color outside the lines.

The November 2010 *Harvard Business Review*'s cover story on military veterans in business noted that Navy and Air Force vets did best in large, formal environments rather than smaller, less-formal ones.

That's thanks in part to all the process management skills they picked up dealing with big, complex systems—airplanes, ships, aircraft carriers. With such large, intricate systems, there's little room for variations in process.

However, Marine, SEAL, and Army veterans were far more successful in environments that required nimble responses to volatile, changing situations. Their on-the-ground leadership training to accomplish difficult missions in confusing, stressful, often crisis situations worked best in areas not requiring a process management background and experience. If given the latitude within a large structure to break rules to accomplish difficult tasks at hand, they were also likely to achieve success above their Navy or Air Force counterparts.

According to research from the executive search firm Korn Ferry, 3 percent of the adult male population has military officer experience and training. That's three times the number of S&P 500 CEOs! There I was, the Special Ops Army infantry officer practiced to attract, retain, reward, and lead highly trained, capable people who could think outside the box.

I could navigate complexity and work well in a team, often in high-stress, life-or-death situations. But could I kedge off as a CEO? I got my first chance to try at age 36.

The ABCs to Advance: A Methodology Refined

I took a hard look at my approach and saw ways to replicate it in other situations. My warzone combat training and experience had taught me how to lead a team through extreme adversity. (After slogging through Vietnamese and Cambodian jungles, I coined this my "Rice Paddy MBA.")

Aside from my Rice Paddy MBA, I realized that a common thread existed in all my early education and work experiences: a passionate interest in group dynamics. I decided to put into practice what I had learned about myself—the ingredients to assemble and lead high-performance teams. I would aim for a CEO assignment and test myself in the volatile world of emerging technologies.

In the CEO role, I became a consummate team builder. My consultative and leadership approach incorporated these practices: asking questions and listening, taking notes, challenging sacred cows, building on the strengths and talent base on hand, collaboratively creating a focused game plan, broadly communicating inside and outside the organization, boldly executing a strategy, visibly measuring results, and handsomely rewarding performance.

I told every member of my varying teams they were part of an elite force as I had been. We had a contract—a bond—that would lift and protect us. It would set a clear standard for behavior throughout our organizations.

I gave this label to my evolving 12-step kedge-off process to reposition organizations run aground: "The ABCs to Advance." The skills picked up over the next three decades helped a lot as I refined my methodology, but the fundamentals remained true over time.

As a CEO for a half dozen science and technology firms (public, private, IPO) in varying stages of growth, maturity, trouble, and renewal, I was able to advance businesses as I built my reputation and advanced my own career. As previously mentioned, the firms were listed among the *Inc. 500* five times, the Software 100 three times, and the Fast 50 and the Fortune 1000 twice. They acquired and integrated businesses and were themselves acquired by industry leaders—for example, Cisco Systems and CA Technologies—for cash or stock for top quartile valuation returns.

In between CEO gigs, I served as a management consultant for firms with their own obstacles to overcome. They needed to kedge off, too.

Success Isn't a Straight Line

For sure, I suffered many setbacks along the way. They humbled me and taxed my ability to bob and weave, rebound from a momentary defeat, and come out on top. A key ingredient I learned in combat applied to civilian life, too. That is, *I couldn't do it alone.* I needed to attract, train, focus, reward, and retain the best people I could find to share my foxhole. That certainly helped keep me alive in Southeast Asia. My mother was right all those years ago: You *are* judged by the company you keep.

The following 22 years as a technology CEO and consultant gave me a plethora of scars of experience. It was time for me to use those scars, take the investor mantle, and coach others to advance, while advancing value at the same time. After serving as an operating partner for Advent International, a blue-chip global private equity firm with $20 billion under management, I was then recruited in late 2005 to spend nearly eight years as CEO of Safeguard Scientifics, a now-60-plus-year-old NYSE holding company. Positioned as a high-flying Internet incubator during the heady days of the bubble, it crashed and burned in spectacular fashion as the Internet bubble burst. Today, after successfully implementing my ABCs, Safeguard has been repositioned, is performing exceptionally well, and is being perceived as a winner. (See Chapter 6.)

My premise is this: If you follow the principles in *All Hands on Deck,* you can avoid, anticipate, or overcome obstacles to *advance,* both on the job and in life. This can work for anyone with ambition and guts. And it can apply no matter your age, your level on the totem pole, or your occupation: business, education, government, the military, non-profit, or athletics.

The following chapters in *All Hands on Deck* give you a "how to" approach to advance in your career. Its principles worked for me. They worked for Captain Knowles. And they can work for you, too.

Phase 1 of the ABCs:
Hatch the Plan

"Many people make the mistake of confusing information with knowledge. Knowledge involves the interpretation of information. Knowledge involves listening."

—Henry Mankell (Swedish author known for a series of mystery novels starring his most famous creation, Inspector Kurt Wallander)

So here you are, brand new in a role or considering one to reposition an organization or department. It has run aground, faces critical issues, and isn't performing up to its potential. The task is lonely, daunting, complete with skeptical eyes staring at you. Hopeful eyes are staring, too.

Can you be the catalyst to lead the organization, department, or team past its current issues? Can you get the ship off the bottom to sail safely once again? If so, where do you start? Follow the ABCs to Advance:

A: Ask questions and listen; then ask for help.

B: Base your plan on what you hear and see, or on what you don't hear and see.

C: Challenge the sacred cows and the status quo.

S: Share the vision to create a collective energy.

A: Ask Questions and Listen; Then Ask for Help

Success stories generally start with the practice of fundamentals. Asking questions at the outset is high on your priority list. Stories of failed navigation through difficulty start with the *absence* of the practice of those fundamentals. For example, Ron Johnson was a rock-star senior executive from Apple Computer, responsible for Apple's hugely successful retail thrust. Recruited as CEO of faltering retail giant JC Penney, Johnson hatched a plan.

This troubled retailer had garnered many a customer by what Johnson called a confusing strategy—offering frequent and heavily promoted multi-product promotional discounts. It was widely reported that Johnson's game plan was to turn Penney into an all-discount all-the-time retailer with a completely redesigned façade. As part of his strategy, Johnson increased borrowing to raise the cash for redesigning all of its stores. Then he executed his plan with guns blazing.

But *wait* a minute. Sales plummeted, losses mounted, the price of its stock sank to rock-bottom lows. Billions of dollars were lost. Thousands of people lost their jobs through layoffs to accommodate the lower sales volume. Vendors and suppliers tanked as well.

What the heck happened? This highly acclaimed leader executed his plan boldly. Why didn't customers flock to Penney's newly redesigned stores? Well, it seems they were confused by the lack of frequent promotional discounts. Customers had valued the coupons and looked forward to these discounts. And they didn't care for the new designs and relative self-service from a once-well-staffed retailer. Customers stopped coming to the stores in droves.

What did this high-profile can-do-no-wrong executive fail to practice? The first A in the ABCs to Advance: *He failed to ask questions and listen.* It looks like he also failed to ask for help. He never conducted focus group studies or pilot programs to get employee, supplier, partner, market, or customer feedback. As a result, he put the organization in a pickle. Observers agree that too much change happened too quickly with little vetting preceding it. The company's board bounced Johnson after the damage was done. First an interim CEO, and recently a new one, have been working to right JC Penney's ship.

ABCs for Captain Knowles

Captain Josiah Nickerson Knowles, on the other hand, put the fundamentals of asking, listening, and getting help into practice right from the get-go. Captain Knowles and crew were shipwrecked on a deserted, inaccurately charted South Pacific island. Anxiety-ridden passengers and crew looked to their captain for a plan to save them. Knowles held back at the outset until he asked questions and listened. Then he asked for everyone's help to hatch a plan with *one overarching goal*: to get out of an impossible predicament. Because everyone contributed, they all felt ownership to the primary goal—survival *and* rescue—and were invested in the resulting plan. Captain Knowles had the rudiments of a plan in his head, but he had the vision to know that the *collective wisdom* of his fellow castaways would brew a superior plan that had full buy-in.

ABCs in Combat

As a young lieutenant sent to combat in Vietnam, I recall being introduced to the unit I was to command and meeting my second in command, a crusty first sergeant on his second tour of Southeast Asian combat duty. As opposed to attempting to impress him with my training, I acknowledged his experience, noting I was trained well but not as accomplished and experienced as he was. Then I asked for his help.

Well, did this hardened combat vet ever light up! "Lieutenant, what a great attitude! You've got it. Together, we'll do right by the Army, do right by our troops, and get everyone home safely," he responded.

We proved to be a terrific team. He enabled me to lead with his wisdom, which eventually became my wisdom, too. *Note to self: Always ask for help!* Before every mission, these well-trained Special Operations (Special Ops) troops would work collaboratively on a game plan to execute a mission. This was the Special Ops practice. A fully engaged, diverse group of people would produce a plan far superior to that of only one or two people. We quizzed one another to flush out the details and contingencies behind every mission. This reinforced what I learned as a child. *Note to self: Collaboration starts with asking for help, then asking questions and listening.*

ABCs in the President's Chair

I look back to being a newly recruited president of a then 20-year-old software company, On-Line Software International (OSI). It had achieved a Fortune 1000 New York Stock Exchange status. Its autocratic founder had stepped aside to use his accumulated wealth to self-actualize and attend medical school.

The company, a former global high flyer, was in trouble. Wall Street analysts referred to OSI as "a tarnished star." It had accumulated major debt to initiate a poorly conceived acquisition, plus it used ill-disciplined, although legal, accounting practices. Its revenue stopped growing. The company lost money for several quarters running and had indiscriminately downsized to save cash.

Adding to the drama, the Securities and Exchange Commission (SEC) launched an investigation into OSI's practices. With cash in short supply, OSI's bank threatened to suspend its credit line. The company's formerly richly priced stock plummeted nearly 85 percent. Gulp!

From that platform, I asked my questions as a brand-new president. I started with the executive staff, one on one, and then moved throughout the organization. I was greeted at first by blank stares. After several moments of silence, I eventually heard this same comment from each member of that executive staff: "Gee, no one has asked me what I thought for so long. I wasn't prepared for the question." Once we got past that initial shock to a modus operandi change, their answers—and their candor—flowed in high fashion. They shared their perspectives freely and, to my surprise, quite objectively. In the face of that acute and complex adversity, they were outspoken in their input.

ABCs for Captain Knowles

Captain Knowles had broken the code to leadership well before my experiences. He continued to ask questions and listen to his fellow castaways. They would hatch a plan to enable their primary goal: survival and rescue for all.

Knowles had spoken to his crew members individually at first. What tools do we need for survival? What skills do we have? Can we break down those skills to assignments on teams? Do we seek help or stay put? Do we all go for help or send a contingent? Who would serve on that contingent? Where does that contingent go to seek rescue? How do we best communicate with that contingent?

Then he conducted group sessions in which he reviewed the summary of answers to his questions to stimulate further discussion.

James Surowiecki put forward the same notions Captain Knowles followed 160 years before his book came out, *The Wisdom of Crowds: Why the Many Are Smarter Than the Few and How Collective Wisdom Shapes Business, Economies, Societies and Nations.* (See the Bibliography.)

As Surowiecki pointed out, three conditions enable a group to develop a far superior plan than any one of the group can develop individually. Captain Knowles followed the three conditions, namely:

* **Diversity:** The crew and passengers of the *Wild Wave* had many different perspectives, sources of information, and sets of experiences and training.

* **Independence of Opinion:** Captain Knowles first arranged his questioning to assist his thinking individually, all within the same day. It happened not simultaneously but as close as he could come to it on a deserted island. He collected wisdom as blindly to everyone else's opinions as possible. He asked for choices to acquire real knowledge and superior, creative thought devoid of peer pressure, "group think," and similar dynamics.

✱ **A Method of Aggregating Information:** Absent 21st-century technology and systems design, Captain Knowles put forward his synopsis of the consensus of thinking. He did so by writing a few words in the sand to provide a prop for further group discussion. His first and second mates would begin the process. Then they added a few of the crew's thought leaders and finally the entire group of passengers and crew.

Who to Ask

In keeping with Captain Knowles' experience and Surowiecki's observations, asking a diverse group of people similar questions can lead to superior input based on several points of view. Those viewpoints are likely picked up at varying angles of observation, some hands on and others at 30,000 feet. Whether determining if I should accept a position or what an appropriate game plan would be once I accepted it, my due diligence to hatch a plan always started with asking everyone under the sun for help. Most people who are asked are thrilled to help. They are quite candid about giving their points of view, with details and specific examples to back them up.

So, given the wisdom of this strategy, whom do you ask?

Insiders: You can find a plethora of people who are knowledgeable about an organization and its issues, problems, opportunities, and more. You'll find them at the higher echelons as well as from the board of directors to the CEO, executive staff, and senior management. Some are in the middle of the hierarchy, responsible to the higher echelons. Others are first-line supervisors or individual contributors in operational or support rolls. Those close to developing or delivering the value proposition to key constituents have a closer operational view than those at the higher ranks.

These insiders *all* have a point of view. Just ask them—from the receptionist to the board chairman, from the team captain to the water boy, from the janitor to the mayor. I've found that many near the bottom of the totem pole have an enormously mature and insightful perspective.

Former insiders: Organizations with issues have likely suffered turn-over in senior, middle, and/or junior positions. People moved on. They, too, have observations and opinions developed over time and further reflected upon after being on the outside for a spell. Seek out key former insiders and ask them the same questions as you ask current insiders.

Recipients of the Value Proposition: A business has customers and perhaps user groups. A government has citizens, special interest groups, party heads, and political supporters. A sports team has fans and sup-port clubs. A higher educational institution has students and parent groups. A healthcare organization has patients, nurses, and doctors. A nonprofit has a targeted constituency. Ask these people the same questions.

A lost customer, patient, fan, student, alumni contributor, political supporter (or whomever) left the organization for a reason—maybe for more than one reason. In fact, they may be receiving that value propo-sition from a competing organization. What an interesting perspective, having seen the good, the bad, and the ugly from the other side of the fence. Ask them.

Partners to Provide the Value Proposition: Commercial enterprises have strategic alliances and business partners, vendors, and those who are in distribution. Nonprofit organizations, government organizations, sports teams, healthcare providers, military units, and most organiza-tions have these partners, too. Ask those individuals the same questions.

Who dropped out? Or who was asked to drop out? Given their expe-riences dealing both with the organization and the decision to leave, they have a learned point of view. They also have experience dealing with competitors who delivered that value proposition, albeit a bit dif-ferently. Ask them.

Competitors Who Deliver That Value Proposition: They could be competing sales or marketing people, factory employees, engineers, or members of the financial or support staff. They could be a differ-ent political party, another sports teams, healthcare providers down the street, members of the campaign staff of competing political can-didates, or nonprofits that have targeted similar donors to deliver to the same identified social needs. Most organizations face competition when it comes to their value proposition. These competitors have an insiders' view as well as an outsiders' view. Ask them.

Former competitors may have totally abandoned the field to make their living in another, perhaps aligned, arena. They left for a reason and they have a perspective. Ask them.

Outsider Observers in the Know: Industry analysts, lobbyists, journalists, advocates, consultants, and unions all develop a view. They see from afar, but they often have a strategic view that's further removed from an organization's day-to-day drama. Ask them.

Certain knowledgeable people have left their field to become involved in a different, perhaps aligned, arena. Put them on your list. Ask them, too.

Thought Leaders: Some carry more weight and influence than others. Thought leaders could be former or current insiders, outsiders, partners, competitors, or observers. When asking questions and requesting help, find out who they are and put them on your "ask" list.

What to Ask

In both profit and nonprofit settings, the answers to only a few questions have given me the baseline to learn quickly what others discovered over a period of months or even years. Over my four decades of asking these questions, I'm struck by how candid the answers have been and how knowledgeable I become by listening.

Question #1: If you owned this operation lock, stock, and barrel—or if you were a dictator and could do anything to enable the organization to achieve its potential based on what you know about it and its environment—what handful of things would you do?

Question #2: What would you have the organization *keep* doing, *start* doing, and *stop* doing to reach its potential and maximize its value proposition?

Question #3: Who are the thought leaders in this field and in this organization? Identify them and seek them out for a one-on-one discussion. Ask thought leaders for their help. Listen to them. And ask them to participate on your informal advisory panel so you can test the premise of a plan hatched from the exercise in Phase 1. I ask everyone Question #3, even if I already know I'm speaking to a thought leader. I've always been surprised by how many have been flattered by my asking. They have given me terrific counsel, which made an enormous and immediate difference to the success of my assignment.

How to Ask

Face to Face: Generally, my best results have been realized when asking Question #1 individually to those on the mid-point of organizational hierarchy on up. I have generally reserved Question #2 for a group of people with dissimilar job responsibilities who sit toward the bottom of the totem pole in an organization's hierarchy. For instance, rather than speaking to a group from the accounting department, I might combine a handful of accountants with several people from other organizational disciplines. That way, I receive more diverse viewpoints, which will craft a well-rounded point of view.

However, it can be interesting to deal with some of them in dual fashion—that is, both individually and as part of a group. This way you can do a subliminal test for consistency as well as sniff out hidden agendas or biases that aren't expressed in the group but were noted individually.

Digital Survey: Welcome to the age of nonstop information. Digital media—with constant instant data feeds, texts, e-mails, tweets, and more—have long replaced a whisper or a note passed under the desk in class. Candid assessments happen at lightning speed. Notions, whether on the mark or way off base, can go viral in a heartbeat. You can tap into digital technologies to ask questions of a larger audience.

Doing a digital survey has its advantages: The transparency of the digital age has an anonymity that can lead to further candor and insightful communiqués. In addition, digital communication can be one-way or interactive, in group fashion or one on one. It can be specific and targeted or broad and far-reaching. It can provide knowledgeable assessments as well as half-baked answers from crackpots. Certainly the potential number of people answering your questions and the sheer number of answers can be cumbersome. However, using a digital survey presents a terrific tool to tap deeply into their knowledge base to help you hatch a plan.

Listen by Taking Notes

Ask questions and *listen* by taking notes (handwritten or in a digital format). When relying on written notes from all my meetings and questions, I keep a special notebook for that purpose only. I've also used a special digital address as the keeper of digitally acquired answers.

In group forums, I've used whiteboards, a pad of paper on an easel, or a PowerPoint projected onto a screen to record the answers to the questions, what to keep, start, or stop. Expose those answers for all to see. Executive coaches use a similar "keep, start, stop" technique in 360-degree reviews. This improves executive awareness of what works for and against that person in how managing tasks are approached. You'll see it makes the warts as well as the gems highly visible. And visibility breeds accountability. You can't fix what you can't see.

My OSI experience occurred before the ubiquitous days of Internet service, but early in the days of e-mail. I traveled in marathon fashion during my first 30 days asking questions in person. I asked them individually and in groups; I uncovered thought leaders; I visited customers, vendors, bankers, and other senior software executives far and wide. Then I asked for their help constructing a game plan that would put stability and luster back into the company.

If I couldn't meet in person, I used a combination of group and individual e-mails or the plain old telephone to gradually provide the baseline for my questions. I filled two notebooks and consumed several gigabytes with their responses. Amazingly, people were pleased to be asked and willingly provided help. Their answers to my questions, coupled with my observations, led to creating an impactful game plan.

That leads to the B in ABCs to Advance.

B: Base the Plan on What You Hear and See, or Don't Hear and See

Your raw notebooks filled with writing and gigabytes of accumulated data all have to be turned into information. Like Captain Knowles, and in keeping with the advice from *The Wisdom of Crowds,* you've gathered viewpoints from a diverse group of people. You've also allowed room for an independence of views. It's time to aggregate this data, make sense out of it, and inject your own expertise to hatch a plan.

The Manual Method

Captain Knowles and I used the same technique. He had answers from his crew of 29 plus 10 passengers; I had mine from hundreds of domestic and international employees, customers, vendors, bankers, analysts, and aligning software company CEOs.

How would you do this?

* Highlight the answers to those questions that strike the same theme repeatedly.

* Place those on the "majority" list.

* For outliers cited once or a few times, place them on a "minority" list. However, don't discard the outlier answers; test each of them with the "advisory board."

This exercise isn't meant to be a popularity contest; it's to form collective wisdom. That collective wisdom will establish the baseline to construct a cogent game plan.

In Captain Knowles' situation, he relied on his first and second mates, Mr. Bartlett and Mr. Trehune, and the ship's doctor. In my On-Line Software example, I relied on a handful of thought leaders who served as informal advisors to give me a sounding board. In most cases, the outliers were just that. Every once in a while, however, I'd find a jewel within an outlier's comment. I learned to leave room for an out-of-left-field view that might be brilliant. In Captain Knowles' case, that jewel was the use of captured birds to enable remote communications. Brilliant!

Captain Knowles constructed a game plan that had group buy-in. After all, the group had to organize to survive and enable rescue; nothing else was important. Members of the group had to assemble teams that divided the work geared toward the endpoint: survival. The provisioning of food, water, shelter, fuel, hygiene, as well as attention to morale, communications, coaching, and supervisory management of critical functions, all required thoughtful organization and proper use of available skills.

This would enable survival, but what about enabling rescue? They knew that island of Oeno was improperly charted about 20 miles from where it was perceived to be. Because the area wasn't widely traveled, who would possibly know they awaited rescue on Oeno?

The Digital Method

The huge benefits of tapping the power of the Internet and social media are the diversity, anonymity for independent thinking, volume, and speed to gather viewpoints as answers to the few questions. The human brain is capable of digesting significant pieces of information, but the digital method will undoubtedly put manual practices on overload. Today, big data analytics are available on demand via cloud computing from a variety of sources. Those sources help evaluate vast sums of information and turn them into a digestible format from which collective wisdom can be drawn.

When my first big software company experience took place 25 years ago, those tools were rudimentary. But with help, I was able to sort several conclusions into "majority" and "minority" columns from my hundreds of e-mail sources. These would help me decipher the information and construct a cogent game plan.

Game Plan: What's Missing?

Base your plan on what you hear and see, and then take advantage of your background, experience, and domain expertise. Listen with your third ear and construct your plan on what you *don't* hear and see. Captain Knowles based his game plan on what he heard and saw, but this method was geared to enable survival only. The complete goal was survival and rescue, but *rescue* was missing from the initial plan. Now what?

That leads to the C in the ABCs to Advance.

C: Challenge the Sacred Cows or the Status Quo

The next step is to test conventions and conventional wisdom. Challenge the way things are done, which are often the obstacles to achieving progress and excellent performance. Change is hard. Inertia is a powerful force. Plus those in power often fight to maintain the status quo, for it's their source of power.

This brings home a teaching by a mentor who'd ask, "Where's the bottleneck?" It's always at the top of the bottle, isn't it? As an example, the U.S. Secret Service is on its third leader in three years as it battles apparent complacency and declining morale. After several security breaches that have threatened the life and well-being of the president and White House occupants, this bottleneck has become highly visible. The gig is up for the status quo.

Captain Knowles faced his form of status quo. "What can we do to enable rescue after this shipwreck?" was the question. All of the mariners' lesson books taught a stranded group to stay put, in one place, close to the shipwreck. Two centuries of survival training had taught a crew to stay together—and it still does today.

But Captain Knowles surmised that, by doing so, his passengers and crew would likely survive, only to die of old age without rescue. So he challenged that conventional wisdom, and with his first and second mates, constructed a plan of travel to enable rescue. One of the two lifeboats could be retrofitted for several people to journey to an adjacent thought-to-be-inhabited island. From there, they could actively seek rescue. That brilliant outlier—using locally captured birds to communicate to the group remaining on Oeno—came in handy.

In the 20th century, OSI had launched each new product during its entire history by using a separate sales force of product specialists. Over the years, OSI launched several products and thus had several sales forces for varying products speaking to the same customer. That customer was generally the information technology department within a big company's mainframe computer organization. For 20 years every product launch they'd considered successful used this approach. This status quo approach, however, didn't facilitate bundling, cross-merchandising, or positioning a suite of products for competitive advantage against a growing cadre of competitors.

So I tapped into my informal advisory board. By challenging the status quo and consolidating the selling efforts under one united sales organization with proper training and tools, we presumed that both efficiency and customer satisfaction would leap. We brought the sales leader and a couple of company thought leaders into the loop. We also sought further input from a handful of long-standing customers who enthusiastically encouraged the initiative.

As noted, change is hard. Jamming it down another's throat can lead to more naysaying than raving fans. So once you construct a game plan, how can you best set the stage to kick it off?

That leads to the S in the ABCs to Advance.

S: Share the Vision to Create a Collective Energy

Once you have a preliminary plan, test it with your trusted advisors. Get the thought leaders behind it. After all, they helped create it. If need be, test it in pilot form. Remember the guns-a-blazing approach of JC Penney's Johnson that backfired? Better to test first!

You don't live in a dictatorship, and you can't execute alone. Instead, you need people who are 100-percent signed up to help you. When leaders share a vision, they create a collective energy. When team members understand their role in achieving that vision, it's energizing and motivational. *You'll need all of that energy and motivation to execute a game plan and kedge off. It's never easy.*

Captain Knowles evaluated and refined his plan along with his confidants and his thought leader, the doctor. Finally, he presented the game plan as conceived by the entire group. They met at their beach encampment at dawn and ate breakfast together. The captain outlined his plan in the sand at their feet as if he were making a PowerPoint presentation on an auditorium's screen. He acknowledged a handful of outliers and embraced the Oeno-captured birds as a remote communications tool. His second mate, Mr. Trehune, was designated the Oeno leader. Then the work of assembling the ingredients for survival was assigned to those with appropriate skills. First Mate Bartlett and four volunteer crew members would accompany Captain Knowles and the yet-to-be-captured birds on a yet-to-be-retrofitted lifeboat bound for the island of Pitcairn—and their ultimate rescue.

In my situation at OSI, I shared our new vision using action words and repeated details of the game plan. From the receptionist to the chairman of the board, I insisted everyone be able to repeat the game plan. My orders included putting it in writing and plastering it everywhere. Keeping the plan highly visible became a part of every conversation. We reviewed our progress against the game plan at every opportunity. We also made sure there was no question the new plan was considered important to the company's future.

Whether it's Captain Knowles' 39 people or a global enterprise employing hundreds or thousands of people, *one game plan executed by all* is more powerful than half-hearted efforts executed by a handful. It requires everyone to sign up 100 percent.

At OSI, I shared the vision a bit differently than Captain Knowles did. I had to recognize I was dealing with a global corporation and hundreds of employees dispersed in several offices throughout the United States, Canada, and Europe. I was also dealing with thousands of shareholders, several analysts, and other stakeholders and interested parties. But the concept of sharing the vision held true.

Unlike Captain Knowles, I didn't present the vision and plan on a sandy beach on a deserted remote island in the Pacific. Instead, I categorized the information I'd aggregated and processed, constructed a five-part plan, and gave each part a label using these five action words: Focus, Leverage, Partner, Expand, Improve. The presentation materials expressed this five-part plan and captured the summary of the answers to my questions.

First, I tested the final plan with my informal advisors. I then held one-on-one discussions with the executive staff. They gathered their direct reports along with the thought leaders who comprised the informal advisory board. The staff arranged an all-hands-on-deck company meeting to include conferencing with the global force across several time zones. We provided written material to supplement the auditorium-style meeting and conferencing of remote offices in varying time zones. We finished with a brunch and took questions as a management team.

The OSI game plan to kedge off looked like this:

* **Focus** resources on the core business,

* **Leverage** the company's strengths to increase competitive advantage,

* **Partner** with strategic alliances and channels of distribution to increase market penetration,

* **Expand** in key areas of complementary opportunity, and

* **Improve** inside and outside communications, cash management, and regulatory practices.

With the plan hatched and communicated, we kicked it off and executed it throughout its initial year and into the next. We terminated ancillary initiatives that didn't fit the product and market strategy. I promoted a couple of stars and recruited a key new player to help execute the game plan.

What was the result? By the following year, our retrained and consolidated sales force had garnered a 47-percent market share in our core business. Our new strategic alliances with key industry players contributed to revenue and market share in previously untapped market segments. A focused selling effort expanded penetration into the federal market. Our company acquired a key new product for an aligning area of opportunity that added to our competitive advantage, profitability, and market penetration. A broad communications thrust added plan transparency to employees, customers, and shareholders alike. We sold underused and non-strategic assets, and we dramatically improved our receivables.

With the added cash, we paid down debt and the bank renewed our credit line. Profits and revenue growth returned, and even beat expectations. Our company cooperated fully with SEC regulators who concluded their investigation and found it clean of fault. Analysts once again followed our company and gave "buy" recommendations to this tarnished star. Business journalists, industry consultants, and trade press writers heralded the company's turn of fortune. OSI was recognized among the top-25 performing stocks on the New York Stock Exchange that year.

Rewards Follow

A thoughtful plan that's well executed by talented people generally produces rewards. Unfortunately, my reward included getting sacked by the founding chairman who maintained dominant boardroom influence and owned 40 percent of the stock. It seemed the individual he had initially wanted for my job was suddenly available.

Looking back, perhaps I didn't sufficiently share the vision and create a collective energy with him. Perhaps I didn't give him sufficient recognition for building the platform I was busy fixing. In fact, I axed some of his pet projects. Perhaps he felt jealous due to the recognition I received. There are ex-presidents and ex-CEOs, but I've never met an ex-founder.

Fortunately, I was well compensated for my efforts and the results, and I left with these lessons learned: Share the vision with *everyone*. Give recognition to *everyone*. Partner with *everyone*. Identify and then neutralize negative forces. Live and learn!

Phase 2 of the ABCs:
Kick Off the Plan

"Great leaders are great simplifiers who can cut through the argument, debate and doubt and offer a solution everybody can understand."

—General Colin Powell

You have enabled your team to construct a thoughtful game plan. It's been well articulated, bulleted in action words, and communicated inside and out. Now what? Nothing happens by itself. With a shared passion to energize your team as you kick off the game plan, some organization and process to provide focus, and the right people with the right skills in your foxhole, you're set. Now kick off that game plan with a vengeance. A half-hearted kickoff can only lead to disaster. Follow the ABCs:

A: Act Boldly to Kick Off Your Game Plan

B: Build on Strengths

C: Control Through Visible Measurement

S: Streamline the Activity Schedule

A: Act Boldly to Kick Off Your Game Plan

What is it about ferry disasters? They seem to occur with regularity. All too frequently, we hear about seemingly avoidable disasters accompanied by failures to follow established procedures or half-hearted kickoffs to rehearsed game plans in case of disruption. It seems the story is always the same. Just change the names and dates.

In April 2014, the South Korean ferry *Sewol* left port in a thick fog. Although its 470 passengers were far fewer than the ferry's capacity of 800 to 900, it carried a freight load well above the safety standard. En route to its port of call—in the fog, navigating a challenging navigational corridor—the ship's captain went to his cabin to take a cigarette break. He left the ship's helm in the hands of a junior and highly inexperienced navigator. This helmsman took a sharp turn in the fog, upsetting the haphazardly loaded and poorly balanced overload of cargo. Before anyone could say "shipwreck," the Sewol was on its side, listing 50 to 60 degrees to its port.

The *Sewol* had 46 inflatable lifeboats on board, more than sufficient to carry its passengers in the event of an emergency. As a quick-acting crew member prepared to engage the lifeboats, he immediately discovered only one lifeboat was operational. Even though regulations called for safety drills every 10 days, those drills never took place. Thus the crew was unfamiliar with the equipment and all emergency procedures. In fact, had the drills occurred, equipment flaws could have been easily discovered and corrected long before needed. Captain Knowles would have been appalled.

The failure to kick off the *Sewol*'s emergency game plan wasn't the only issue on that fog-filled April morning. A South Korean Coast Guard cutter, with its captain and crew of 14, responded immediately to the *Sewol*'s emergency call. In such an emergency, their game plan was considered basic and well established.

Specifically, they were to board the troubled ship (in this case the *Sewol*), enter the wheelhouse, and, via the ship's public address system, command passengers and crew to gather on deck to evacuate the sinking ship. Seems simple enough. But the cutter's captain thought it would be too difficult to enter the sinking *Sewol* or its wheelhouse. So the seemingly complacent Coast Guard cutter's crew made no attempt to enter the wheelhouse.

Investigations later showed it would have been easily possible, even if the door or windows needed to be broken to do so. Instead, the cutter captain announced on the *cutter*'s public address system that *Sewol* passengers should abandon ship and jump into the ocean for rescue. However, only the *Sewol* passengers on deck could hear this announcement. Among the first to jump in were the *Sewol*'s underwear-clad captain and his crew members.

Emergency protocol calls for captain and crew to see first to their passengers' safety and well-being. It's a sacrosanct maritime practice. So much for protocol and a well-known game plan!

Within the hour, the *Sewol* rolled over and sank. Of the *Sewol*'s 470 passengers, 290 were missing, *most of them school children.* At least the Korean court imprisoned *Sewol*'s captain and several crew members for their failures in this situation. The Korean Coast Guard's culpability seemed under-recognized by comparison.

No Room for Complacency

Any athlete or coach in competition, any soldier in combat, any politician facing an issue, any doctor looking to cure disease, any educator wanting to influence apathetic students, or any businessperson seeking to right a disrupted situation must have one thing in common: a strong game plan, *boldly executed.* That means any time they're tentative in kicking off their plan, they're likely to get hurt. There's no room for vacillating in indecision, complacency, or mamby-pamby actions.

A game plan—to have a shot at succeeding—needs to be kicked off at the outset with these qualities: overwhelming energy and enthusiasm, a confident attitude, and a steely resolve shared among the leader and all players. Half-hearted responses to launching a game plan often ends in a compounded disaster—first the problem itself and then compounding it by poorly kicking off a known-to-be-effective game plan.

Winston Churchill regrouped his forces after a devastating, morale-crushing defeat at the hands of German forces in Dunkirk in the early days of World War II. Talk about running aground! To kick off a rebound effort, his message to the British people—and the world at large—had to be bold. He single-handedly shifted an attitude of defeat into an attitude of hard-fought victory through these eloquent yet simple words: "We shall defend our island whatever the cost may be, we shall fight on the beaches, we shall fight on the launching grounds, we shall fight in the fields and in the street, we shall fight in the hills; we shall never surrender." Then he backed that up *with a detailed plan* to help swing the tide.

Captain Knowles' Game Plan

Only 82 years before Winston Churchill's famous speech that ignited British resolve, and 156 years before *Sewol's* compounded disaster, Captain Josiah Knowles (with his passengers and crew stranded on a desolate Pacific island) had hatched a plan. If that plan to lead them to survival and rescue had a breath of a chance, it required they act boldly. Knowles, who was keen to show a command presence among his forces, always set the example by his attention to attire and personal grooming. He cleaned himself up, put on fresh clothing, and trimmed his beard and hair before meeting with his team to outline the game plan.

Captain Knowles presented that game plan with forceful, positive, and enthusiastic resolve. Why couldn't a handpicked team sail 100 miles to an adjacent island to seek rescue? He asked for examples from his crew of them doing exactly that in a small craft. After all, these were experienced, hardened sailors. All agreed the goal was readily achievable.

They talked about the sea worthiness of a lifeboat, and the material and skills needed for survival, while proactively seeking rescue. The team adopted Captain Knowles' positive attitude and agreed they "had what it would take" to accomplish their primary goal of survival and rescue. And they acknowledged they had the mettle to handle the unforeseen. They would kick off their game plan with a boldness that would shake the small patch of earth they inhabited, while using rats and menacing hermit crabs to enable that survival. This wasn't a pie-in-the-sky effort; rather, they agreed to a rational undertaking that would build on their strengths.

That leads to the B in the ABCs to Advance.

B: Build on Strengths

People and organizations alike have strengths and weaknesses. The most successful are the ones who build on their strengths versus lament their weaknesses. Knowledge is power. Acknowledging each of them enables the kickoff of a game plan to lead with its strongest suit.

Captain Knowles conducted his 19th-century version of a SWOT analysis (Strengths, Weaknesses, Opportunities, and Threats) to kick off his game plan for survival and rescue. To summarize:

* Among the strengths were the capabilities of his diverse roster of passengers and crew plus the availability of two lifeboats.

* Their remote geography on a wrongly charted island was certainly a weakness.

* The use of Oeno's birds helped patch the remote communications weakness.

* The opportunity to be rescued by voyaging to adjacent islands was far superior to waiting for a ship to enter wrongly charted waters.

* Threats to survival could be managed by the crew's capacity to work together.

* The presence of rats and crabs moved from the list of threats to the list of strengths. On an island where hunting for game required luck as well as skill, the rats and flesh-biting crabs could be easily captured, providing an abundant source of protein to sustain life for the three dozen men in the near future.

✳ The threat to the voyagers attempting a passage to
the second island 600 miles away to seek rescue was
extremely real. However, the captain and crew agreed
the risk was worth taking if they had any shot at all for
being rescued.

SWOT Analysis as a CEO

At the kickoff of any game plan, I always made it a practice to
conduct this SWOT analysis with my various teams. "Group think" is
far more powerful than isolated and individual effort. Like Captain
Knowles, I often found that, whereas perceived strengths were obvious,
items considered threats were, in fact, strengths or opportunities to be
exploited. And any game plan worth its salt builds on the strengths that
exist. Strengths could be a customer base, technology, organizational
reputation, capability, differentiation, key personnel, strategic partners,
stakeholders, or investors.

Building on strengths cannot only make a difference in achieving
goals, it can add to the organization's confidence that the undertaking
would be achievable at all.

Cayenne Software Example

My teams often took a perceived weakness or threat and turned
it into a unique strength that facilitated our success. In one example,
Cayenne Software, a newly public software company (I had just signed
on as CEO) had missed the quick pace of technological change. Wall
Street, the trade press, and industry insiders considered the Software
100 Company another fallen technology leader that hadn't kept up.

Wait a minute! What about its 1,000 global enterprise customers
comprised of the world's largest companies? These customers loved
Cayenne Software's technology. They considered it bulletproof and
industrial-strength for mission-critical applications. Newer competitive
products were right for departmental applications but lightweight and
not proven for mission-critical ones. Those happy customers said they'd
buy this industrial-strength product line if it were moved ("ported" in

techie terms) to the new platform within a year. The weakness became the strength that needed a bit of engineering work. The decision to continue was hard and the naysayers spoke up. But the company's fortune turned when those large global customers bought the old technology delivered on the new platform. Cayenne's profits and stock value returned.

IBM's Situation

Three decades ago, IBM faced a similar dilemma when mainframe technology matured and gave way to new hardware. Its response was not only to offer the new hardware but to also embrace the needs of its customer base with new IT service offerings. Revenue gains for new services soon exceeded revenue declines from its maturing mainframe products. Profits and stock value quickly returned.

Today, IBM is facing that same issue. As Yogi Berra said, "It's déjà vu all over again." This time, though, enterprise systems and software revenue are dropping in favor of big data analytics and cloud computing. Some say IBM has done a great job bringing to the market those new offerings, which have grown into multibillion-dollar revenue generators. However, those increases have yet to offset the declines of the maturing enterprise systems and software offerings. Transitions take time. They're still hard, and the naysayers still speak up.

Surebridge's Struggle

In another example, Surebridge, an early software-in-the-cloud pioneer, hit the wall after the Internet bubble burst. By early 2002, it seemed to struggle with the disarray of the bubble's burst. Its private equity investors were groping for a game plan to stay afloat. At that time, I switched positions from board consultant to CEO.

Although the firm had a handful of large businesses, those customers were unhappy with the company's ability to service their needs. Competition for those customers from bigger vendors was rabid. The weaknesses were obvious to all. However, Surebridge serviced more than 1,000 small to mid-sized businesses—better known as mid-market customers—where the competition thinned out.

Building on this market as a strength enabled the company to reposition itself as a leader in the middle market. The company politely fired its handful of unhappy large clients and focused on five vertical segments within the mid-market. Add-on sales to those customers contributed to revenue growth, and the gain in new customers where light competition prevailed enabled Surebridge to grow revenue, achieve profits, acquire other companies, and build additional value. Acquired for a premium, Surebridge has become a unit within the Fortune 500 communications giant Time Warner Cable.

A thoughtful SWOT analysis that lists everything at your disposal and categorizes it in those four quadrants—Strengths, Weaknesses, Opportunities, and Threats—will empower you and your team to define strengths upon which you can build to kick off your game plan. With that, you can identify the momentum indicators that will make your progress visible.

That leads to the C in the ABCs to Advance.

C: Control Through Visible Measurement

If something is important, it should be made visible for everyone to see. If it isn't seen or measured, it can be perceived as unimportant.

In baseball, for example, batting averages, ERAs (earned run averages), RBIs (runs batted in), errors, wins, losses, and alike are all measured and visible. They're considered important statistics to every player's performance. My son's little league baseball coach was the only coach who passed out each player's statistics before each practice session and game. Those kids paid attention to the numbers. They worked to improve them and eventually won a championship.

Every situation has its key statistics to highlight momentum—or its absence. My best teachings include defining the right statistics and making them highly visible to my teams.

Gather Statistics and Make Them Visible

What might have happened if the ferryboat *Sewol*'s captain had posted results from the drills conducted every 10 days engaging the 46 inflatable lifeboats? The boat might still have had an accident. After all, stuff happens. But he would have averted the tragic loss of life as a result of the disaster.

By comparison, Captain Knowles' crew practiced and drilled in the event of a storm-driven wreck. He measured the time it took his crew to prepare to abandon ship with the provisions needed to sustain living. He always posted the results, and they comprised a piece of his logbook. Clearly, statistics were important to him and thus important to his passengers and crew. What happened in the frenzied sea as *Wild Wave* was breaking apart? All hands were able to abandon ship within minutes, and the crew suffered zero fatalities. Big difference.

Provisioning to sustain life on Oeno was certainly critical to *Wild Wave*'s passengers and crew. How much food, water, firewood, and so on were needed to sustain life? Once that was measured, people were assigned specific tasks, and their results were posted daily. Captain Knowles knew how many miles a day he needed to average to go from Pitcairn to Nukahiva before running short of provisions. He ensured that key components required to progress toward the goal of survival and rescue were measured *and made visible,* posting them daily on the lifeboat *John Adams.* He held people accountable.

In the case of late-to-market Cayenne Software, its engineering leader measured progress in porting the technology to the new platform every single week. They posted statistics on bulletin boards, and sent memos and e-mails throughout the company. When the ported new product was finally delivered, the company posted graphs and charts quarterly, tracking the rise in new product revenue against the fall of old product revenue. Eventually, those lines on the chart crossed and growth in new product revenue finally exceeded the decline in the old one.

Surebridge, the cloud computing company, posted its results monthly as well. Add-on sales to established accounts, new sales to new accounts, sales productivity, gross margin, and profitability—all were made visible to everyone from the board of directors to the receptionist. In a private versus public company setting, more information sharing is possible. This all helps keep an organization on track through measuring and making visible areas deemed critical to success.

The point is this: There was no question what these company leaders considered to be important by the statistics they tracked and made visible. And they immediately recognized those responsible for the delivery of any momentum indicator.

That leads to the S in the ABCs to Advance.

S: Streamline the Activity Schedule

You've accomplished Phase 1 by hatching the game plan. You're en route to kicking off that game plan. You're armed with a bold can-do attitude, your strengths, and a system to provide controls and make progress visible. Now, you're about to embark on the most important two days of your assignment that can pave the way for a crisp and forceful execution.

Your objective becomes tightly integrating your strategic game plan into operations and aligning your team to execute in a high-performance way. Follow these activities to the letter:

The Team Off-Site Agenda

Hold an off-site meeting with key members of your team to get them aligned and highly focused on executing your game plan. Plan on being together for a couple of days. Share the agenda with participants before going off-site. You may or may not benefit from employing a meeting facilitator; you might act as the facilitator yourself. Judge the situation, get some feedback, and make your decision. Because I've done this several times, I usually choose to act as my own facilitator.

A team of 10, a hundred, a thousand, or tens of thousands—even millions—can accomplish great feats if it's focused with everyone executing the same plan. Naturally, you can't hold an off-site meeting with a million people. You can, however, take your key constituents—the top one to three dozen members of your team—and gain 100-percent alignment. These people are key to passing that alignment throughout your organization.

Where do you start? Captain Knowles used the only media at his disposal: a stick pen and a sandy beach. Over time, others have employed a poster-sized pad of paper, an easel, a crayon or magic marker, and tape to attach the planning posters on the meeting room walls. Today, people use a computer and a projector to craft the wording of meeting results and make them visible to all.

I've often started retreats with a breakfast or lunch, allowing team members to break bread and answer the opening question: "What do you hope to come out of this meeting in the next couple of days?" I suggest writing down those answers so you can refer to them at the close of the session.

The Team's Survival Exercise

The opening exercise of your off-site retreat will set the stage for the remaining time together. A whole host of group survival team-building exercises are available that will occupy your first hour together. They range from lost-at-sea shipwrecks to nuclear attacks to lost-in-the-desert or jungle plane crashes. These group communications and decision-making tools work well for a wide spectrum of ages, skills, and education levels. The exercise I've favored over the years is desert survival in the aftermath of a plane crash.

It takes five minutes for each individual to rank 15 items from the plane crash, in a range from most to least important to the group's survival. It then takes 15 minutes for the whole group to rank the same items. Reaching consensus is more difficult and time consuming because of dealing with conflicting opinions. Your job as facilitator also means acting as the timekeeper and observer to score and then debrief the exercise. (Meeting moderator tools to guide you are readily available for these exercises.)

Invariably, the group scores exceed individual judgment. During the debrief, discussions can cover these points:

＊ How decisions were made,

＊ Who influenced the decisions,

* How these people provided the influence,

* How better decisions could have been made,

* If people listened to each other (why or why not),

* How conflict was managed, and

* Which kinds of behavior helped or hindered the group.

The big takeaway came down to what Captain Knowles learned years before Jim Suroweiki wrote *The Wisdom of Crowds*—that is, collective wisdom is more effective than one individual's input. If the group spent fivefold the time, its score would not likely be meaningfully improved. They were most likely to rank the key items for their survival near the top of the list.

Hence, our team has just a couple of days to gain alignment to execute its game plan. Get on with it. Seeking perfection has a time and place. Righting disruption needs to come with a sense of urgency to right the ship. If a grounded sailboat doesn't kedge off soon, its weight resting on the bottom could well break the vessel apart.

Your grounded organization needs to get off the bottom, so don't wait! You need alignment to execute now!

Vision Statement

If you don't know where you're going, any road will take you there. Does your organization have a vision statement around which people can rally? All the great ones do. What is yours? Steve Jobs started Apple with a clear vision in the 1970s to put a computer on every desktop. That vision has certainly morphed as the company evolved, but it served as a clear rallying cry as Apple developed to be what it is now.

I've found that constructing and agreeing to a vision statement is either very easy for some organizations or very difficult for others. This could be an exercise that takes a half hour, a half day, or, if it's really dysfunctional, days and days. Right now, you don't have days and days. It's the foundation of your alignment exercise, however. Spend the time here and now and you'll save yourself heartache and time as time goes on.

Mission Statement

Your mission is your organization's charter. It's the boilerplate of your organization's communication both inside and out. It should be highlighted on your Website and in every press release. It defines who you are, and what you provide, to whom, how, and why. It needs to be crisp and in words that your grandmother can understand. Write your mission in simple, plain language with no acronyms or industry jargon. Aim it for Main Street comprehension and consumption.

Go to Market Strategy

Whether it's a for-profit business or a nonprofit organization, you have a target audience for your goods, services, or value proposition. Who do you intend to reach? Do you target a specific type of industry vertical or a demographic? Which ones? How do you reach and deliver to your target audience? Directly? Through channels of distribution? Brick-and-mortar retail? On-line? Multiple approaches? Put this in bullet points to define what, who, and how.

Competitive Positioning

Define your value proposition. Why do you win in the mind's eye of your target audience or market when it's your value proposition that they want? If not, why do you lose? Which organizations have a competing value proposition? Why do they win or lose? With all of that as information, graph this out. Define your vertical and horizontal axis and put a picture on this competitive positioning that will visualize your advantages and differentiation.

Elevator Pitch

The question comes often and from different directions. It could be from your Aunt Martha, a would-be shareholder, a prospective customer or employee, a voter or donor, or whatever. You're in the elevator and going to your floor in less than a minute. Can you crisply outline who your organization is, what it does, and how well it does it, and give credible evidence that it's the real deal before the elevator door opens and your interested party gets off? Maybe you can. Can everyone in your organization? Can they say the same thing, or will their explanation look like a different organization altogether from what you just described?

Who said, "A camel is a horse designed by committee"? There's no room for a camel in your meeting room. Your team must craft a crisp few sentences that can be articulated in plain language in less than a minute and that your Aunt Martha can understand. Your elevator pitch will pique her interest further and may entail a call to action. "How can we help you?" "You should be a shareholder, (a student, a donor, a customer, a distributor, a ticket holder, etc.)." This elevator pitch is for every member of the organization to memorize and give to any interested party. That consistency of pitch is so powerful when every member of an organization says the same thing about what it does and how it does it. And it's key to alignment.

With an elevator pitch in hand, you can have some fun by testing every member of your organization, from members of the board to the receptionist, from the mayor to the janitor, from the coach to the water boy, from the executive director to a junior associate. Aligned organizations pitch and position themselves with consistency. Every member of an aligned organization knows who they are and what they do, and can articulate it with their own style, but their messaging is consistent. They're talking about the same organization. There's no confusion.

Game Plan

You've already constructed a game plan in Phase 1, shared that vision, and created some collective energy around it. You constructed it with action words and in bullet points. Refresh everyone's mind-set and post the game plan once again for all to see.

Primary Goals (the BHAGs) to Focus the Energy

Some organizations highlight one overarching goal to set them free from disruption. In Captain Knowles' case, survival and rescue for one and all was the one and only goal around which the team coalesced. That was one big, hairy, audacious goal that was coined as a BHAG by Jim Collins and Jerry Porras in their book *Built to Last: Successful*

Habits of Visionary Companies. Captain Knowles scoped that out nearly 150 years before Jim Collins's birth. Working toward any more than a few goals makes a statement that nothing is important.

Business enterprises and nonprofit organizations alike have shareholders or stakeholders, customers or targets to receive their value proposition, and employees to deliver it. I've found that no more than three goals—first articulated by the organizational leader, then discussed with the off-site attendees—can provide the fodder for the alignment of resources that are prioritized to achieve those goals. One goal needs to consider the shareholder or stakeholder. It could be revenue and profitability, market leadership, organizational stability, or any specific goal that will reward that organizational supporter. One goal should consider the customer or receiver of the organizational value proposition. Every situation is different. Is it some measure of customer satisfaction or return on investment? Lastly, what goal specific to the well-being of members of the organization will settle the disruption you're facing? Is it turnover, employee satisfaction, being named the best employer in the region? Whatever it is, to be credible to an action plan to stabilize a disrupted situation, it needs to be highly visible and articulated and shared by the leadership to enable the alignment that you're seeking.

In my situation with Surebridge, the cloud computing company disrupted by the burst of the Internet bubble, it completed three acquisitions in quick succession. Goal #1 was to grow to $100 million in revenue with 30-percent margins before taxes, interest, and depreciation. Goal #2 was a specific measure of customer satisfaction and retention as indicated by formal customer surveys. Goal #3 was for all employees, customers, and shareholders to believe that they were employed by, doing business with, or shareholders of one unified organization, and not the several different ones that came together to form the one.

Critical Success Factors (CSFs) to Prioritize the Actions

With those goals articulated, any off-site team can then look at the items that are critical to achieve those goals. Articulate your few goals and ask—functional area by functional area—what the team considered absolutely critical to its success in the specific functional area of responsibility to achieve goals #1, #2, and #3. People from other functional areas should be allowed to chime in to add their point of view. Review them once you're done and ask if what you've highlighted is absolutely, have-to-do critical, or is just nice to do. There's no room for doing what is nice to do if resources are required to focus on what is absolutely critical.

Goals and CSFs Chart

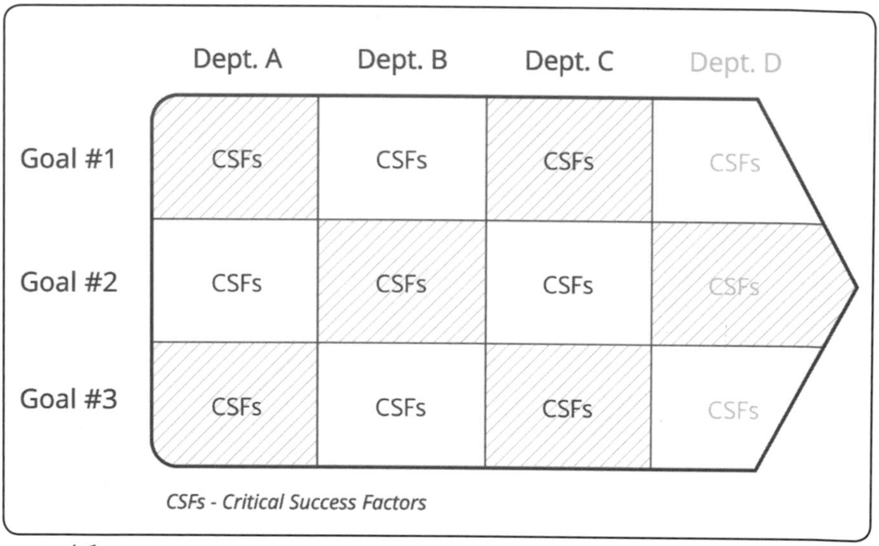

	Dept. A	Dept. B	Dept. C	Dept. D
Goal #1	CSFs	CSFs	CSFs	CSFs
Goal #2	CSFs	CSFs	CSFs	CSFs
Goal #3	CSFs	CSFs	CSFs	CSFs

CSFs - Critical Success Factors

Image 4.1.

Captain Knowles put forth one primary goal. His passengers and crew then formed key work groups. Survival required some very specific groups. The quantity of food, water, and shelter for three dozen people was specifically calculated and was obviously considered critical. Hunters of food, gatherers of water, firewood and alike, farmers and fisherman who could add to the food source, cooks, preparers and preservers to feed the castaways, builders of shelter—all articulated what they needed to do to enable survival and rescue. The doctor also put together a team to assist his functional area of responsibility: the physical and emotional well-being of all. Among responsibilities of this team was disease-free sanitation of this newly formed village.

Captain Knowles formed a functional team to enable rescue. The teams coalesced on its CSFs and held accountability to the group for their delivery to enable that one primary goal of survival and rescue. Everyone had a role to enable the primary goal, and everyone's activities were dedicated to achieving those CSFs.

Action Plans

Some things are more important than others. We saw that, at the outset of the off-site meeting, when we ranked 15 items in order of importance to survival. The same holds true when considering what specific actions need to be taken to achieve any one critical success factor. Ask yourselves a prioritizing question. What three actions are most important now to achieve a specific critical success factor? Those are the action items where visibility needs to be given to measure progress.

High-performance teams know their jobs and also appreciate the roles of others, and what is required of them, to accomplish the tasks at hand that are deemed critical. Cross-functional support is often critical to success. It's easier to achieve when all are working toward the same set of goals. Make those action items visible. By doing so, it adds to the feeling, for all members of a functional area, of being held accountable.

Momentum Indicators

One culprit of failed performance after a kickoff is poor visibility of the things that count. It's alarming how frequently that basic premise is absent from the organizational woodwork. Wharton management professor Lawrence G. Hrebiniak noted in his book *Making Strategy Work: Leading Effective Execution and Change* that researchers found less than 15 percent of organizations routinely track key indicators of performance. Instead, only the progress toward early goals is visible. This lack of introspection makes it easier for organizations to ignore poor progress. Ignoring failure makes it that much harder to identify execution bottlenecks and take corrective action.

Track several indicators that will show your team is on the right track to achieve its critical success factors. Those key indicators can and must be identified. For instance, Surebridge, my cloud computing company, had specific revenue and margin targets, productivity metrics, customer satisfaction standards, and employee survey data. These were made highly visible to track progress to goal achievement.

But every situation is different. Define what is specific to your situation. These momentum indicators will help keep your organization on track. Visibility breeds accountability. Accountability breeds success.

Captain Knowles' passengers and crew defined exactly how much food, water, shelter, and other specifics they required to survive. Incorporated into their CSFs were the quantity and daily measurement of needed output in order to survive. The captain also defined the daily progress his traveling team needed to make in their quest to seek rescue. Those statistics Captain Knowles didn't call "momentum indicators," but he ensured they were defined, tracked, and posted for all to see. This enabled group members to see immediately if they were either on the right track or heading for trouble.

Momentum Indicators

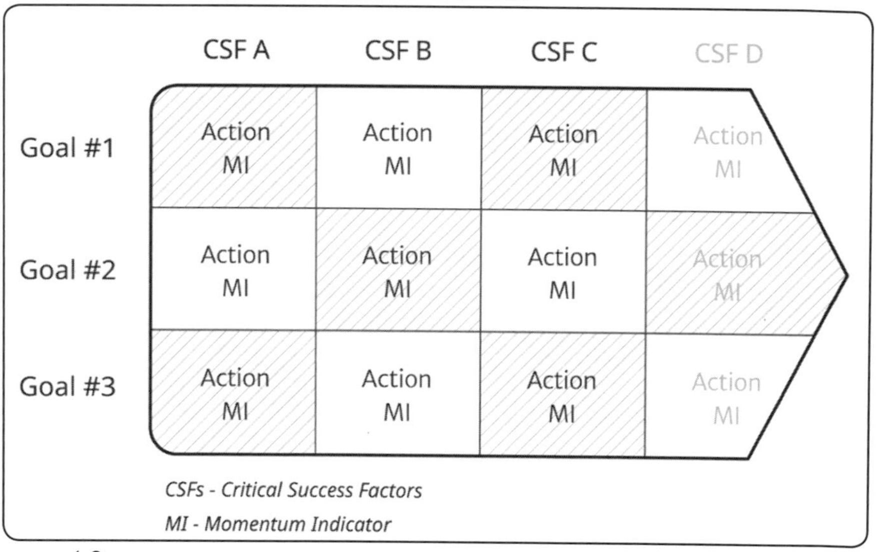

	CSF A	CSF B	CSF C	CSF D
Goal #1	Action MI	Action MI	Action MI	Action MI
Goal #2	Action MI	Action MI	Action MI	Action MI
Goal #3	Action MI	Action MI	Action MI	Action MI

CSFs - Critical Success Factors
MI - Momentum Indicator

Image 4.2.

Skill Sets Assessment

The goals are established. You've identified the critical success factors by functional area to achieve the goals, and you've prioritized a handful of immediate action items to accomplish those CSFs.

This is a great time to take stock of your team's capability. Do you have the skill sets on board within your organization to accomplish those CSFs? It becomes obvious to off-site team members when they look at the skills around the table as they relate to their articulated work requirements. It should be put up for discussion. Are your skill sets appropriately assigned to the right functional areas and the right action items for their capability? If so, you're cooking. If not, what can be done to put the strengths of your human resources on the tasks that build on their skills and capacity? Do you need to recruit from the outside, transfer from within, or conduct specific training sessions for certain people in certain functions? That must be a piece of the action plan to better enable successful goal achievement.

Captain Knowles didn't have the luxury of being able to recruit from an outside organization for what he needed. He could, however, assign various people to functional groups based on their skills. Where skills were missing, he could train people for specific tasks to better prepare them to contribute to any actions deemed necessary to achieve a CSF. For instance, not everyone was trained in sanitation, but the doctor made sure his crew was cross-trained to prevent disease. The close quarters of a ship provided a natural training ground for the island encampment. He also held classes with the entire group to convey individual roles and responsibilities that would ensure the health, well-being, and survival of everyone.

Culture Definition

Culture is an overworked and misunderstood arena in which definitions vary and everyone is an expert. Experts will agree, however, that culture generally refers to the shared values, attitudes, beliefs, and code of behavioral standards within an organization. Corporate culture is rooted in an organization's goals, strategies, structure, and approaches to a work force, customers, investors, and the greater community. With much of the off-site meeting focused on alignment around an organization's vision, mission, strategy, goals, critical success factors, and prioritized action plans, culture must become a piece of your off-site agenda.

Disruption occurs for a variety of simplistic reasons. And it can be overcome through basic and fundamental activity. Changes to the outside environment can lead to a disruption that is beyond one's control. However, some changes are predictable and occur in slow motion. When the outside environment isn't at fault, it's more often dysfunction at the top that leads to disruption. Remember: The top can mean the top of anything: a department, a region, an organization, a city, or a country. They all have a bottom, a middle, and a top. In an organization, the top isn't only a CEO, an executive director, a mayor, or whatever the title might be. It's also a board of directors.

As my mentor asked me so many times: Where's the bottleneck? It's always found at the top.

Culture Also at the Top

An organization's culture has no first and last name. "It's the way we do things around here." Yet, there are times when the culture has caused a disruption. So it needs to be challenged and reshaped as part of a plan to kedge off the bottom and sail safely into open ocean once again.

The off-site meeting presents an interesting time to speak to your organization's leaders, as well as thought leaders, about the kind of organization to be created and its values. This exercise will help define your culture in a perfect world. You may be close; you may be light years away. But you *can* improve your culture.

It starts with defining what you want it to be.

Have you noticed? People don't generally do what they're told to do. They often do what incentives lead them to do. And they will follow both positive and negative examples of their leadership. Your crew, you included, must be prepared to "walk the walk" of the desired culture and lead by example. Just "talking the talk" without "walking the walk" makes you or your crew the bottleneck to progress, so either change or be gone.

Desired behavior can be encouraged not only by example, but by recognition to help build and reinforce an organizational culture. For example, at Surebridge during a management off-site meeting hosting people from four merged organizations, we spoke of each company's individual cultural norms. We asked what was most desired and what was least desired. We also highlighted research about the cultural norms shared by similar science and technology firms that were successful.

The collective wisdom of this team opted to define itself as high quality, innovative, results-oriented, customer-responsive, and respectful in the way people treat each another. The combined company of several hundred employees articulated its cultural values in a series of communiqués both inside and outside the firm. Various departments conducted a 360-degree review on each other's behavior over a 90-day period. They then gave recognition rewards to those who best exemplified the behavioral standards of this newly articulated culture.

Within the course of the year, that culture was fortified within the organizational woodwork. The more the culture was defined and rewarded, the more it became ingrained.

As execution progressed, Surebridge was well on its way to achieving all of its goals. Revenue, although it had not yet reached $100 million, was 70 percent in place. Its margins exceeded target. Customers and employees who were surveyed described themselves as "happy campers." Within two years, a larger public company acquired Surebridge for 15 times its cash flow, which was considered a major valuation premium. Payment terms were two-thirds cash and one-third stock. The stock came with a lockup and couldn't be traded for six months. Within that six-month period, the acquirer's stock more than doubled in value. The acquiring firm was then itself acquired by a Fortune 100 firm.

What were the reasons for this valuation growth? What was the attraction of this formerly disrupted cloud computing firm? Its visible capacity to achieve results, its rich talent base, and its winning culture. For its 2001 bubble-bursting vintage, its return on investment achieved top decile, having performed in the top 10 percent. It outearned 90 percent of the other investments made during the same disruptive time frame. Not too shabby, thanks in no small part to the work done up front to define and support its culture. That made the difference.

Phase 3 of the ABCs: Execute the Plan

"An average plan, violently executed now, is better than a perfect plan next week."

—General George S. Patton

You've constructed a thoughtful, well-supported game plan. Your team is properly aligned around a key goal or two. The critical success factors are acknowledged and action plans are defined to accomplish them. Your value proposition is solid. You've established visible momentum-indicator metrics to highlight your progress, and your culture will support your efforts. Now what? There are countless stories about failed strategies. All too frequently, however, it wasn't the strategy itself but its execution that was flubbed. Among the culprits of failure, you'll find an ill-disciplined focus, a diffusion of applied resources, and poor communications to reinforce the focused effort.

As Wharton management professor Lawrence G. Hrebiniak noted in his book *Making Strategy Work: Leading Effective Execution and Change,* MBA-trained managers might know how to construct a strategy but often fail to carry it out. His findings concluded the biggest factor might be executive inattention. Once a plan is decided on, surprisingly little follow-through happens to ensure it is executed. Leaders take their eyes off the implementation ball.

There are two schools of thought about the best way to improve execution. One emphasizes putting the right people in your foxhole ("Superior people yield superior execution") whereas a second emphasizes process over people. Researchers suggest the organizations that deliver results combine both approaches.

To be among the success stories, as you execute your game plan, follow the ABCs.

A: Assert Yourself at the Focal Point

B: Borrow From Alliances and Partnerships

C: Communicate Progress and Results to Keep/Get on Track

S: Spread the Rewards of Wealth and Recognition When Things Go Your Way

A: Assert Yourself at the Focal Point

Stand for something and execute with a take-no-prisoners style—aggressively. Nothing substitutes for applied force when it comes to execution. Here's an example that seems like ancient history now.

After the bubble burst in 2001, Hewlett-Packard (HP)'s high-profile celebrity CEO combined the company with Compaq to create the world's biggest computer hardware supplier. Thereafter, observers claimed that HP leaders then executed a different competitive game plan every week. First, they emphasized quality as their competitive differentiation. Then they moved to delivery, and then substituted price. Next stop, they featured service. Among a whole host of issues was not standing for *anything*. Goodbye, rock star CEO.

Then HP said hello and goodbye to a few more CEOs in rapid succession—and HP is still rebounding from this. In fall 2014, under its fourth CEO in a decade, HP announced a plan to divide the company into two pieces. One would address consumer needs, with the other addressing business enterprise needs. To kick it off, the consumer piece unveiled 3D technology that is 10 times faster and at a fraction of competitors' prices.

Similarly, Captain Knowles had to bob and weave like a fighter in a ring. His primary goal was survival *and* rescue for one and all. Not only did that require him to spit in the face of conventional wisdom and set out for the island of Pitcairn, it required a doubling down of effort to leave that uninhabited island in an in-need-of-repair lifeboat and venture to Nukahiva on its way to the Sandwich Islands. To add angst to an already-difficult endeavor, half of *John Adams*'s volunteer crew refused to board her on the second leg of the journey.

As a result, Captain Knowles had to assert himself at the focal point to enable the goal: getting rescued. Without his assertive plan execution, the skeletal remains of a dead crew might have been discovered on two different islands long after they died.

Prime Response's Repositioning

Assertive resolve takes several forms applied at different and difficult times. As the Internet bubble was filling up later in the 1990s, I believed I, too, could participate in this phenomenon and capture the American dream. That's when I took the helm of Prime Response, a British company with a whiz-bang new Internet offering on the horizon. An investor had just acquired the interest of one co-founder and added capital to help fund its execution.

The company's pre-Internet-enabled marketing automation product had earned market leadership in Europe and was newly penetrating the U.S. marketplace. Its first generation of software, however, was riddled with bugs. As a result, the customer support requirements were extensive. Its European software engineering presence could handle customer support requirements on that continent, but Prime Response botched its support of newly acquired U.S. customers several time zones away from its software engineering resources. In fact, the company botched the formation of its organizational structure. It looked like two different companies on two different continents, each with its own strategy, branding, and the like.

As CEO, I followed the first two phases of the ABCs: I collaboratively hatched a game plan, added needed talent, reorganized, and aligned the team. I also introduced a uniquely positioned Internet offering with reckless abandon. As a go-to market strategy, we tightly focused our sales resources on large business to consumer (B2C) service enterprises. We recruited and trained a specialty sales force to compete like an ultimate fighter, tough with finesse. I called this cast of characters in our aggressive sales force the Ivy League Street Fighters. (It never mattered where they went to school.)

At the time, bubble-era *Wall Street Journal* headlines were riddled with the firings of major companies' CEOs and VPs of marketing who failed to embrace the Internet aggressively. Their exit interviews voiced concern they were being asked to abandon their brick and mortar business—where 90 percent of their profits originated—for an unproven Internet channel. If they stopped paying attention to their primary business, they'd also get fired. What a dilemma.

Prime Response introduced its new Internet-enabled software offering as the first and (then) only provider that combined off-line, on-line, and wireless capacity using an integrated database of customer behavioral activity. Messaging aggressively asserted that customers could save their jobs by "bringing the clicks to the bricks," while other vendors' products forced users to "abandon their bricks for the clicks." Prime Response trumpeted testimonials from newly acquired, high-profile customers in financial services, communications and media, transportation, travel and leisure, retail, and e-commerce and technology that were darlings in their arenas. That leap to market leadership in a hotly competitive space paved the way to its initial public offering (IPO) from highly credentialed investment bankers.

Who expected a pushback from one of those important customers, a consumer technology direct marketer (named CTDM to protect the innocent) that threatened the completion of the IPO?

We were in the middle of a two-week IPO road show where my chief financial officer (CFO), chief technology officer (CTO), and I were presenting our company to institutional investors. That's when CTDM's marketing VP contacted Prime Response through his corporate law department. CTDM had purchased Prime's marketing automation product for $300,000 several months before and sought to return it, demanding a full refund. CTDM also demanded its name be removed from the IPO filing documents. The documents were already filed.

A contract review had made it clear not only was the $300,000 sale final, but CTDM had also granted full permission to publicize its name. Both our VP of sales and general counsel met with the marketing VP and his in-house lawyer to no avail. Enormously disappointed to not have a resolution in hand, they passed on this dilemma to me. Our investment bankers and their legal staff scheduled daily, early-morning updates to check the status. We knew that if CTDM made major noise, the IPO would fail.

In blitzkrieg fashion, I learned that CTDM's IT department had made an operating systems change within its infrastructure. That change had made our software incompatible. Oops! Fortunately, within 90 days, our software product was scheduled to release an upgrade that would make it compatible. So I offered a deal on the pending implementation of the new upgrade, but that didn't matter to the marketing VP and his lawyer. Their demand for a refund became threatening. We arranged another conference call.

Surprising to all, after that call, CTDM signed a release that withdrew its earlier demand. It accepted the new software release and gave permission a second time to use its name in all promotional documents *including the IPO*. What an astounding turnabout! The investment bankers and their lawyers, along with my board of directors, were elated. My staff was open-jawed. "How on earth did you pull this off?" they asked.

Simple!

During a collective wisdom session with Prime Response's CFO and CTO while waiting to catch a flight for yet another round of intense IPO presentations, we hatched an offer CTDM couldn't refuse. My cell phone call to CTDM's VP of marketing early the next morning happened only 10 minutes before taking the podium to speak to about 50 would-be institutional shareholders. The call was short and to the point: CTDM's purchase contract, along with its permission to publicize its name, was undisputable. But CTDM held an intimidating hostage; they'd break up the IPO if we didn't give them a full refund.

What was the offer that couldn't be refused? I said I had a lawsuit document in my pocket (a bluff) that would tap CTDM's deep pockets for treble damages to a forecasted $1 billion market value of our firm after the IPO. Its malicious intent to disrupt that IPO, according to my legal staff, would be fodder for a highly visible and damaging lawsuit. "Say goodbye to your career, Mr. Marketing VP. Your big-kahuna employer will hold you accountable, as well as the lawyer on your staff."

Alternatively, I explained, my company's treasury would gain nearly $100 million in IPO proceeds. It needed $300,000 of CTDM's products (which was true). We offered to buy those products from CTDM within 90 days of the IPO's completion instead of from one of its competitors. The VP said, "Uh, I'll get back to you." He did later that day, with a full retraction of his earlier demands.

Prime Response's IPO was 11 times oversubscribed and traded at three times more than its initial offering price on a first-day pop as a public stock. Captain Knowles was right: Assert yourself at the focal point. There's no room for a weak effort.

That leads to the B in ABCs to Advance.

B: Borrow From Alliances and Partnerships

The word *borrow* has a financial overtone. But it means much more than cash from the sale of equity or a loan from a bank. In this definition, it means resources you don't have but could surely use—often from alliances and partnerships. If you don't have them lined up, the question becomes: Where might you get them? If the Lone Ranger wants to ride again and again, he'd best not do it alone.

In Captain Knowles' situation, he and his crew were left alone to survive. To augment their capacity to achieve their dual goal of survival *and* rescue, all they could do was assess the surrounding terrain and "borrow" what resources they could. Here's what they found: rats and crabs to augment wild game and fish for food; various birds for remote communications; and stone tools and nails from burnt shacks for life-boat repair. These were their only sources of alliances and partnerships.

Looking at my situation as CEO, before its IPO, Prime Response was running low on funds to enable its growth. And it was running low on resources to implement its systems within a growing cadre of customers. So it struck an alliance with a global IT consulting firm, Accenture (formerly Andersen Consulting). The alliance included joint marketing of the product to its global customer base and the company acquiring equity ownership in exchange for four million dollars. The funds would provide the bridge financing to fund Prime to its IPO in proper financial shape. The added cash and marketing reach also stimulated an already-rapid growth rate and provided additional credentials for its successful IPO. Prime Response was no Lone Ranger; it could not have done that alone.

Successful organizations set up beneficial alliances and partnerships with holders of strategic and financial resources. That's as true for companies as it is for governments, sports teams, hospitals, schools, a nation's military, even individuals and small teams. The lesson is to augment your capacity to execute by using alliances and partnerships that provide certain strength you lack.

Ask what that strength is, where it can be found, and what your appeal might be to a would-be partner. Then seek out that partner. If it falls in your lap by accident, consider yourself lucky. But your best bet is to make your own luck and proactively find suitable partners.

You can augment this without the huge lead time of a sales effort. For example, do you need thought leaders to give you advice? Want to tap into their rolodexes? Then assemble an advisory board. Also ask your board of directors for help. You could recruit a new player with the right skills and add him or her to participate on your board. Are you lacking key skills and need them right away? Contract with consultants who have the domain expertise you need today.

Most of all, don't try to do everything yourself. You're good at a few things. Let others help your effort.

That leads to the C in ABCs to Advance.

C: Communicate Progress and Results to Get/Stay on Track

Assume there's no such thing as over-communication.

Frequent communication is paramount for a well-executed game plan. Communicate inside and outside the organization on regular intervals. Use any event as a catalyst to reinforce the messaging. Repeat the game plan over and over and over again. Review progress on stated actions to accomplish the critical success factors (CSFs). Keep your eye on achieving the goal (or handful of goals) your team constructed at the off-site meeting. Then communicate. Following are suggested ways to do that:

Inside Communications

Game plans can fail simply because not all the people involved know about them. The link between those at the strategic and operational off-site retreat, and those at the middle and bottom of the organization, need frequent touch points. That's how to ensure the plans are shared and everyone involved understands the accountability of their actions to accomplish the goals at hand.

You might package the off-site results as a form of marketing collateral, and then require each unit manager meet with his or her team to review its entire content. Frequent management meetings scheduled regularly signal to the entire organization that both commitment and consequences are genuine.

Game plans can also fail due to a resistance to change. Citing the goals, the CSFs, and the actions make the need for change or buy-in to the plan plainly stated. There's no room in the foxhole for nay-sayers to the actions needed to succeed. An open, two-way path of communication can flush out any sound reasons behind the resistance. Once you understand any issue, you can deal with it to enable a proper execution. Remember: Knowledge is power. And a powerful execution needs an open path of communication.

At those frequent meetings, use visible momentum indicators to assess performance. They can be posted electronically as well as on varying walls, bulletin boards, and more. Visibility breeds accountability.

Shortening the time frame between momentum indicator reviews provides quick performance feedback up and down an organization. In this way, you can better assess the effectiveness of execution, and identify and correct any problems.

On the *Wild Wave,* Second Mate John Trehune ensured that teams of passengers and crew reviewed the momentum indicators to enable survival every day. The status of food, water, firewood, sanitation, and general health was all reported at daily camp meetings. At one point, after several weeks of no rainfall, they could visibly see how their storage of water was insufficient for survival much longer. It would be a tense problem if it didn't rain within another 10-day span. So they jury-rigged a makeshift salt-water purification system to fill the gap.

At Prime Response, we put forth three major goals: 1) to fix customer support, 2) to launch as one unified company a hot new product that gained market leadership in its niche, and 3) to finance the growth. Those goals, the CSFs, and the action plans were part of every communication taking place at weekly global management calls, unit management meetings, and quarterly executive operational reviews. The frequent communication of those momentum indicators focused the effort and played a major role in achieving those goals. We showed that frequent visibility bred instant accountability and successful execution.

The process wasn't a slam dunk, but the whole organization participated fully in the game plan's execution. Our communication sessions provided a venue to recognize, reward, and reinforce those exhibiting the cultural values that also played such a major role toward our successful execution.

Outside Communication

Disruption is generally seen and known both inside and outside an organization. Customers, shareholders, stakeholders, partners, donors, voters, patients, parents, or those who are prospects for future dealings need reassurance a game plan exists to create a successful future.

I suggest you package your game plan for external consumption to domain experts, consultants, analysts, and even local, national, or trade press. Just by articulating you have a game plan and a strategy aids in the perception and reality that your organization is a meaningful player in its arena. Yes, it intends to be taken seriously.

Be sure to collateralize and launch a serious external communications program. Tell the outside what's going on and how you're dealing with events. Otherwise, observers will make up their own accounts. Don't give those unfriendly to you more of an opportunity to fill a void with information of their own that suits *their* purpose, not yours.

Upon arrival in Tahiti, Captain Knowles told the press about *Wild Wave*'s shipwreck and the crew's efforts for survival and rescue. He enlisted the U.S. Navy's assistance to inform U.S. authorities and the castaways' families of their survival and rescue story. They also provided regular updates as progress unfolded. As a result, the captain, passengers, and crew gained immediate recognition and credibility.

Both Prime Response's and Surebridge's messaging to the market, consultants, financial analysts, and alike echoed the internal messages being sent. They each had a game plan, great people to execute it, and ways to make measurable progress visible. Their breadth of communication bred confidence and credibility. When glitches to progress appeared, corrective actions became part of the communication. In the presence of consistent messaging, it was far more difficult for competitors to spread false and damaging information about the company. That transparency spread a reputation of integrity, which added to the company's credibility, its appeal, and ultimately its competitiveness.

Executive Communication

In combat, I dealt with life-and-death stakes. I learned to deal with reality straight up, with no hearts and flowers, and that set the tone. My teams discussed the ins and outs of our missions with incredible candor. By doing so, we were able to deal with the ugliness around us and come out on top of *it,* rather than it coming out on top of *us.* I took that lesson from combat with me to civilian life. It has been just as true with any team's style of communications with one another. Leadership that encourages a frank assessment of reality among key staff has a much better chance to get the company off the bottom and sailing safely once again.

During the bubble's tailspin and the recessionary dynamic that came with it, companies were beginning to combine on a daily basis. IPO bankers quickly made the switch to become merger and acquisition bankers. In the computer software arena, best of breed products had given way to product suites. My Prime Response team confronted that harsh reality and preemptively sought an appropriate combination partner. It identified, courted, and merged with a provider of complementary customer relationship management (CRM) products that targeted the same vertical markets that we did. The stock of both companies sank 90 percent as the bubble burst and a recessionary economy was in full bloom. Each firm had the proceeds from an earlier IPO to make it a cash-rich, well-heeled vendor. Luckily, the combination made sense to the investment community and to customers.

Inside of a year, the combined company performed well, and its stock traded at five times its previous value. What would have been the outcome if an assertive posture weren't taken during the bubble, at the IPO, or at the bubble's burst? One can only guess. But confronting and dealing proactively with reality generally produces rewards; anything less generally produces disappointment.

Had we not assessed this reality and dealt with it aggressively, we might have been left without a dance partner in an industry that consolidated quickly.

Boardroom Communication

Boardrooms generally hold a variety of viewpoints and sometimes conflicting agendas. A board needs leadership, too.

To keep a board on the path to building value, it's helpful to share the vision of a game plan and pound home the plan, goals, critical success factors, and momentum indicators. This keeps everything on the same page of execution. Too often, a board can drift with well-intended out-of-left-field influences that have nothing to do with the game plan.

Looking back, I learned one of my biggest lessons from one of my biggest mistakes. At that time, Cayenne Software had just completed a dramatic turnaround for mission-critical applications. My old venture-capital board members left in quick succession. "Thanks very much. Nice job!" they said. "Here's some money. Here's some stock. Now we're going with our new money and not staying with our old money. We can sell our stock position in your company much better by not being a board member."

They fully understood the whole game plan. And we all understood that a turn of fortune would be short-lived. Why? Because those companies with competing low-end products were engineering more capability and selling 70 percent of our functionality at 50 percent of our selling price. Getting into that low-end game as a late entrant had poor success prospects. The game plan called for finding an appropriate buyer for the higher value once the turnaround effort succeeded.

I quickly recruited a new board to fill the vacant seats. They were intelligent, respected professionals in business, consulting, and banking. So what was amiss?

First, none had any background in that kind of software business. Every meeting was a learning experience, but I wasn't learning. Instead, I was educating. No value there. Second, my new board needed more help to focus around a game plan than the people within my organization. I took it for granted that board members had circled around the game plan and didn't realize that they hadn't. Third, the board members didn't see the need to find a strategic buyer and wanted to talk about what the company might look like 10 years out. My reaction was: "I told you that up-front. *Come on!*" They seemed to be having fun sitting on a public board. To them, it was prestigious at the country club to cite a board membership. Fourth, they seemed to embrace the status quo. "Let's not make any bold decisions." What happened when I brought forward a would-be buyer or potential acquisition of a company or product line that would build value or attract a would-be buyer? Their desire to maintain the status quo made it obvious that, after five years as CEO, I could go no further. Either they all had to go or I had to go.

So I went, leaving behind the wrong skills in the boardroom fox-hole. And within a year, that 180-degree turnaround circled a full 360 degrees. The soon-to-be-distressed company was acquired by a former suitor for a pittance compared to what it would have paid a year previously. That discount was a big price to pay for my failure to effectively communicate with a new board and get its buy-in. That failure squandered the rewards of wealth and recognition that had been previously earned.

Two years later IBM acquired, for more than $700 million, a small European software firm with a unique product offering that my team had previously proposed as a $30 million acquisition. It fell on deaf ears. Expensive lesson, indeed!

Fundamental communication to keep a crew on track needs to be repeated over and over again at all levels, including the board. Since that experience, I've started my board meetings with the BHAGs (big, hairy, audacious goals; coined by Jim Collins, author of *Good to Great*) and the game plan. In addition, I've strived to keep conversations limited to those items that build value and accomplish agreed-upon goals. It sounds like this: "Let's all reaffirm our commitment to the game plan and goals. Want to talk about anything else? After the meeting is over!"

That leads to the S in ABCs to Advance.

S: Spread the Rewards of Wealth and Recognition When Things Go Your Way

You've hatched a terrific game plan. You've shared the vision and created a collective energy. You've kicked off that game plan with a vengeance. Your team members were 100-percent aligned. You've crisply executed the plan, enlisted help, and communicated inside and out. You've given momentum indicators full visibility. You've hit glitches along the way but, all in all, things are breaking in your favor. Progress toward those goals is quite evident. Your team's morale is heading higher and higher.

With all of this going on, it's tempting to take a bow, isn't it? Well, if you do, take it in the privacy of your dressing-room mirror. You'll keep the focus on successfully accomplishing your goals much better by not taking that bow personally. Instead, pass the credit to those in your foxhole who helped you. Just because things are beginning to break your way now doesn't mean your goals have been achieved. You're on the right path. Celebrate progress but don't declare victory prematurely.

Focus on incentives. People are less likely to do what they're *told* to do and more likely to do what they're *incented* to do. Incentive programs—whether they're in the form of riches or recognition—should be established on the front end of your execution. They'll help keep those in your foxhole focused on getting to the Promised Land.

Take the opportunity to use cash in the form of salary raises, bonus payments, stock options, or other tools to reward successful performance toward accomplishing goals.

But in good times or bad, riches don't always hold the key. Promote those who made a difference and exemplified the cultural values your organization holds dear. Provide recognition awards and peer group praise to those who contributed to your progress and success. Use career development experiences such as special assignments, education, time off, or flexible hours. Those non-cash rewards are sometimes preferred over money. Just as you continually communicate to your team, continually reward those who enable the pathway to success. And consider this: High-performance teams generally find it motivating when you move out those who couldn't be counted on to hold up their end. That's part of creating a successful team, too.

How did rewards play out for Captain Knowles and his crew? Second Mate John Trehune, as the Oeno camp captain, recognized everyone in the encampment who hunted and gathered to enable survival. Captain Knowles pressed his co-owners of *Wild Wave* for his crew's back wages so he could pay them for transportation to their homes and families once rescued. Praised as "the greatest captain of them all," he played the role of humble servant and passed recognition to his first and second mates, along with the ship's passengers and crew. Sharing recognition and praise with his fellow castaways added to his appeal as an extraordinary leader. It bred loyalty from all directions: passengers, crew, peers, ship owners, the press, and the general public. Clearly, this helped him advance.

At the end of the day, incentive programs that include wealth and recognition will keep your team's execution continually focused on achieving the organization's goals. There is an innate human need to be appreciated. Sharing wealth and recognition not only reinforces the desired behavior, it establishes a following of strong contributors. Captain Knowles' crew stayed with him from voyage to voyage. Among the rewards was the opportunity to advance.

In addition, Captain Knowles provided visibility, praise, and recognition within the maritime community. He made recommendations that helped his passengers and crew alike continue to advance in their fields. Both John Trehune and James Bartlett became sea captains themselves. Some of the crew continued as highly sought-after members of the maritime community, becoming second or first mates, and later captains, too. Others became maritime instructors or consultants; many moved to other walks of life. All were favored by being branded as *Wild Wave* survivors.

Next, you'll meet modern-day leaders who have lessons to teach business leaders, just as Captain Knowles has done.

SECTION III

Stories of the ABCs to Advance in Action

Interview questions:

✳ How did you get to be the person you are? What's your story?

✳ What was your career progression before joining this organization?

✳ What was the situation before you entered the organization that led to its issues?

✳ What attracted you to this situation when many would run away?

✳ How did you hatch the plan to address this situation?

✳ Once the plan was hatched, how did you align your team to kick off the plan?

✳ With the game plan hatched and kicked off, what was your approach to execute?

✳ What obstacles did you encounter along the way? How did you deal with them?

✳ What was the end result of the execution?

✳ What's your reflection as you look back?

✳ How did the experience help you advance?

6

Peter J. Boni:
Back From the Brink at Safeguard Scientifics

"Keep pounding away and the
breaks will come."

✳ How did you get to be the person you are? What's your story?

Three things stand out: 1) a dysfunctional childhood, 2) a formal education, and 3) military combat experience.

Surviving a Dysfunctional Childhood

Between first grade and the start of high school, I bounced into and out of 11 different schools in several states. This created constant change and upheaval in my schooling and living circumstances. To adjust, I learned to build a sort of order within myself in the midst of all that disruption.

Image 6.1: Peter J. Boni. Photo copyright Safeguard Scientifics. Used with permission.

My father, a talented tool and die maker, chased defense contracts for a living. I was a working-class city kid, first in East Boston, then in the South Side of Chicago. Our family also shuttled to southern states a couple of times. Like chickens, little boys have a pecking order about them. The new kid on the block has to fight his way to school. Tiring of fighting, I learned to be charming to avoid the fight. However, if it had to be, I could be pre-emptive and go after a bully on my terms.

When I turned 11, my father got sick and couldn't work for the remaining four years of his life. Our family had no money coming in, and I mean *no* money. My mother was highly resourceful; on what sale rack or in which second-hand store she found my clothes, I'll never know. At 11, I started to notice girls. But what girl would ever look at me wearing what I was wearing? I was embarrassed. I needed to make my own money to buy my own clothes, yet who would hire an 11-year-old and for what amount of money?

When he was healthy, my father welcomed me to his basement work-bench so he could teach me to use his tools. Both creative and mechanical, he had various tools, including six different screwdrivers for six different kinds of screws. He had small, medium, and large hammers, big-headed or small-headed nails, long or short nails, various wood or metal saws, chisels, planes, two vices, and wrenches for different-sized nuts and bolts.

I hated everything about woodworking! His small motor skills were as graceful as a ballerina's; mine were as clunky as a chain saw. My mechanical aptitude was as big as his smallest nail. To make a living, he said, I had to figure out how to use these things. Something inside me said I could sell whatever anyone made, but I had no aptitude for or interest in making anything myself.

In whatever backyard we had, my father was a passionate gardener. Too many tomatoes and other fruits and vegetables always spilled from his bountiful garden for our small circle of family and friends to consume. At 6 years old, not a bit shy, I'd put this excess garden booty in a basket, knock on doors around the neighborhood, and sell the fruits and vegetables. I asked my mother how much they charged at the grocery store for them. She said, "Well, the store gets 25 cents for a good tomato. You should charge 15 or 20 cents." I protested. No way! Dad's tomatoes were so much better, bigger, riper, and sweeter. I saw how he nurtured them—the planting, fertilizing, watering, and protecting them from predators required knowhow and passion. Therefore, I should ask *more* than the quarter the store charges. Plus, I'm *delivering* the goods!

My mother and I settled on my charging the same price as the grocery store for his superior fruits and vegetables, delivered. Out the door I went, basket in hand. My father's jaw dropped at what he termed my "moxie." Without saying it, he and I both realized I'd make my own way in this world without working with my hands. To this day, I respect and appreciate those who do.

With that as my business background, at 11 years old, I took the bus to the wholesale district on Maxwell Street on Chicago's South Side. I was armed with my stash of birthday and Christmas cash, and accompanied by a few friends for advice and muscle. We had an adventure dodging the alcohol-laden, unwashed bums on the wrong side of the tracks.

I bought caseloads of varying household trinkets—gardening supplies, hand hoes, flower, plant, or vegetable seeds, whiskbrooms—you name it. Equipped with my army of sixth-grade boys to carry a half-dozen cumbersome boxes back home on the bus (what a sight that must have been), we repackaged the goods in my living room. In that moment, I had no notion I was starting a business; I was simply creating a job for myself and money for my family.

Those days, stores always carried large quantities, and I heard my parents complain about buying more than they needed. So I used a non-familiar formula: specialty low-cost packaging and the convenience of door-to-door delivery in small quantities. I'd even take custom orders. I repackaged the goods with a half or a quarter of the content local retailers offered, and I charged a per-unit premium.

A Young Entrepreneur

Picture a motivated, poorly dressed 11-year-old walking door to door with a basket of goods in the local neighborhood and adjacent areas about 25 hours a week after school and on weekends. Back then, before having two income earners was common in families, someone always answered the door. Due to sales and depleted inventory, I went back and forth to Maxwell Street on the bus often. I stood my ground with a tough crew of grown men to buy my merchandise at prices that gave me a profit. I struck up positive relationships with my suppliers as an entertaining cash customer. I shared what I was doing and why, and I asked for their help. I must have touched a soft spot in this hardened, crusty group of wholesalers, as they gave me advice on repackaging and the right quality of goods to buy and resell. (Note to self: *Always ask for help when I need it. People give it willingly.*)

Lo and behold, I finished the month with what seemed to be real money, back in the day when a hundred bucks was closer to a thousand in buying power. I bought my father new shaving gear and my mother a skirt and blouse. And I had enough to buy myself a wardrobe at Marshall Field.

That set up my first date. Cute, freckled Debbie trooped with me on the bus to Marshall Field to take advantage of the after-Easter sale. She helped me make the right clothing selections for my mother, and I bought Debbie a "thank you" prize of Frango mints. Later that week, I took my cadre of friends out for an ice cream soda party to thank them for helping me target and repackage my product lines. I had risen to hero status. (Note to self: *Always recognize those who help me.*) I finished with a $20 stash of cash to tuck away, double the $10 I had when I started.

I repeated this simple formula after again noticing what adults complained about. When Christmas came, I took half my stash ($10) and returned to Maxwell Street to visit a stationery wholesaler. There I bought a whole carton with several hundred Christmas cards. I had noticed that, when the adults wrote out their Christmas cards, they were always short a few. Cards purchased individually were expensive; the alternative was to buy packages of 10 or 20 and get stuck with too many. So I repackaged the Christmas cards as a five pack and knocked on doors during the last two weeks before Christmas. Several in my cadre of sixth graders acted as sales agents in their neighborhoods. I gave them half of the profit on every box they sold. Success!

My $10 turned into $50 so I could afford my holiday outfit, a few Christmas gifts, and then some. I did the same over Valentine's Day, only to be humbled and disappointed. Sales were so low; I had enough leftover Valentine's Day cards to cover my personal needs for the next four years. Adults didn't send out Valentine's Day cards like kids did! (Note to self: *Have a better handle on the target market.*)

One or more of my friends must have told my teacher, Mrs. Kane, about these escapades. After class one day, she commented on my being an entrepreneur. "Entrepreneur? What's that?" I had no idea. I thought it meant I was well dressed.

"Oh Peter," she said. "Go look that up." I did. It's no small wonder I made a living all those years later by bonding with those who designed and made things. I had an internal sense to package, price, go to market, get positioned competitively, and scale my activities. Along the way, I learned to lead. I eventually applied these traits to the science and technology industries where chaos, confusion, upheaval, and disruption reigned due to rapid growth and constant change. That suited me well, with big thanks to learning how to survive a seemingly dysfunctional childhood.

Gaining a College Education

In spite of the constant disruption in my schooling, I excelled in school. That was important to my father, so it became extremely important to me. He often related a story of how he had run out of money and never finished his Depression-era mechanical engineering education. I became keenly aware that a tool and die maker, even as a highly skilled machinist, falls subject to all the economic whims resulting from a recession's impact on production. As part of the production crew, he was subject to the layoffs that come with lower-tier production schedules. What a major effect that had on his life—and on mine, I thought at the time. "This won't happen to me," I resolved.

Thanks to that influence, coupled with being in the same high school from start to finish, a peer group of fellow athletes and scholars, plus mentoring, scholarships, loans, and my own work ethic, I graduated from the University of Massachusetts at Amherst. Armed with a psychology major, a management minor, and a growing interest in high-performance team dynamics, I felt ready to conquer the world. That college diploma—the first among those in my working-class family to receive one—has opened more doors for me than I ever could have imagined.

Experiencing Life-Altering Combat in Vietnam

I graduated from college with what some might term the unfortunate luck and timing of being draft-eligible at the height of a war. The U.S. Army had other plans for when I might start to pursue my own ambitions. What were my choices in the aftermath of the 50,000 to 60,000 men per month draft call resulting from the Vietnam War's escalation, thanks to the Tet Offensive in 1968? I could go into the Army, go to Canada, or go to jail. Run that by me again! What were those choices? Being an American, Canada as a choice was out. And I had no interest in spending time in prison. So the Army became my only rational choice.

Why let some stupid lieutenant kill me? I knew where I was going. I took the officer's test and went to Infantry Officers Candidate's School (OCS) in Ft. Benning, Georgia, to become a lieutenant myself. My 10 months of training included weaponry, strategy, tactics, martial arts, navigation through jungle and mud (Georgia is the home of the Oki Fanokee Swamp), mountaineering, parachute jumping— all complete with physical and mental stress. Succeeding through more of the extremely taxing training required what training officers called "Socratic Resolve." They were referring to Socrates' quotation: "Nothing in the world will take the place of persistence. Talent will not. The world is filled with unsuccessful men with talent. Education will not. Nothing is more common than an educated derelict. Genius will not. Unrewarded genius is almost a proverb. It is persistence and determination alone that are omnipotent." Our 200-person OCS class graduated about 100 men, a 50-percent attrition rate.

As reported in *The Army Times* in 1968, casualty rates for Regimental Infantry Lieutenants in combat were alarming. However, the casualty rates for Special Operations Infantry Officers were lower in a statistically meaningful way. That might seem counterintuitive, sure, but I took statistics at college. Special Ops wasn't a place where anyone could simply volunteer. You had to apply, be tested, qualify, get recommended, and pass even more rigorous training. Thankfully, I earned that opportunity. My first duty assignment was in Ft. Bragg, North Carolina, the home of the JFK Center for Special Warfare, where I specialized in Psychological Operations (PSYOPS). That saved my life, and, to a degree, defined it. How? It defined my sense of teamwork—that is, working with highly competent people covering each other's backs to accomplish the mission at hand.

So feeling exceptionally well prepared, off I went to war. Deep inside, I was a scared kid—well trained but so very scared. We were all scared kids doing what we could for each other in the name of "the mission."

Strategy: Win Hearts of Villagers

I spent 15 months winning hearts and minds in remote, jungle-embedded villages along the Ho Chi Minh Trail, on both sides of the Vietnamese/Cambodian border. I often worked alongside CIA paramilitary, with units from the 25th Infantry Division providing security around the villages. We were tasked to make friends with the locals, gather intelligence about where the bad guys were, and then seek them out. This tactic was known at the time as "search and destroy." Our strategy involved disrupting both the enemy's supply chain and the morale of its people.

How difficult would it be to win hearts and minds in Iron-Age villages on the edge of thickly vegetated jungle where defoliating airdrops of Agent Orange fell and sometimes missed the intended targets?

Here's how I was trained to approach this. Upon entering a village, I would determine if it was friendly and then seek out the village chief (essentially the mayor). We learned if a village was friendly or hostile by seeing the demeanor of the children. If they came up to the GIs with smiles and joy, it was friendly. If they were shy or didn't approach, the village was likely to be hostile. I remember in one unfriendly village amid the stony, black-eyed glares of wary children, its village chief explained that Agent Orange, airdropped two years before, missed its jungle target, striking far too close to the village and killing some of the villagers' crops. A farmer's water buffalo died. A number of villagers were sickened by the accidental spraying. A baby was stillborn. These villagers had been offered no apology or restitution. In fact, no one seemed to know or care.

With that as the backdrop, why should this chief or any of his people embrace the idea of giving U.S. soldiers information about the location or frequency of North Vietnamese supply patrols?

The Army put at my disposal a few-hundred-dollar slush fund in local currency, the Vietnamese Dong. I was held accountable for using that money as restitution or compensation, as I saw fit, to help win hearts and minds. Without admitting any wrongdoing I approached the chief, offered to "make it right," and apologized on behalf of the U.S. Army. I paid him $150 in Dong for the destroyed crops, water buffalo, and general suffering.

My team then began what we called a MEDCAP (Medical Civil Action Program). A medic set up shop on a borrowed table in the village center and attended to varying villagers' ailments with his arsenal of medicines and bandages for rashes, cuts, bruises, coughs, and more. The line of people wanting the medic's attention kept growing throughout the day. I noticed a small, seemingly undernourished 4-year-old boy with a cleft palate. He was shy and unsmiling, with sad, droopy eyes. He stood alone. Members of my team discussed his situation. The Army had teams of plastic surgeons working on wounded GIs. Why couldn't they work on this kid? In a short radio contact, I presented the idea to my colonel. He bought the idea and made arrangements for the boy's surgery. Together, we re-visited that village a couple of days later to meet with the village chief and the boy's parents. We offered a helicopter ride to a Saigon military hospital for the boy's complementary corrective surgery. Offer accepted.

A few months later, when my unit had operations that once again caused us to visit that village, a few dozen cheering children equipped with smiles had their hands out to receive GI gum or candy. Among those kids was a handsome four-year-old boy with bright, clear eyes and an engaging smile. He followed me throughout the village for the remainder of the day. He also held my hand as we walked, and he climbed onto my lap during my visit and discussions with the village chief. The chief looked at the boy glowingly and voiced his admiration. Young Bao's normal-looking lip was ever so slightly scarred. I noticed he had gained weight and grown a couple of inches.

At the village chief's thatched house, my troops traded Army C-rations with the locals for recently prepared Vietnamese cooking—chicken, fish, and rice. Under the guidance of their village chief, villagers talked openly through our interpreter about the comings and goings of enemy supply missions to and from the Cambodian border. I left that village with an appreciation that one could be sensitive, compassionate, and strategic at the same time. Mission accomplished.

In my tour of duty, I achieved a few huge goals I'd set for myself—that is, accomplish my mission with merit while experiencing minimal casualties, including my own. I had no guarantee I'd see my 25th birthday, but I came home with all my arms and legs and also with my head on straight.

The sociological climate in America at the time was not only anti-war; it was openly hostile to anybody in a military uniform. To this day, I'm angry about being attacked by anti-war protesters while at a restaurant in full uniform the day I returned stateside. I buried the whole experience deep inside me and didn't talk about it.

It took me 10 years to realize the impact of that 15-month experience on my psyche and how it would affect my managerial approach. And I came to grasp why casualty rates were so much less for those in Special Ops. We had been given an enormous degree of autonomy combined with the benefit of highly specialized training. Some missions required the precision of a surgeon's knife rather than the bluntness of a sledgehammer. We experienced fewer friendly fire incidents and less collateral damage than other troops. You could say our men were highly motivated, well trained, and equipped with a can-do attitude, with commanders who were better than the average bear.

In the process, I had developed special skills to lead and deal with a team through adversity. I've coined this my "Rice Paddy MBA" in leadership through adversity, learned in a jungle, remote villages, and rice paddies. These skills became the fabric of my managerial and leadership approach. Given that I was an athlete and leader in school, I didn't need to go to war to drive these lessons home.

What was my biggest lesson? That I can't do the seemingly impossible alone. Yes, I learned the power of being collaborative with an elite force of specialists. Our missions were complex, but our collective wisdom bred a superior plan to accomplish any mission. Since then, I know to keep the right mix of high-caliber people in my foxhole. If they're not high caliber—if they can't be trained or don't have the right talent for the task at hand—then it's important to get them out of my foxhole— fast. Professional lives are at stake, including my own.

Collaborative Style

A collaborative style worked well with this elite, expertly trained, highly competent team of people. We had diverse skills, dissimilar backgrounds, and education that ranged from high school to PhDs. We shared a natural sense of dependence and trust as well as a common sense of mission, goals, and purpose.

I learned that high-performance decision-making could happen at all levels within an organization if the mission and goals are well articulated. Within a combat unit, every person understands the meaning of a mission and his or her role to execute a game plan to achieve it. In a combat environment, reality needed to be faced straight-up with a mind-set to think outside the box. I was trained to communicate in a crystal-clear, can-do fashion. I saw firsthand how well-defined roles and responsibilities facilitated well-coordinated timing and precision. And I learned that good leaders enable members of their team to lead as well.

Combat is the most stressful, dynamic, and difficult environment imaginable. You're forced to make choices—life or death decisions, really—without having all the information. Sometimes when the shells are flying, not making a decision is the worst decision you can make. You know that, if you stand still, you'll certainly get shot.

I took the concept of decisiveness under fire into civilian life. I also transferred the moral courage to do the right things, the focus on accomplishing the most important mission-critical things, and an enormous sense of responsibility for the welfare of the team. Those skills—and the perspective I gained by leading a highly competent force through the fear, chaos, and confusion of hostile enemy fire—better prepared me for righting organizations that had run aground.

So many sectors of the worldwide economy are missing an enormous opportunity if they don't seek out those who have recent combat experience in the Middle East. The lessons I learned in Southeast Asia and the accompanying skills are also found in more recent veterans across several countries. Intangible values like duty and honor translate exceptionally well to civilian life. Who else would you want in your foxhole to contribute to your organization?

✳ What was your career progression before joining Safeguard Scientifics?

After the Army, I returned to civilian life, first in sales and marketing, and then progressed to the executive levels of general management. For the first 10 years, I worked within larger companies. Turning points for my career were moving from industrial products to high-technology products, and then moving from large to smaller and mid-sized companies as CEO. I largely advanced by righting disrupted situations or organizations and restoring their growth. Then, after running a half-dozen companies in varying stages of maturity, trouble, and renewal for more than two decades, I applied my skills to private equity and venture capital. (See Chapter 2.)

Fast-forward to 2005 when Safeguard Scientifics sought me out.

✳ What was the situation before you entered the organization that led to its issues?

Safeguard Scientifics was in its sixth decade when I took over as CEO in late 2005. A holding company thought to be on the verge of bankruptcy, it had choking debt and ownership in low-growth business units that were consuming cash that Safeguard didn't have to spare.

Its stock had lost 99 percent of its value after the Internet bubble and September 11th–induced recession. The resulting less-than-$1-per-share stock price and high debt relative to the company's overall net worth—called the debt to equity ratio—jeopardized Safeguard's public listing on the New York Stock Exchange. Most of the business community and the community at large had written Safeguard off as a yesterday company, a loser that might not survive.

The morale was Grand Canyon low; the debt was Mount Kilimanjaro high. At the same time, the aftermath of earlier Enron scandals forced the Sarbanes-Oxley reporting requirements on all publicly traded companies. Safeguard's staff employed Nazi-like tactics to ensure its cadre of majority-owned firms followed these new regulatory and reporting requirements. Hence, Safeguard was highly unpopular within the ranks of its portfolio companies—so unpopular, it was unable to obtain a positive reference from their management. Having a lack of fans didn't bode well for putting new money to work and acquiring interest in any other prospective company.

From Acclaim to Ruin

From its founding in 1953, Safeguard Scientifics acquired ownership interests in a variety of companies, served on boards of directors, and worked to add value to those businesses in some fashion. It then sold its stake in these firms, hopefully at higher values. That replenished the cash coffers and enabled its profit model to fund reinvestment all over again. Some onlookers called the company a publicly traded venture capitalist.

Its five-decade evolution from an industrial products' heritage through a mix of technology industries to an Internet incubator garnered it wealth and acclaim. Its stock grew throughout the 1980s and 1990s from a long-languishing $3 to $5 per share to $100 per share after a 1-for-3 stock split at the height of the Internet bubble. Safeguard's Forbes 400–listed founding CEO never sold one share of his stock; rather, he borrowed against it. He and the company shared the fruits of their wealth through highly visible philanthropy.

But a bubble eventually bursts. And it did! In April 2000, only 30 days after the stock market's March 2000 crest, it burst with reckless abandon. The plummeting stock from the bubble's explosive meltdown left both Safeguard's founder and the company holding a debilitating, unpayable debt. This positioned them at the brink.

In a highly visible move, the board dismissed the founder, who wound up in financial ruin. The press had a field day featuring the demise of an Internet superstar and its portfolio of what they termed "dot bomb" companies. They turned to praise the vision of Federal Reserve Chairman Alan Greenspan for citing "irrational exuberance" and Warren Buffett for disparaging bubble-rich Internet stocks.

Ultimately, Safeguard's board, which included many seeming friends of the founder, resigned one by one. They left in place a new board to figure out what to do. How could they get the company to rebound—if it could rebound at all?

Failed Effort to Rebound

A newly recruited crew on the management team and the board of directors embarked on a majority ownership strategy of a mini-conglomerate. They sold, closed, or combined several of the "dot bombs" and completed a $200 million convertible bond offering to restructure their debt. That enabled Safeguard to acquire majority interest in a group of business services companies.

Naturally, Safeguard was seeking stability after the burst of the bubble. Unfortunately, its new strategy did not achieve the stability the company needed. Service businesses can be especially volatile and tough, especially in a down economy. Therefore, the board's strategy had two unintended consequences.

First, the new service businesses were in low-growth sectors that provided no recurring revenue. They also had high capital equipment requirements during a time of stagnation in the business sector.

Second, the valuation metric for IT services firms, which comprised the majority of Safeguard's reported revenue, was the lowest of all public companies at the time. Wall Street applied a one-size-fits-all valuation method to Safeguard. That put the lowest common denominator of value on Safeguard's overall business. It didn't matter if one third of its revenue came from other types of businesses that held a higher metric of valuation. The value that plummeted after the initial burst took a second plunge.

By 2005, Safeguard Scientifics was considered by onlookers to be an unattractive, dead, or dying company with little free cash, no friends, and no future. Facing a new century, Safeguard the winner had been branded a loser.

✳ What attracted you to this situation when many would run away?

When it comes to disrupted situations, I have a contrarian, disciplined, and enterprising mind-set. My background and experience uniquely gave me the perspective to view this dire situation as an opportunity. After more than two decades as a high-tech CEO repairing companies in varying degrees of disruption, and another decade as a management consultant and venture capital/private equity investor, I seemed to be right for the part. And the part seemed to be right for me.

The company's valuation appeared rock-bottom low. (When the chips are down, the stock market sometimes over-punishes a firm that has run aground.) That overly depressed price per share would be the basis for measuring any repositioning success. It would also be the strike price for any newly issued stock options to me or to my team of talent that needed to successfully reposition it.

I wasn't ready to declare it an impossible situation. I practiced the OODA loop (Orient, Observe, Decide, and Act) learned in the Army to quickly assess the situation. There were a few jewels in this chest of portfolio companies in which Safeguard held mostly majority ownership. If they could be culled and polished, it seemed they would generate sufficient cash returns to enable the gradual retirement of the debt and leave additional cash to reinvest in a more rewarding strategy. What the company needed was that strategy *and* the right team of people to execute it.

Safeguard Partner Companies 2005

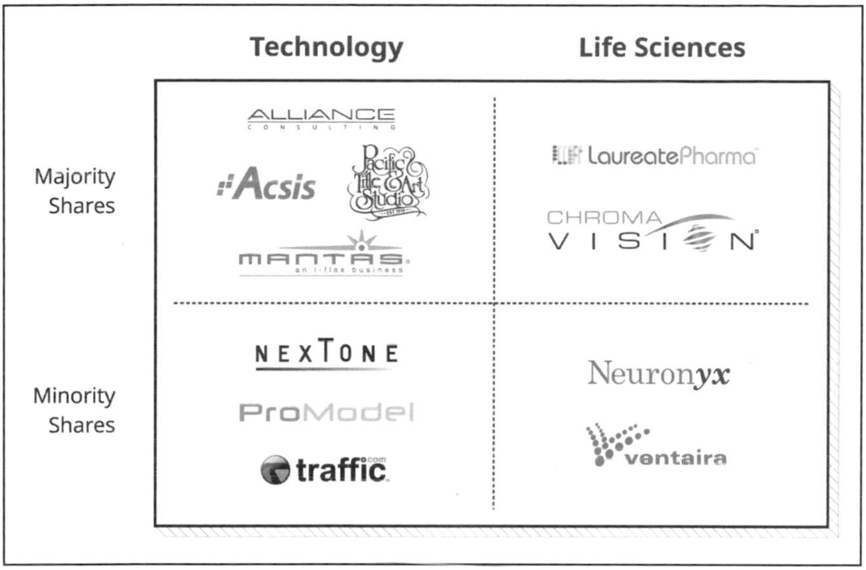

	Technology	Life Sciences
Majority Shares	ALLIANCE CONSULTING ::Acsis Pacific Title & Art Studio MANTAS an i-flex business	LP LaureatePharma CHROMA VISION
Minority Shares	NEXTONE ProModel traffic.com	Neuronyx ventaira

Image 6.2

✳ How did you hatch the plan to address this situation?
Phase 1 of the ABCs: Hatch the Plan

Passion, focus, and people.

Over the years, I have observed three primary attributes that separate successful ventures from those that didn't quite achieve their potential:

First, team members need a passion behind their vision of a compelling value proposition—one that targets a substantially sized constituency.

Second, they need a focus organized around a clearly articulated game plan to deliver that value proposition to that constituency.

Third, they need the right mix of people—rallied and led as a high performance team—to execute that game plan.

If Safeguard Scientifics was to be coaching its portfolio, it had better practice those fundamentals itself and excel at them. What did I do?

I employed the techniques to lead high-performance teams, my "Rice Paddy MBA" to navigate through the adversity at hand, and a successful approach called *The ABCs to Advance.* Using them, we had to kedge off from a serious grounding that was nearly a shipwreck.

A: Ask Questions and Listen; Then Ask for Help

At age 11 while living on Maxwell Street, I asked those around me for help. They helped. This approach worked in the Army, too, and throughout my career. After recruiting help from everyone I met, I asked dozens of questions, took notes, and followed up with more questions and notes. Specifically, I asked people inside and outside the company: current and former employees, company portfolio personnel, shareholders, and stock analysts as well as vendors, bankers, and members of the press. You name them and I asked them!

Sometimes I asked questions one-on-one; other times I asked in groups. My "why" questions were followed by "what" and "how" queries. Their opinions often originated from firsthand assessments about what happened to Safeguard, why, and what to do about it. I call that "collective wisdom on steroids." Collective wisdom kept me alive in combat and has served me well thereafter.

B: Base a Plan on What You Hear and See, or Don't Hear and See

I sorted the many answers to my questions into two groups: the common themes and the outliers. Then I formed a small informal advisory board to help me vet some would-be game plans based on a variety of views. From that exercise, we constructed a game plan that made sense. It became the basis for the plan that was shared with a larger advisory board of thought leaders.

At this point, I saw an organization without consistency or accountability. No one articulated the same plan the same way. People who prospected for and scoped new companies for investment weren't the same ones responsible for making the investment, nor were they responsible for the performance of the companies where Safeguard Scientifics did invest. Thus, the deal team had no ownership in the outcome, and their compensation plan reflected that disconnect.

Whatever the organization thought its strategy might be, I found little passion behind taking majority stakes in low-growth businesses for the sake of stability. Ultimately, those businesses weren't stable at all.

C: Challenge the Sacred Cows or the Status Quo

The sacred cow was the Investment Company Act of 1940 (aka "The 40 Act"). To remain compliant with The 40 Act so the Securities and Exchange Commission (SEC) wouldn't consider Safeguard a regulated investment company (with complex reporting and tax requirements), Safeguard was required to own the majority—more than 50 percent—of each company in its holdings. There was room in The 40 Act for Safeguard to hold non-majority assets, but it was thought these needed to be an extreme exception to the rule. Hence, Safeguard Scientifics was seeking to be a majority owner of its businesses.

How can one find an emerging growth company with a management team or investor group building a hot growth company that's prepared to sell a majority stake at a *lower* valuation? At a *higher* valuation, that was possible. Slow-growth companies with tired investors and management looking to sell out for a lower price could be found. But those types of firms were the kind that Safeguard already owned. No big value-uplift available there. In addition, there were extremely high-potential investment opportunities that were so costly (based on strict adherence to The 40 Act), they were unaffordable to the likes of Safeguard.

That majority ownership interpretation of The 40 Act was the sacred cow that needed challenging.

To examine this sacred cow, we contracted a law firm specializing in the Investment Company Act of 1940. That led to our evaluating every conceivable business model. Should Safeguard continue its operating company path? Should it become a regulated investment company or an asset management company? Could it succeed in a holding company model? Should it take itself private or keep its listing on the stock exchange? What kind of resources would be available to enable success? Would the external environment for that business model enable success?

S: Share the Vision to Create a Collective Energy

I tried the evolving game plan on for size with a handful of those who answered my questions. These "thought leaders" both inside and outside the company could help me spread enthusiasm for the plan. That led to some refinement and buy-in from the team and Safeguard's board of directors, as well as the support of the onlookers. Among the benefits of collective wisdom is a team passionately committed to the plan. Knowing I couldn't execute alone, I wanted the added passion of team members resolved to achieving *their* plan.

Ultimately, we embarked on a holding company strategy to:

* Build value in the few jewels within the legacy businesses,
* Cash out of those businesses when the risk-adjusted timing was optimum, and
* Use the resulting capital to gradually retire the debt and make new investments.

"Cashing out" meant finding an exit path for our ownership, either by selling a company outright or by taking it public, most likely through an initial public offering (IPO).

Rather than buying only majority stakes, we sought to acquire "influential" stakes. That was further defined to be ownership of more than 20 percent, where Safeguard Scientifics would be the largest institutional shareholder. For instance, if Safeguard owned 25 percent of a firm, then Safeguard would occupy 25 percent of that firm's board or have 25 percent of the voting rights.

We would seek those stakes in firms at varying stages of growth. This would include a selected few that were pre-revenue and preparing to go to market, some at initial revenue, others expanding after capturing market adoption, and those gaining high traction as early market leaders. If exits would help drive value, then being able to either enter or exit a business at any stage in which value could be realized was integral to the game plan.

We would add value by providing operational support as well as capital in these firms with greater growth potential and higher valuation metrics but lower capital equipment requirements. The firms would have the potential to generate oversized returns.

We would target segments in healthcare and technology industries, industries that tend to be counter-cyclical. That means when one industry is on a roll with premium valuations and mergers and acquisitions (M&A) activity, the other tends to level off. If the driver of Safeguard's value was IPO and M&A activity, why not be balanced? The healthcare and technology industries were synonymous to product lines. The ownership stake in any company was synonymous to a product within a product line. When a company was sold for a profit, therein was the business profit model.

Both industries also played well into the operational background of the team and the eastern U.S. geography. That's where the name Safeguard Scientifics was in its sixth decade and it had earned a branded footprint. Dusting the tarnish off a formerly strong brand is far less costly than building an entirely new brand.

By distilling this collective wisdom into bulleted action steps, we shared this game plan both inside and outside the company. We prepared to kick off the plan and then its execution. We motivated many people by the mere fact of having a game plan, let alone a cogent plan.

✳ Once the plan was hatched, how did you align your team to kick off the plan?

Phase 2 of the ABCs: Kick Off the Plan

> "If you don't know where you're going, any road will take you there."
>
> —Chinese proverb

A: Act Boldly to Kick Off the Game Plan

The deal teams were immediately reorganized along industry lines: healthcare and technology. I gave them cradle-to-grave accountability. Each team was tasked to:

* Find the prospective firm where we wanted to put our money,

* Negotiate and close the deal,

* Guide the business through its evolution and performance, and

* Ultimately return cash to Safeguard via well-timed, more valuable exits.

The exits could come as an IPO or, more likely, an outright acquisition. Safeguard's legal, financial, and operational support staff was available to assist where needed.

The board's compensation committee approved a compensation program that properly rewarded a deal leader's achievement of building and realizing value. It recognized portfolio performance versus goals, cash returns back to Safeguard, and the impact those returns had on the price of Safeguard's stock. That was a competitively important component because it helped me attract and retain the best and the brightest.

Rather than employ financially trained investors as key talent (e.g., many venture capital and private equity investors), Safeguard would have a composite of people with C-level operational skills. This included former healthcare and technology industry CEOs, CFOs, and heads of sales, marketing, technology, and the like. Other investors sitting on portfolio company boards might cite a case study they read in business school when a portfolio company was facing an issue. Safeguard's people on boards could cite the scars of experience on their backs, making it possible for them to coach a firm facing issues or help them avoid potential issues.

With the right mix of people in place, we were almost ready to kedge off. But first, to get everyone on the same page, I organized an October off-site meeting for Safeguard's top dozen people. This would kick off my third month since I started with the company. First on the agenda was a team-building exercise to highlight the benefits of collective wisdom. Why? We didn't have two years to agree on a plan; we only had two days.

B: Build on Strengths

Even in a down-and-out situation, strengths rise to the top. In Safeguard's case, some strengths were found within the ranks of the company. Certain people on that team had the right background and skill sets to execute the game plan and were already inside the company. I promoted one insider to head the deal team's technology sector. With his solid background, experience, skill, and mind-set, he was up to the challenge. He also had the support of people both within Safeguard and inside its technology companies. We recruited deal team talent from the outside in the healthcare sector at first and then from the software sector a bit later.

A key strength and differentiator would be the operational component of the game plan, the operational resources to lend a hand, and the operational background and experience of Safeguard's people. Which would an entrepreneur prefer to have on board: an ex-CEO who had firsthand experience of the challenges faced by an entrepreneurial management team, or a 30-year-old Ivy League MBA armed with case study knowledge? By coming to the table with more value than just the cash, we believed Safeguard Scientifics could be far more attractive as a real business partner.

As noted, Safeguard's holdings included a handful of jewels. We put our focus behind the few companies in the portfolio where we believed value would be created. We worked with each business unit to clearly articulate and share its game plan to grow value. We upgraded some of our portfolio managers and added staff where it would make a difference. We sought to sell or close portfolio companies in which their value was scant, at best.

We identified the branded footprint of Safeguard Scientifics as a strength. After five-plus decades as a public company, it would take far less time and cost to polish a tarnished brand than build an entirely new one. Safeguard touted a number of noteworthy successes. For example, an early investment in fledgling Jerrold Electronics morphed into what became Philadelphia-headquartered media giant Comcast. An early investment spawned multi-media retailer QVC, now part of

John Malone's Liberty Media empire. Novell, Cambridge Technology Partners, Internet Capital Group (now Actua), Kanbay, DocuCorp, and a host of other highly prominent and valuable global technology firms were all Safeguard success stories.

Innovation was part of Safeguard's branded footprint. Its use of a subscription rights offering or selected stock placement was responsible for some highly acclaimed IPOs in the 1980s, 1990s, and early 2000s. That was before the bubble burst and Wall Street changed its rules.

We treated Safeguard's Mid-Atlantic geography as a strength. Historically, whatever venture capital the region attracted tended to come from outside the region. But Safeguard was a regional insider, and the healthcare industry was a prominent contributor to the regional GDP. More and more technology businesses were spawning around healthcare and financial services industries, which were also prominently featured within the region. Digital media firms were disrupting old media firms— also located in the Mid-Atlantic! Therefore, why go to Silicon Valley or Route 128 to compete with other venture capitalists who have their own regional-branded footprint? Besides, enterprise software concerns with a cloud computing business model were setting up shop where the enterprise customers were located, largely on the East Coast.

C: Control Through Visible Measurement

Working with each business within the portfolio, we identified the key momentum indicators for each business unit. When placed on a digital dashboard, it was visible to see whether the business was making progress executing its own game plan or having issues. Visibility breeds accountability. Various graphs, charts, posters, and digital communications made every measurement visible.

Based on the goals we developed at the strategic off-site (more information is in the next section), the team identified several metrics germane to the tasks at hand to successfully reposition Safeguard. The goal: to become a winner for the next decade of the new century. The event helped focus our activity on the things that mattered most. With finite resources, we couldn't expend energy that didn't matter to the desired outcome.

These metrics remained visible throughout our repositioning efforts. At every weekly staff meeting, every monthly operations review, and every quarterly off-site gathering, we reviewed where we stood, gauging our performance against these momentum indicators. We did the same thing for each of our portfolio companies.

Once again, visibility breeds accountability.

S: Streamline the Activity Schedule

Vision, mission, and elevator pitch

At the off-site meeting, we started by wordsmithing the vision statement, our charter, and a 60-second elevator pitch. We delivered the elevator pitch the following week to every person in the company, including members of the board of directors. We then tested them to memorize it and recite it verbatim. I've learned that messaging is more powerful when everyone in an organization says the same thing about what it does and how it does it. That's as true in Safeguard's 30-person organization (including its 12-person deal team) as it is in a 300,000-person organization. Everyone referred to Safeguard as the catalyst to build great companies.

Competitive positioning and targeting strategy

To summarize, we defined, validated, and agreed on our positioning and targeting strategy. We refined our competitive positioning and our go-to-market strategy versus venture capital or private equity firms and strategic buyers. Then we visualized that positioning and differentiation in a diagram.

Safeguard was set to provide more operational savvy support to its companies than a traditional venture capital or private equity investor. In the traditional scenario, if a management team and its investor group sold to a strategic buyer, the monetary upside was usually left behind, although they did benefit from having operational support from the acquiring company.

Choosing Safeguard Scientifics as an investor in a company enabled managers of that company to pocket the uplift in the company's worth as it built value while also gaining operational support. For shareholders,

Safeguard's stock ownership provided far more liquidity to its investors than the traditional venture capital or private equity investor, called Limited Partners, or LPs. Safeguard investors could buy as little or as much stock as they wanted on the public exchange, sell it at any time, and buy back in again if they chose. By comparison, the LP had to be qualified, commit a large sum of cash, and wait several years to see the money returned—hopefully with a profit.

Safeguard Competitive Positioning

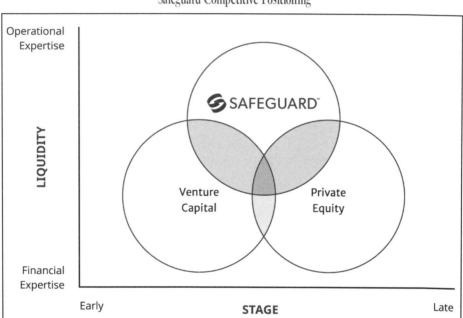

Image 6.3.

To lead our future growth, we targeted very specific segments of the healthcare and technology industries that were higher in growth and valuation metrics but lower in cash consumption. Through front-end research, we identified five strategic themes that were driving growth in both industries. The defined growth drivers were maturity, migration, convergence, compliance, and cost containment.

Our population is maturing; so is the IT infrastructure. Information technology is converging into healthcare products and services.

Also converging are therapeutics, diagnostics, and medical devices. Regulatory compliance is driving buying behavior, and cost containment is the watchword across the gamut of industries. Given all of these factors, it was far easier to grow the company with the wind at our back.

Primary goals (the BHAGs) to focus the energy

At our off-site meeting, we strove to become the perceived winner for the next decade of the new century and outlined three BHAGs (big, hairy, audacious goals)—a term coined by Jim Collins, author of *Good to Great*—to drive our activities.

Our first BHAG was meant to restore lost value to shareholders, to achieve a $1 billion market cap. Because the valuation at the time was less than $100 million, that 10x increase seemed like a tall order. After a 99-percent decline, however, a 10x increase wasn't so out of reach.

Our second BHAG was meant to restore Safeguard's reputation within its portfolio of companies. How could it compete to acquire new interests if its current portfolio saw no added value in its relationship with Safeguard Scientifics? We sought to be 100 percent referenceable. But we had to ask: "100 percent is up from what?" and "How do we measure it?" So we engaged a firm to do a survey that put metrics around Safeguard's performance and perception of adding value within its portfolio. The first measure came up below 50 percent—a failing F grade. Pretty poor! But that became our baseline to measure improvement.

The third BHAG was meant to restore employee and constituency pride in Safeguard, which the business community had largely written off. A more qualitative goal was to be recognized as a winner by the second decade of the new century.

Critical success factors to prioritize the actions

For every BHAG, we had to define its critical success factors by functional area. What did we absolutely have to do? The answers guided our actions. It also enabled a further skill-sets assessment and resource allocation that would ensure the right skills were present to accomplish those critical success factors.

To grow Safeguard's value and come close to that $1 billion target, we deemed it critical to grow the value of the companies we currently owned. We could then realize that cash value through an outright sale or an initial public offering. Of the 11 firms in the portfolio, that opportunity existed for only three. But all three had hair on them that needed to be combed with a steel instrument. The remainder would be closed or packaged and sold at the first opportunity. Substance over style ruled the day.

Ultimately, Safeguard Scientifics needed to apply new money to build highly successful winning companies that would generate outsized returns. We realized two additions to the deal team's talent bench needed to be identified and recruited. We opted to leverage outside talent by developing an Entrepreneur or Executive in Residence (EIR) program that would hire experienced and accomplished part-timers looking for a company to run. Their task would be to work within the deal teams to find, qualify, and close exciting new opportunities.

We also had to provide shareholders with more transparency by making opportunities for growth visible to them. This meant continually highlighting our progress via a steady flow of what we called "momentum indicators"—not only for ourselves but within the companies that made up our portfolio. The valuation metrics used by Wall Street to determine value had to be higher than the lowest of the low. Due to Safeguard's high concentration of IT services revenue, the lowest of the low was the current valuation metric.

The individual to institutional shareholder ratio was 75 percent to 25 percent. Many shareholders were angry holdovers from the bubble's burst, whereas institutional holders were mostly short-term-minded hedge funds. We needed a complete shift to 75-percent long-term institutional holders. A following among certain stock analysts would help attract those targeted shareholders.

To become 100-percent referenceable, Safeguard needed to provide coaching, guidance, and support to its companies. Highly referenceable partners are collaborative, not dictatorial. They help the company, not just themselves.

We needed to alter the entire approach of building value in our company. To achieve mutual goals, it had to be far more collaborative and helpful going forward. This was in contrast to totally relying on the limited inside resources of a 12-person deal team and a 30-person holding company. So to accomplish a turnabout from a failing grade, it became critical to assemble a high-quality advisory board. Members of this board would interact with us, our portfolio of companies, and even our prospective companies. Their collective wisdom, Rolodex, and industry knowledge, we believed, would make a significant difference in our attaining a 100-percent grade. They might even provide Safeguard Scientifics with additional competitive advantages and differentiation.

That responsibility rested with the deal teams. Both the healthcare and technology teams went to work to recruit the right mix of people and set up ways to put their talents to use.

Launch a communications program

To be considered a winner in the new century, we deemed it critical to not only garner a few successes but to launch a targeted communications program aimed at several constituents. So Safeguard targeted the healthcare and technology industry segments, which were the source of outbound deal flow due to our own outreach. We targeted the venture capital or private equity players where our would-be syndication partners and farmland for inbound deal flow would reside. The public stock market's attitudes about Safeguard Scientifics spilled over into the perception of the community at large. The investor relations component, critical to the success of achieving the $1 billion BHAG, had a larger role in the third BHAG.

If perception is the ultimate reality, we needed to form and properly staff a corporate communications program that could integrate the entirety of this messaging to all these targets in coordinated fashion. That required a personnel change to staff a new department with these critical success factors defined as its mission.

We reduced this exercise to a matrix presentation document that we shared with our whole staff, the board, and key outsiders who signed non-disclosure statements. We considered this step an extension of sharing the vision to create a collective energy. It created the ultimate road map to prevent distraction from working on anything that wasn't critical to survival and our eventual successful repositioning.

Define and reinforce the culture

We asked ourselves what kind of work environment we wanted and what would be best for our extensive portfolio. Successful science and technology firms claimed a few common cultural traits we wanted for ourselves: *quality, innovation, action-orientation, responsiveness to customer needs,* and *respect for the individuality of the workforce* (called QuAICRR, and pronounced like a duck's quack.)

Then we defined *quality* as the caliber of our people and our approach. Innovation was termed as new and different versus more and better. Thinking outside the box was okay. Paralysis by analysis was unacceptable. We had to decide and do it. Our customer was our portfolio, which we deemed a "Partner Company." What did any company need from us?

As part of the revitalized culture, we wanted Safeguard to be a fun place to work where everyone could be themselves and feel comfortable. It had to have a high-performance personality and set an example for our Partner Companies. They'd be encouraged to define the cultural norms that would enable their own achievements.

Conscious of the attributes found in high-performance teamwork, we worked to put them into practice within Safeguard Scientifics. We wanted to set the teamwork example for our portfolio, including swift conflict resolution. Of course, we were bound to disagree from time to time, but we were committed to find solutions, make compromises, and then move on to the next set of issues.

Compensation plans circled around the concept of the "three musketeers": all for one and one for all. We'd share both our victories and our defeats as a team.

✳ With the game plan hatched and kicked off, what was your approach to execute?

Phase 3 of the ABCs: Execute the Plan

"It's better to lead from behind and put others in front, especially when you celebrate victory when nice things occur. You take the front line when there is danger. Then the people will appreciate your leadership."

—Nelson Mandela

A: Assert Yourself at Focal Point

In the kickoff phase, it was important to act boldly. Any time I've been tentative, I've been hurt. The same holds true as we executed the plan. I learned in my days in uniform that dogged resolve to overcome obstacles make or break missions. A battle plan *must* apply proper force. If conditions on the ground significantly change, the battle plan must be quickly assessed and adjusted if need be. If not, then it's critical to aggressively assert yourself and you're likely to win.

At Safeguard Scientifics, we notched some early wins, faced plenty of challenges, endured a few defeats, made mid-course adjustments, and nurtured our team to get through the rough spots. It wasn't easy. But it was fun.

The impact of early wins

Among Safeguard's majority-owned companies was Laureate Pharma, a bioprocessing manufacturing-outsourcing company that Safeguard had bought in its entirety for $25 million in 2004. It was a startup that spun off from a divesting parent company. The purchase included two manufacturing facilities. Laureate provided outsourcing services to drug companies that had no manufacturing capacity. With little revenue and few customers, Laureate couldn't use two complex bioprocessing manufacturing facilities. Safeguard's CFO seized the opportunity through his Rolodex and sold one of the manufacturing plants for $25 million. With that immediate cash return, the cost of

Laureate Pharma became zero—not a bad basis for measuring a rate of return when the business could be divested.

It was December 2005. I had only been on the job for four months.

Companies sold to build cash reserves

Mantas was a majority-owned analytics software firm whose technology Safeguard purchased from a defense contractor in 2001. Its management team commercialized the business by focusing the technology on fraud detection applications that targeted both the financial services and telecommunications markets. While growing at a double-digit percentage, profitability remained distant.

Recognizing that the post–9/11 Patriot Act mandated anti-money laundering requirements, we opted to divest the telecommunications component of the business. We focused our efforts on enabling compliance of anti–money laundering laws. Global financial giants such as Goldman Sachs, Allianz, and a "who's who" roster standardized Mantas' product line. The business grew to $35 million rapidly and began earning 20-percent pre-tax margins.

We hired an investment banker to test the waters for a sale. Oracle determined this business was strategic to its interest to increase its own penetration in the financial services sector. Its $127 million cash purchase of Mantas in 2006 gave Safeguard Scientifics $88 million for its majority ownership. The price was nearly double the market valuation metrics for other perpetual-license software firms at the time. We signed those papers quickly.

Traffic.com was a carryover from Safeguard's "dot bomb" portfolio, but this one was a real business. It gathered and localized traffic data for drivers and gave them updates via the Internet and over the vehicle's GPS system. Safeguard held less than a 5-percent stake and wasn't highly engaged with the company. Traffic.com realized a successful IPO and then was quickly acquired by GPS leader NavTek. It was then swallowed by the Swedish mobile telecommunications darling at that time, Nokia. Safeguard booked a small amount of cash in the transaction. Victory has many fathers. Safeguard took a bow and moved on.

Pacific Title and Arts Studio (Pac-Title) was a Hollywood-based film production facility with a 70-year heritage of servicing film studio requirements. Safeguard Scientifics had acquired 100 percent of it when Pac-Title made an early move to enable the digitization of film.

Pac-Title had garnered a stellar reputation within the Hollywood ranks. However, without a recurring revenue stream, it was always scrambling for new work to pass the breakeven point. Its market was narrowly defined and small. Each new order came with an oversized capital equipment requirement that consumed whatever positive cash Pac-Title generated. Then in 2007, the Hollywood Academy of Motion Pictures recognized Pac-Title's leading-edge service with a coveted Oscar for Technical Achievement in Film. With that recognition in hand, Safeguard's operational team found a $16 million cash buyer for Pac-Title a few months later.

These early exits infused $130 million of cash into Safeguard within 18 months. That funded the acquisition of "influential" stakes in several new and exciting companies in healthcare (diagnostics, medical devices, specialty pharma, and IT healthcare) and technology (digital media, financial technology, and enterprise software, all with cloud computing business models). These offered exciting possibilities.

Business growing to ripeness

While the investments in the new portfolio were gaining market traction, the performance of Safeguard's majority-owned legacy IT consulting company, Alliance Consulting Group, responded to its management's focus on financial services and pharmaceutical markets. The business grew from $50 million to more than $125 million in revenue. It posted modest earnings, making it ripe enough for a sale at the prevailing lower valuation metrics for that type of business. At that point, we hired an investment banker to find a buyer.

At the same time, Safeguard Scientifics worked with Laureate Pharma's team to further focus its competitive positioning. Initially, Laureate was losing the sale to prospective new customers more frequently than winning them. After a win-loss analysis and further study of competitors, we found an underserved niche—drug companies that were either in clinical trial or in the early stages of market release. Companies like this often required specialty packaging and lower volumes. That is where Laureate would focus in order to differentiate itself from its bigger competitors. Because most of the competitors in the drug manufacturing industry had been high-volume commoditized solutions with little packaging customization, the focus Laureate had on a new, well-defined market niche enabled its rapid growth en route to profitability. As its revenue grew from nothing to nearly $30 million, the company made money and became nicely positioned for a valuable exit.

My back-of-the-envelope calculation indicated we could fetch $150 million for both Laureate and Alliance. That by itself could be used to pay down some of our debt coming due by 2011. It would also provide funds for further investments to build a new portfolio.

Safeguard owned 60 percent of Chromovison Medical Systems, a medical imaging company that targeted cancer diagnostics firms. Chromovision went prematurely public because of an earlier Safeguard rights offering to enable its IPO. The company's product line was technically viable, but the market was too narrow a niche. How do you grow to become a $100 million business when you dominate a $10 million niche? But rather than treating the company like a dog and selling it, we had another idea. We would reposition the business.

Chromovision's newly recruited CEO, Ronnie Andrews—a strong leader who built a dedicated and passionate corporate culture—pivoted the company to reposition the imaging technology. Rather than selling equipment to cancer diagnostics firms, Chromovison became a cancer diagnostics firm itself. It had a new target audience of medical practitioners.

Ronnie and his newly recruited head of sales targeted a unique distribution channel of community pathologists, a channel that the big competitors LabCorp and Quest were bypassing. They were eager to partner with a firm that could give it a better than fighting chance against the industry giants who were squeezing them out.

Putting breast cancer first, Ronnie expanded Chromovison's product line to include the diagnostics of the five major forms of cancer. It then rebranded the company and changed the name to Clarient. It provided superior service and was the first to offer a FDA-approved image delivered over the Internet. Adding to its value proposition, Clarient embraced novel biomarkers that could personalize the diagnostics with recommended therapies. This produced superior clinical results based on the knowledge of a patient's molecular and protein makeup, popularly termed "personalized medicine."

At that point, Clarient's growth went on a rampage. Its stock moved up from the doldrums and doubled in value. The company divested of the original imaging product line to a $12 million cash buyer so it could further fund and focus efforts on the new core business.

But to continue to feed that pronounced growth, Clarient needed Safeguard's cash infusion via a $25 million loan. Its rapid growth caused financial and operational control issues. Safeguard Scientifics transferred several people from its own operational and financial support staff to Clarient to help keep the wheels on this racing train. Because success breeds a following, bankers gathered around Clarient. Healthcare industry analysts and the trade press began writing about it, and would-be acquirers sought to learn more about the company. It also became known in the trade as a desirable place to work.

With those successes under our belt, our advisory board in full swing, our corporate communications messaging hitting both Wall Street and Main Street audiences, and a few analysts giving Safeguard buy recommendations, the stock nearly tripled. T. Rowe Price, a leading mutual funds company, acquired a long-term stock position, and several others followed. Within 18 months, the company's stock ownership was 50-percent institutional, with a growing cadre of long-term holders.

Team dynamics

Team dynamics within my management ranks weren't all I had hoped they'd be. As a Bostonian, I often quoted famed Celtics' basketball coach Red Auerbach. During the winningest time in the Boston Celtics history during the 1960s, the cigar-chomping coach said in timeless fashion, "They say you use your five best players, but I found you win with the five who fit together the best."

Following that advice, I traded two highly talented and competent people, the CFO and the general counsel, for two highly competent and talented people who meshed markedly better with the others on the team. They produced a far improved chemistry to enable the high-performance teamwork we needed.

Meanwhile, survey data showed that Safeguard's failing grade of referenceability with its portfolio, called "Partner Companies," increased from the failing grade of 50 percent to about 85 percent, a solid B. Improved, but not the 100 percent to which we aspired.

Enabler of entrepreneurship

On another front, the Philadelphia community at large was noticing that this was the dawn of another day for a new Safeguard Scientifics. With Safeguard's corporate philanthropy long dormant, we sponsored an initiative to bring the National Foundation for Teaching Entrepreneurship (since renamed the Network for Teaching Entrepreneurship) into the Philadelphia school system. What better way to reinvigorate a brand than to position Safeguard as a community leader solidly behind the fabric of what it features itself to be—an enabler of entrepreneurship.

Too few organizations, especially fledgling ones, take seriously the responsibility to individual communities. Shareholders, customers, and employees get all the focus and attention. Safeguard's reputation and the community hugely benefitted from its passion and energy focused on improving the lot of poor, inner city kids by sharing its knowledge, its value system, and a bit of its cash. Recognition from the community enhanced the branded footprint of being a perceived winner, not only on its way back but also giving back. Safeguard's people were filled with satisfaction knowing they were making a difference.

Wow, I thought! Not bad for a couple of years of effort. Step aside, people, Safeguard Scientifics is on its way.

✳ What obstacles did you encounter along the way? How did you deal with them?

Nothing prepared any of us for the financial crisis and resulting credit crunch that hit global markets in 2008–2009. What a land mine that put to the test all of our Socratic resolve. Napoleon defined a military genius as "a man who can do the average when all around him are going crazy." That sums up what was happening!

Safeguard's management team navigated this complexity, stayed focused on its goals, thought creatively, and stood toe to toe to overcome so many obstacles during this global meltdown. It was a scary time for everyone. We guided our Partner Companies to:

- ✳ Conserve cash,
- ✳ Operate aggressively and predatorily to gain and hold customers, and
- ✳ Seek accretive, cashless acquisitions to take out weaker competitors.

We certainly needed to give each other a morale boost from time to time, but we all shared ownership in the strategy. We believed that, overall, we were on the right path to achieve our BHAGs, but the external environment was tumultuous.

My public company CEO circle all said the same thing; their boardroom relationships and decision-making experienced the stress and uncertainty of a potential cash crisis and a deteriorating stock value. Add to that fears of a shareholder lawsuit and a half-baked effort to examine strategic alternatives. Times were tense.

Despite these challenges, we'd put together a detailed plan to streamline the activity schedule and define critical success factors to achieving our goals in the kickoff phase. That gave us the focus necessary to overcome the obstacles appearing before us. It took a year to come out the other end of this chaos in a stronger position.

Indeed, success would never follow a straight line.

First Signs of a Slowdown

The sale of Alliance, which looked so promising earlier, looked more and more like a "no sale" as it began to experience falling revenue from the ensuing recession that struck at the heart of its financial services customers. Previously interested parties either lowered the amount they'd be willing to pay or backed out completely.

Safeguard's stock, which showed strong early gains during the early success of its repositioning efforts, felt the pinch along with the rest of the market. The downward pressure accelerated as analysts and investors began their flight for safety. They feared that, with corporate M&A potentially in the doldrums for an undefined period of time and with the credit crunch underway, those with debt on the balance sheets would experience a liquidity crisis. Perhaps these businesses couldn't be sustained at all. Fear, uncertainty, and doubt indeed tend to have negative impacts on Wall Street. At that time, any company with debt on its balance sheet became a leper.

Shareholders and analysts began calling with their pocket calculators in hand. With cash at X, expenses at Y, capital needs for the current vintage of Partner Companies at Z, and the debt coming due in 2011, if there is a standstill in M&A and no credit available, what is Safeguard's plan? Their calculations under that scenario rendered that Safeguard would hit a cash wall. We didn't have a definitive answer, and we needed to develop one fast.

A Bold Response: The Bundle

In the absence of a healthy M&A environment—and with a bunch of cats and dogs left in Safeguard's legacy businesses when I arrived—the "bundle" concept seemed to be worth exploring. Baseball teams enter into bundled trades frequently. That means they bundle the trade riders whose talent isn't deemed critical to the team's current season. They hope to trade that bundle for talent that is deemed essential.

So why couldn't Safeguard do that? It would trade a bundle of companies, anchored by a star, in exchange for a bundle of cash deemed critical for our current situation. The star was Laureate; the others were five legacy firms that Safeguard hadn't yet closed or sold. These firms didn't fit the current strategy and weren't strategic to Safeguard's future. So trying to sell them one at a time, especially in the impossible M&A climate, seemed futile. We had tried with Alliance and failed.

Amid a cadre of skeptics within the team and on the board, I took the lead and knocked on the doors of secondary funds with a basket of firms in hand. To myself, I even nicknamed Laureate my 30-cent tomato. My code name for Alliance was Maxwell, after my childhood visits to the Maxwell Street wholesalers who treated me so well. It took a few months, but not only did that basket of fruit capture interest, it garnered two offers. We signed a term sheet to sell the bundle for $130 million.

Safeguard Partner Companies 2005 —Sold, Closed, or Rebranded

Image 6.4.

Safeguard's general counsel drove the due diligence process and final negotiations with the buyer. These were contentious. Obviously, the financial crisis wasn't a passing downturn; it would become deeper and longer term, bordering on catastrophic. The price of the bundle kept dropping by seven figures each time it was discussed. As a contingency, we entertained conversations with a few firms that had shown interest in acquiring the star, Laureate, on a stand-alone basis. That was what we called our Plan B.

Five months later, the financial markets continued to melt down due to the failure of Lehman Brothers, the credit crunch, and the bailouts of AIG, General Motors, Chrysler, and Fannie Mae and Freddie Mac. Big banks were quaking under pressure with the economy, unemployment, and the housing market in a free fall. Add to that an election of a new president and the stock market dropping 500 points a day, we closed this bundled transaction for a grand value of $106 million. That included Alliance's and Laureate's $30 million of bank debt.

We didn't have to resort to Plan B.

Shareholder Pressure During the Financial Crisis

Our back was off the cash wall, so to speak, and we had cogent answers to the X, Y, and Z calculation questions regarding cash. Liquidity and survival were no longer immediately questionable. But in the background, global financial markets were in turmoil. Safeguard Scientifics had shown it could build value in the legacy businesses and yield cash. But it was too soon to show that its team could identify and build a new portfolio that could realize increased value. A handful of those newly acquired firms that did exemplify its current strategy had actually failed, whereas others were scaling quite successfully.

An analyst's report referred to Safeguard's bundled sale as a "fire sale." We answered the critics with the teachings of legendary management guru Jack Welch of GE fame. He noted that if assets weren't strategic to your company's future, you should convert them to cash and put that cash into assets that *are* strategic to your future.

At that time, though, nothing seemed to matter—not the cash, not the Jack Welch logic, nothing. Safeguard's stock kept dropping like a stone, along with the rest of the world's stock markets. Earlier gains that put Safeguard's stock performance well ahead of the S&P 500 and the Russell 2000 were wiped out. The stock performed alongside the indices—that is, in the tank. With increased cash on the books from the bundle and an out-of-proportion drop in the price of Safeguard's stock, some of the large institutional shareholders increased pressure on the company to use that cash to support the stock via buybacks in the open market. However, our board members were dead set against any cash proceeds going to fund a buyback. Cash, in their view, enabled the company to execute its business model. Acquiring stakes in companies, building value, and then realizing that value when the time was right was the lasting way to build shareholder value.

Because Safeguard's trading volume had dropped along with its stock price, they also had concerns that those advocating a buyback would be the first ones to sell their stock. Hence, Safeguard would be placating a shareholder only to use its cash to buy out that same shareholder!

Boardroom Angst Added Drama

Safeguard's outside board of directors was comprised of an experienced group with diverse skills. Its members had both operating and financial backgrounds. Their ages ranged from a low of 55 to a high of 74. Holding seats were three each former science and technology CEOs and CFOs, a Big 8 Audit Partner, an entrepreneurial technologist, a mergers and acquisitions (M&A) specialist, and a venture capitalist. As a group, they were as unprepared for an unprecedented meltdown as anyone else. Both the board and management had worked in harmony until the financial crisis hit. But the stress of an unprecedented global financial markets meltdown took its toll. Frankly, all knees were shaking, mine included. But my job required me to be steady under fire, deal straight-up with the ugly reality, and put forth the best game plan possible. The goal was to build shareholder value. But that was seriously eroding with the nonstop *Wall Street Journal* headlines reporting declining profits, layoffs, business failures, and predictions of pending financial doom.

A Dose of Reality

The statistical momentum indicators we'd identified helped measure where we were in accomplishing our BHAGs and critical success factors on this disrupted terrain. Still, on the positive side of reality, the bundle alleviated cash concerns, at least for a time, although if this downturn lasted past 2011, then we'd have cash issues. Crystal balls didn't work in 2008 or 2009. Do they ever?

In addition, Safeguard's then-current roster of Partner Companies, in spite of this unprecedented global downturn, had just posted 30-percent aggregate revenue gains year over year. Using recurring revenue business models, they accurately predicted an increase in that aggregate growth by more than 30 percent going forward. Those strategic growth drivers were working.

Doing Something Right

Yes, the company was making BHAG progress. In fact, the most current Partner Company survey gave Safeguard Scientifics a 95-percent approval rating. Though not at 100 percent, this measurement reinforced the fact we were doing something right.

And Safeguard's top-20 institutional holders were using this stock dip to enlarge their ownership position. They were buying more stock at discounted prices and lowering their overall cost of ownership. Saying this another way, *they were supporting the company.* Long-term financial institutions—better known as professional institutional investors—now owned more than 65 percent of the company.

The science and technology industries, Partner Companies, Wall Street, and community at large (as reinforced by a positive cash balance, survey scores, and press coverage) considered Safeguard to be on its way back. Two "buts" hung in the air: its down-and-out stock price and its debt-laden balance sheet.

On the negative side of quantifiable reality was that Safeguard's stock, if it didn't rebound, could sink so low that it might get thrown off the New York Stock Exchange and wind up on "The Pink Sheets," sometimes called "penny stocks." They're low in value, lower in trading volume, and they seldom break out. Plus the company would still be burdened with the cost of being a public company. It's possible to be thrown off an exchange and then return to being listed, but that entails a good deal of legal and financial effort. We knew all parties would be best served to avoid that drama. We also knew if Safeguard delisted altogether and became private, the debt was to be due immediately. We didn't have the cash to pay it off.

Reverse Stock Split Not an Option

Some firms with their backs to that wall engineered a reverse stock split. This reduced the number of shares a firm had outstanding, which also mathematically increased the price per share. In Safeguard's case, a $1-per-share stock multiplied by the 120 million shares outstanding equaled a market capitalization of $120 million. If it had 20 million shares outstanding (a 1-to-6 split), shares would trade at $6 per share.

Historically, the success rate of the reverse split maneuver was poor. After the burst of the Internet bubble, with so many companies going public prematurely, several struggling firms engineered a reverse split to enable them to remain listed. Most of them continued to deteriorate in value. Ultimately, they were dropped from the public exchange anyway. Investment bankers did point out, however, a success formula existed in the midst of this poor record. A company needed positive dynamics versus negative dynamics. If that company timed the reverse split around a flow of good news that accentuated its positive dynamics, its stock price could avoid the continued price erosion. It could even increase.

Another negative side of quantifiable reality was the debt. Safeguard had cash for the moment, but its debt wasn't going away. The due date was in early 2011, only two years out. We had the Al Gore "lockbox" mentality to stash the right amount of cash away in installment fashion until the debt came due.

The downdraft on the global stock market also was weighing on convertible bonds. Safeguard's bonds from a 2004 offering barely traded, but when they did, they were trading at 20 to 30 percent off face value.

Making Lemonade

Our CFO had a notion about how to take this lemon and make lemonade. His was a three-part recipe: 1) take the cash out of the "lockbox," 2) acquire the discounted bonds on the open market whenever possible, and 3) get the help of a banker to solicit those bonds (as opposed to waiting until a holder wished to sell them).

With major financial institutions fearing their own liquidity, many were taking losses just to raise cash. Safeguard could benefit by buying that discounted debt.

So after the cash infusion from the bundle, the board and management unanimously approved the CFO's formula for making lemonade. Over the next year, nearly three quarters of the outstanding debt was scooped up at distressed prices averaging 75 cents on the dollar. Let's call that a good deal that helped transform Safeguard's balance sheet. This proved to be a far superior use of cash than buying back stock.

Unfortunately, after agreeing on the debt buyback, management and the board unanimously agreed on nothing else for six full months, including a proposed reverse stock split. The fear of a long-term outright depression was hanging in the boardroom air. That put in question the sustainability of Safeguard's business model in the absence of corporate M&A activity or an IPO market.

Evaluate Strategic Alternatives

A board is responsible to public shareholders for value creation. Was the board blaming Safeguard's business model for the tanked stock price? Were board members afraid of shareholder lawsuits if stock values didn't reclaim lost ground? Were they looking for a contingency if a 1929-like depression reappeared?

It might have been a composite of everything. My marching order was to review every business model under the sun and come forward with recommendations based on a variety of scenarios. I saw this as an effort to comfort the frail in the face of fire, so I pushed back. Every business model under the sun had been reviewed a few years back. We had made thoughtful decisions then. Plus we were visibly posting positive momentum indicators showing that measurable progress was well under way. Did Walmart look to change its business model because its stock got whacked? Or did its leaders focus on being the best retailer it could be?

My management team wondered if I would survive the process of board management and communications. Would I get fired for insubordination or just turn the keys over and quit?

Analysis and Debate

Fortunately, the Steady Eddies on the board helped me get over my pushback in the name of fiduciary responsibility. Special committees, investment banking advisors, Safeguard management, and the board met to discuss the merits and pitfalls of every alternative presented. After analysis and debate, the committee concluded no silver bullet existed. We would execute the game plan on the table.

This whole process seemed to me to take an eternity, although it actually took six months—from the back quarter of 2008 to the second quarter of 2009. I had other things on my list of critical success factors that could build value and make a difference. Demonstrating positive momentum within the Partner Companies and the prospects for strong investment returns while cleaning up the debt were paramount.

Those things called for aggressive execution by members of our management team. We rallied to convey to our board a plan that would thwart the market forces that dragged down valuation and added board-room angst. The plan would also respond to investment advisors who were practically screaming at us to reinforce our balance sheet—the rule of the day for the investment community.

Yes, we were on the right track with our business model. But high debt and low net cash were killers to a stock in this crisis-laden climate. If we could more thoroughly clean up the debt, we'd experience valuation gains that better reflected our progress in repositioning the business.

The time was also right to revisit the concept of doing a reverse stock split.

Clarient, the Reverse Split, and the PIPE

Investment bankers made the case that Safeguard's 60-percent ownership was preventing Clarient's stock from increasing in value. If ownership was less than 50 percent, more value would be generated. They provided statistics and studies to back it up. They also claimed to have institutional targets wanting to buy whatever Clarient stock Safeguard would sell as part of a secondary stock offering. An extra $60 million of cash on Safeguard's books could enable a breakout.

Magic Number

What a terrific time to announce a reverse stock split! Here were the positive dynamics in a negative situation: the infusion of cash, the validation of Clarient's healthy and attractive business, and the resulting balance sheet relief. The price of Safeguard's stock would be valued at more than $5 per share, with $5 proving to be a magic number. Many institutions and stock analysts wouldn't buy, own, or give coverage to companies with stock priced less than $5 per share. Several investors were targeted by Safeguard's communications efforts. They saw the positive momentum indicators and kept watching. But they wouldn't pounce at a stock price less than $5 per share.

This reverse split was the topic often debated inside and outside our boardroom and among shareholders. The statistics overwhelmingly said that defensive reverse splits led to further erosion in a company's stock price.

However, this was an offensive situation, not a defensive one. Safeguard's management packaged the entire proposal to time the Clarient secondary offering with the Safeguard reverse split. We took the strategy to the board. In support, an investment banker presented documented cases to validate the proposal to board members. When reverse splits were announced with positive dynamics and positive news, it was stated, growth in value resulted. Approving the proposal in the name of shareholder value was recommended.

The facts ruled the day. The board passed the measure. In March 2009, when the stock market had seemingly reached bear-market bottom, Clarient launched its road show for a secondary stock offering. It would sell a piece of Safeguard's interest to institutional shareholders. The completion of Clarient's secondary stock offering and Safeguard's reverse stock split were announced simultaneously.

What happened? Safeguard Scientifics pocketed $60 million in the transaction. Clarient's stock price jumped more than 50 percent in the first month. That value uplift spilled over to Safeguard's stock as well, to the tune of a 200-percent rise from its bear-market bottom. After the reverse split, it stood at $10 per share.

Jarring Speed Bump

Just a few months after Clarient's well-executed secondary stock offering and jump in stock value, the company hit a jarring speed bump. Billing and collections to Medicare, handled by a third-party contractor, incurred administrative delays that also created revenue recognition delays. That came as a surprise in their earnings release.

Surprises aren't treated kindly, especially in a scared and hostile financial market. As a result, Clarient's stock lost a third of its market value overnight. New holders of Clarient's stock were vocally upset. This glitch had a cash consumption effect on the business as well. Did Clarient have enough cash to fix the billing issue? To do so, it intended to establish its own billing mechanics as well as fund its growth.

Clarient's board took action. They believed the business carried enough substance and positive dynamics that a private placement of the sale of newly issued stock—termed a PIPE (private investment in public equity)—could attract sufficient cash to get the company over the hump and back on track. It would also pay down the debt provided by Safeguard. This would, in turn, enable Safeguard's balance sheet to improve by another $25 million. They engaged a banker and quickly got the process underway.

A Hugely Positive Deal

A few weeks later, in summer 2009, Oak Investment Partners—a highly regarded investment group I knew—called me out of the blue. The voice mail said, "Let's get reacquainted." This group, too, was looking for investment opportunities in the diagnostics sector. Did Safeguard Scientifics have a situation that might be a fit? Actually, Oak heard of the deal through the banker but reached out to me for an insider's angle. Talk about timing!

Within weeks, Clarient and Oak Investment Partners signed a term sheet for a $40 million PIPE. It was priced 10 percent above the market for the stock, without the sometimes-customary and punitive warrants that could further dilute earlier shareholders. In a negative market, this was a hugely positive deal.

Inside Safeguard's boardroom, analysis and debate over the deal and its impact on Safeguard's future extended. This led to a scramble to study the impact of that proposal versus any intellectual alternatives. Bankers got involved to do validation studies and evaluate long-term results. If the deal delays continued, Clarient's management and board feared Oak Investment Partners might scuttle the transaction. At that point, Clarient bankers had no other term sheet on the table for consideration. We had to consider this question: What might be the effect of a shareholder lawsuit if Safeguard was behind the collapse of a seemingly good deal for Clarient's—and even Safeguard's—shareholders? Prior to our final board meeting to consider the deal, I told my family that I'd either come home with my business card still valid or a severance check. It was becoming personal. With alternate scenarios finally vetted and deemed weak, Safeguard's board approved Clarient's transaction with Oak.

The Breakthrough: Success Breeds Success Through Socratic Resolve

By thinking outside the box, staying focused, and creatively and aggressively addressing the obstacles stemming from the global financial crisis, we practiced the ABCs and came out on top.

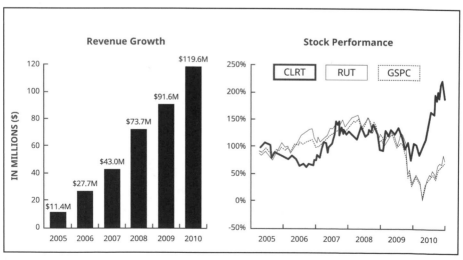

Clarient Revenue and Stock Performance

Image 6.5.

During the ensuing few months, Clarient fixed its billing issues, and its profit margins returned to targeted levels. The growth and health of its balance sheet attracted buy recommendations from several analysts. By the end of the year, its stock doubled while Safeguard's stock continued to grow. This happened (in part) due to the attraction resulting from newly initiated analysts' coverage and their buy recommendations.

Slow Improvement

The crisis had bottomed out. Through it all, we remained focused. Slow improvement hung in the air. For 2009, Safeguard's aggregate Partner Company revenue grew 40 percent during the tough recession. Partner Company surveys scored Safeguard's performance at 100 percent, an A+. Both Safeguard and Clarient, with far improved balance sheets, saw stocks realize nearly twice the gains as the S&P 500 and Russell 2000 indices. Safeguard's new roster of Partner Companies was hitting its stride.

By mid-2010, Clarient attracted GE's attention and not by accident. Goldman Sachs had pitched Clarient's board earlier about having a relationship with GE. In Goldman Sachs's estimation, Clarient would scratch GE's itch.

GE had twice attempted and failed to gain leadership in a diagnostics business. Clarient was a leader, had a strong team, and complemented GE's imaging technology that was considered leading-edge. GE Healthcare announced its Clarient acquisition by year end. The approximately $600 million purchase price tallied a fivefold improvement in value from the time Chromovision repositioned itself as its Clarient brand. That was the largest valuation multiple paid for a diagnostics company in 12 years. Safeguard booked more than $200 million in cash as a result of Clarient's success. It marked the largest cash return in its almost 60-year history—more than it returned from Novell 20 years previously.

As the financial crisis slowly abated, many in my public company CEO circle shared that dynamics inside their boardroom had slowly returned to their old normal. Board members gave me a glowing performance review but noted that my "board relations" needed improvement. As I reviewed the board's performance, I noted my disappointment that these experienced, talented people allowed a crisis to dilute their focus on executing a game plan—one that they'd all approved. We all vowed to do better. Three of the directors didn't stand for re-election at the 2010 annual meeting.

Safeguard Partner Companies 2006–2012 —Life Sciences and Technology

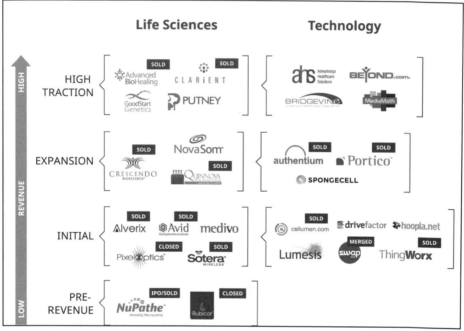

Image 6.6.

By spring 2011, Partner Company Avid Radiopharmaceuticals posted a big win. The FDA approved its test to diagnose and predict neurodegenerative diseases such as dementia and Alzheimer's. With Safeguard's help, Avid previously cultivated Pfizer and Eli Lilly as early investors. Both considered this area potentially strategic to their future. Eli Lilly, using its inside track, acquired Avid for $300 million, with another $500 million to be earned based on milestones and revenue achieved over a three-year period. The first milestone of $100 million was quickly earned and gave Safeguard a four times (4x) cash-on-cash gain, which means for every dollar put in, four dollars were earned.

A couple of months later, Partner Company Advanced Biohealing (ABH) announced it had filed for an IPO. ABH provided a cellular-based, regenerative artificial skin to promote healing in severe burn and diabetic foot-ulcer patients. (See ABH's case study in Chapter 8.)

Safeguard Scientifics, along with a syndication partner, acquired ABH from a European owner who couldn't figure out a workable U.S. pricing and reimbursement strategy. This owner closed the business. Then the syndication rehired all the people and recruited a new management team. Safeguard's deal team worked with the new management team to outline its new go-to-market strategy.

Safeguard Partner Company Aggregate Revenue Growth

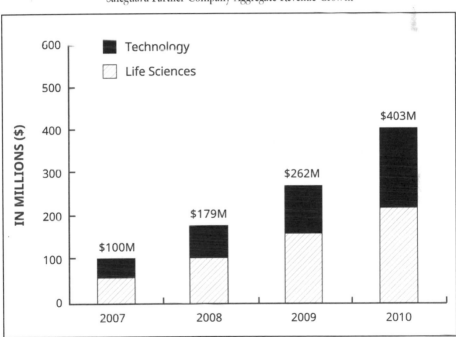

Image 6.7.

Four years later, ABH's business soared to a forecasted $200 million revenue and showed high profits. Two years before, Safeguard introduced ABH to Shire, a global specialty pharmaceutical giant, as a would-be partner that shared a strategic interest in regenerative medicine. The night before the IPO priced, Shire announced the cash acquisition of ABH for $750 million, which was 25-percent greater than the midpoint of the IPO pricing range. Safeguard had earned a 13 times (13x) cash-on-cash return, the third largest in its history. The deal multiplied $10.8 million into nearly $140 million in a little more than four years.

Not long thereafter, McKesson announced its $90 million acquisition of Partner Company Portico Systems. This IT healthcare firm had software to automate the insurance reimbursement process in a way to enable compliance with patient privacy laws. This scored Safeguard Scientifics another four times (4x) cash-on-cash return.

B: Borrow From Alliances and Partnerships

The critical success factors identified from the kickoff stage enabled some bell ringing. The addition of Executives in Residence (EIRs) to supplement the deal teams provided useful supplemental resources, not only to source new deals but also to add value to existing Partner Companies. One EIR joined Clarient as chief operating officer (COO), and he contributed in major fashion to keep the fast-traveling train on its tracks.

Two advisory boards comprised of two dozen highly accomplished people from either the healthcare or technology industry met twice a year in person and through various conference calls as well. They assisted in culling through and qualifying a growing deal flow. At advisory board meetings, prospective partner companies gave quick pitches to the board and participated in meetings and social events. This became a selling event in which any prospective partner company could see the differentiation and competitive advantages of Safeguard's approach in full display. Members of Safeguard's board of directors participated in these events and became selling agents themselves.

Alliances with would-be syndication partners also flourished. Within a few years, Safeguard Scientifics plowed through a deal flow that exceeded 1,000 companies annually. From that flow, we averaged investing $50 million in eight new high-potential Partner Companies a year.

The deal teams encouraged all Partner Companies to seek alliances, partnerships, and alternative channels of distribution. The concept of leveraging the resources of others applied to everyone's business, not just Safeguard's. And the strategic partners of Avid and ABH were ultimately the ones who acquired the companies at such fruitful valuations.

The EIRs, advisory boards, syndication partners, and other alliances worked in geometric proportions. Rather than a 30-person company executing Safeguard's game plan and strategy, 100 times that many people—all equipped with the elevator pitch for consistency in messaging—worked on its behalf.

While we were borrowing resources, Safeguard's chief financial officer (CFO)—with board approval—extended the time frame when the remaining debt would become due. The CFO partnered with a banker to restructure the majority of the convertible debt at a higher rate of interest, a three times higher price per share should it be converted, and three years longer to pay it off. This came with an option to purchase the debt before it could be converted to stock. That took a huge weight off of the near-term uncertainty we felt.

C: Communicate Progress and Results to Get/Stay on Track

The communications team organized a continual flow of information to insiders and outsiders alike. Some was internal and confidential to outline progress toward goals; some was external and made public to highlight issues, opportunities, and progress. Some was one-on-one; some was held in group meetings; some was via multi-media releases. All the communiqués—internal and external—made the progress on the momentum indicators visible. It all had an impact to either alter or reinforce our behavior to enable the achievement of our BHAGs. The communications team arranged for the entire executive staff to attend media training. This assisted in consistently and professionally delivering the message points.

The visibility given to the momentum indicators spilled over to the boardroom. This helped get through the rough spots during the financial crisis. It also equally spilled over to Wall Street analysts who gave

Safeguard write-ups and valuation more appropriate to its achievements. And it spilled over to Main Street, which generated the view of Safeguard Scientifics as a resuscitated winner in the new century.

Given society's shift toward social media, our communications team embraced social media communications as an early adopter and integrated digital media into the mix. Team members offered communications and messaging consulting throughout the Partner Companies to enable people to enhance their own messaging and communications.

Innovators take the leading edge. Clearly, brand recognition for Safeguard and its Partner Companies had notched up. Many of them enhanced their own recognition as a market leader in their industry segments.

S: Share the Rewards of Wealth and Recognition When Things Go Your Way

It's reinforcing to share the wealth and recognition when breakthroughs occur. It's tougher to share the blows when things go awry, never in finger-pointing fashion but in the spirit of improvement to achieve our BHAGs.

Stock options were vested based on achievement, and their value increased based on the performance's impact on valuation. Cash rewards also contributed to that sharing when performance wins came to fruition. We used stock awards not only for company team members but also for Safeguard's board of directors, advisory board members, and EIAs as well.

When Safeguard or any of its Partner Companies received recognition for any achievement, the team member directly responsible for the accomplishment took a public bow via the communications program. Recognition also came from Safeguard's board and compensation committee. Congratulatory "atta boys" were deservingly distributed. So were bonuses and increases in stock ownership.

Victory has many fathers. We all took a bow and saw an improvement to our net worth, not necessarily at the same time.

During that time, unforced turnover within Safeguard's ranks was lower than low. One senior member of the team resigned in the third year of the repositioning due to a change in his life. Outside of that, the team starting this transition was the same team credited with the repositioning. That lack of turnover helped us make our achievements even more likely to be realized.

What leader wouldn't be happy with a 3-percent unforced turnover and a 97-percent retention of his "keepers" over an eight-year period?

✳ What was the end result of the execution?

BHAG #1 is still a work in progress as $1 billion was a lofty target. It's supposed to be audacious! While I was at the helm, we got halfway there and achieved a five times increase in its value (5x valuation increase).

Four more Partner Companies were acquired shortly after my retirement. One of them, Thingworx, was recognized as "deal of the year." Safeguard Scientifics realized $750 million of cash proceeds (thus far) from the roster of Partner Companies, three IPOs, and top-tier returns from the acquisition of several Partner Companies by big guns. That cash also enabled a repayment of what was choking debt, Safeguard's stock hit a decade high, and its trading volume increased six times its valuation. The number of analysts covering events expanded from one to seven. Net cash equaled the former debt of $200 million. That's a $400 million reversal for fortune that achieved record levels. While the debt-to-equity ratio on its balance sheet moved from 1:1 to 1:8, its institutional shareholder base grew from 25 to 75 percent, and its stock far and away outperformed the Russell 2000 and the S&P 500 over the same timeframe. Let's call that a good run.

To summarize, my high performance team entered a near-bankrupt situation and found a way to generate the cash to retire the debilitating $200 million debt. We also invested $330 million to acquire influential stakes in two dozen firms. They've been built to become highly valuable, market-leading Partner Companies that are performing exceptionally well. Those Partner Companies grew aggregate revenue by 50 percent the year after I retired. They will eventually either seek an IPO or get themselves acquired by the right strategic buyer.

Safeguard Scientifics Seven Year Stock Performance

Image 6.8.

The substance exists for Safeguard to realize future gains. The value of a share of stock has exceeded $20 per share and continues to rise. Stocks go up and down based on short-term considerations in the macroeconomic climate. All the momentum indicators are running in the black. Safeguard has formed a proven team to pull it off.

Goal Achievements

How has the company fared in meeting its Big Hairy Audious Goals?

BHAG #1—to restore lost value to shareholders—remained achievable. BHAG #2—to restore Safeguard's reputation within its portfolio of companies—had been achieved. So had BHAG #3—to restore employee and constituency pride in Safeguard Scientifics.

For three years running, Partner Company surveys scored Safeguard at 100 percent. And for the past few years, various constituents in Safeguard's audience recognized it as a leader. As an example, for three years out of four, a venture capital/private equity trade organization awarded Safeguard "Deal of the Year" for its Clarient, ABH, and Thingworx achievements. Ernst & Young also recognized me as a Master Entrepreneur in its Entrepreneur of the Year competition.

I believe that recognition of any one of the team spills over to anyone who was part of it. Hurray for the Three Musketeers!

✳ What's your reflection as you look back?

Among our key board topics was succession planning, as my time at the helm was coming to an end. At first regarding this as a five-year assignment, I never anticipated the biggest financial crisis since the Great Depression would rear its ugly head to derail our team's stellar work. It seems I was the right guy for that time of instability and disruption.

With our platform stable and almost eight years under my belt, I put some gains in my pocket and left room in my schedule to spoil my grandchildren. My inducement stock options with an eight-year lifespan were expiring. Remember: At heart, I'm a mercenary. Without a reload, I was history.

It took a high-performance team to drive Safeguard Scientifics to achieve a heralded transformation. A thoughtful plan that's well executed by talented people produces rewards. My succession was planned to leave high-quality, capable, well-trained people in place to achieve far more. I know how to build and lead a team. We accomplished a great deal, and that speaks for itself. I'm also skilled at simplifying complex situations; I can find the few buttons needing to be pushed to make a difference and remain focused on them. Then I can communicate those buttons in simplistic fashion and rally a team around them.

As I look back, a board of directors has a tough job, especially in the face of crisis and adversity. Its members have to challenge everything, turn over every rock, and test the conviction and the substance behind every premise. That's their job.

It's hard to be on the receiving end of that scrutiny when the shells are flying. These questioning personalities that appeared during the financial crisis enabled a collective wisdom to unfold. Ultimately, given the circumstances, our company made the best moves it could. That didn't happen by accident. Everyone involved should be recognized and share in this victory.

In the aftermath of Safeguard's successes—the cash, the increased market value, the strong Partner Company scores, the community and industry recognition awards—I became Mr. Know it All. Yes, I was still aggravated by boardroom dynamics that I interpreted as unsteady under fire. I violated the "swift resolution of conflict rule" for a high performance team. Was the board trying to help me or give me the guff of a schoolyard bully? (My childhood baggage showed up!)

Know that I'm as reflective on my failings in the face of this assignment as I am my victories. Our team members shared the aggravation I felt; many adopted my confrontational, Mr. Know it All attitude in the face of their challenges. After all, we called so many good plays, why was the next one any different?

But failure is an orphan. I have to raise my hand and be held accountable.

Costly Mistake

Our team championed, and I approved, a deal to acquire a sizable stake in a company that sold into a huge, untapped market. They had disruptive competitive positioning and major differentiation. The board's capital management committee, loaded with operational professionals, encouraged caution, citing tactical and logistical concerns that gave them pause.

As already noted, I'm a big believer in collective wisdom. As it related to this situation, I failed to benefit from that collective wisdom coming from my board. I didn't listen. None of us did, but setting the right tone for creating and benefitting from collective wisdom was my job. That cost us. That new company failed for all the reasons the board cautioned and some others that we didn't see. Perhaps Safeguard's value would be somewhat greater if that cash had been put to better use.

Fortunately, we live in a great country where you're allowed to learn from failure.

Second Guesses

Not taking boardroom advice in this situation put back in vogue second-guessing on other deals. I took questions and comments from the board's capital management committee, which provided governance oversight to capital deployment activity, as unfounded second guesses. If I hadn't been Mr. Know it All, that second-guessing might not have added new angst to what was an improved dynamic in the aftermath of the financial crisis.

But was this second-guessing or a committee doing its job, albeit with less confidence due to the judgment exercised? Its members challenged and tested the conviction and substance behind every premise. In my mind, anyone trying to help me is a friend. Friends give advice and counsel, not guff. But I couldn't tell the difference.

In the aftermath of all the behavioral angst during the financial crisis, I was taking challenges personally. Remember that line in *The Godfather*? "It's not personal, Sonny; it's business!"

Four Wins

Not long after I retired, four of Safeguard's Partner Companies subject to a good deal of that second guessing were acquired by big players. These four wins returned between two times to four times cash, added an additional $120 million to Safeguard's tally of cash returns, and increased Safeguard's stock to a new decade high.

Stock analysts have subsequently rallied around several of Safeguard's Partner Companies, with forecasts of another 50-percent increase in stock value when these winners find their own exits. What about new investments that have yet to see the light of day? Definitely, success can breed further success.

I admire what a high performance team can achieve! Never underestimate the importance of the human dynamic. And never lose humility when you do achieve it.

✳ How did the experience help you advance?

I've refined and used the ABCs to Advance for almost four decades. Most recently, it enabled me to advance to a new stage in my life.

When I decided to retire, I reflectively spoke to my board about my childhood baseball hero, Willie Mays. He could run, jump, field, hit, steal a base, and win ball games like the champ he was. He hinted that the time was coming to hang up his glove, but season after season, he returned for one more year. But many don't remember him for his feats; they remember him for dropping the ball in center field, overthrowing or underthrowing to third base, tripping on his way to first base, or hitting to the infield rather than over the infield.

I also spoke about Winston Churchill, a giant of a personality who rallied his nation when desperation reigned during the early days of World War II. Once peacetime came, his people voted him out of office.

I never want to be remembered like the aging Willie Mays. He should have gone out on top. And like Winston Churchill, I'm suited to be a wartime chancellor, a wartime consigliere.

Today, Safeguard Scientifics is in a new place with the talent needed to build to that new tomorrow. I love peace inside of my personal and family life. But I find peace on the job a bit boring. Professionally, I'm energized by ongoing challenges.

A Platform to Give Back

I feel like I'm advancing to this new stage at the top of my game. When I was in my teens, my father died with two bucks in his pocket and nothing in the bank. I'm likely to have a bit more.

After retiring from Safeguard in May 2013, I formed Kedgeway (*www.kedgeway.com*) as a platform to write, consult, speak, teach, invest, direct my philanthropy, and sit on a board or two. This is how I share my experiences—my formula to *advance*—as well as what I learned from the mistakes I made along the way. I want to help a whole new generation of ambitious people who have a desire to *advance.*

I'm proud of a number of the people who worked side-by-side with me on my teams over the years. I'm especially proud of those who have advanced to lead organizations of their own as an owner, senior executive, president, managing partner, or CEO. Some of Safeguard's Partner Company executives are case studies by themselves.

For example, Ronnie Andrews, who provided leadership as CEO of Clarient, went on to become a senior executive within GE Healthcare.

He was recruited to become president of another leading healthcare technology concern, Life Technologies. Life Tech was singled out as an acquisition target by healthcare gorilla Thermo Fisher. Andrews learned so much from leading the acquisition of Clarient by GE that he headed the acquisition activities between them, too. With the deal concluded, he then served as a senior executive within Thermo Fisher, responsible for a multi-billion-dollar business unit. Ronnie will likely continue his advance.

Clarient's COO Dr. Mike Pellini entered the company from an EIA role inside Safeguard. Also working as a senior exec within GE Healthcare after Clarient's acquisition, Foundation Medical—a venture-backed genetic early-stage diagnostic company—recruited Mike to become CEO. Not only did he succeed in building the company, he took it public. Foundation Medical's IPO achieved a $1 billion market cap. Mega-healthcare company Roche has since purchased 53 percent ownership for $1 billion, leaving Foundation Medical with an exceptional partner to commercialize its product offering and plenty or runway to achieve additional value.

Simon Moss, who worked as a software sales executive before becoming CEO for Safeguard's Mantas, built and sold the company to a firm that was majority owned by Oracle. He's now CEO for another Safeguard Partner Company, Pneuron. Simon has advanced from salesman to sales manager to first-time CEO to experienced CEO with a successful track record. He's also a young man with years remaining to advance in his career.

Kevin Rakin is a South African immigrant with a background in finance and then general management. As a fairly inexperienced CEO, he built Advanced BioHealing to become a market leader before selling to its acquirer, Shire, on the eve of an IPO. After working as a senior executive with increased responsibility within Shire, Kevin started his own investment firm. He used millions of dollars of proceeds earned as ABH's CEO and more millions raised from institutional investors who were impressed with his track record. Now seeking other ABH-like opportunities where he can add value, he's earned terrific credentials to do just that. (See Kevin's case study in Chapter 8.)

Network for Teaching Entrepreneurship (NFTE)

The Safeguard Scientifics experience introduced me to an extraordinarily rewarding situation within the Network for Teaching Entrepreneurship (NFTE).

NFTE provides entrepreneurship and business training to poor inner-city kids as a way to empower them to complete their education and prepare for their future. They're set to capture the American dream! Based on research, NFTE graduates are more likely to improve their three Rs, finish school, develop career aspirations, seek additional education or training, enhance their leadership skills, and increase their locus of control. In fact, they out-earn their non-NFTE peers by a whopping 50 percent.

I've joined NFTE's national board to assist efforts that have been proved to be so impactful to more than 500,000 disadvantaged youth.

I was once a poor, inner-city kid who worked hard and made mistakes, but I had the good fortune to have the right people in my foxhole. I've benefitted from a mentor or two along the way. And I got lucky.

Today, I'm excited to take my part in mentoring NFTE kids to reposition and realize their potential—to enable them to *advance*.

Dorvin D. Lively:
Reforming Maidenform

"Make the best use of what is in your power, and take the rest as it happens."

—Epictetus

✳ How did you get to be the person you are? What's your story?

In the third quarter of the 20th century, I grew up in 19th-century-like conditions in an impoverished section of rural Arkansas. You might say I'm a generation or two removed, since I grew up in ways my parents' or grandparents' generation did. I came second in the stack of three sisters, with one several years older and the other two a bit younger than me. We lived on a farm with no running water or indoor plumbing. That's right: We used an outhouse. We actually hauled water from a spring a mile away. We lived day to day.

Image 7.1: Dorvin D. Lively. Photo copyright Bill Truslow Photography. Used with permission.

In a crazy sense, I didn't know this was primitive for the early 1970s. A number of people in the area lived in similar ways. While growing up with a simplistic childhood, many of my peers expected to continue to do the same as their parents and grandparents. I wanted something different.

Do What it Takes

My sisters and I were raised with love and respect. We never doubted we'd have enough food on the table, but we didn't have toys, clothes, or the bicycles that many of our friends had. There were times my mother didn't have the money for groceries, so we survived on what we had. For example, we grew vegetables in a small garden and I helped my mother can them in the summer for wintertime. Our family Christmases were simple and small. New clothing and footwear were rare. I had to have holes in my shoes before they were replaced. My mother patched the knee holes on my blue jeans, and I'd wear those to school. (It's funny that knee holes are today's hot fashion.)

Although we lacked materially, my family supplied the security of a powerful foundation filled with love, support, and a firm value system. My mother in particular planted a sense of subsistence within me that I knew I could apply toward my future. My father taught me recreational hunting and fishing. And they both taught me the art of survival. I can say I know how to grow, trap, preserve, and catch my own food. I can also apply entrepreneurial instincts to earn an income. While others might not have a clue, I'm confident I can survive—even thrive.

Throughout high school, I worked on our family farm and helped with the cattle. In the low-income farm country of rural Arkansas, I also worked for various farmers in the community, hauling hay in the summer and such. Whatever they asked, I did. To supplement my earnings, I raised and sold hogs. After selling a litter of pigs, I reinvested the money, bought feed, raised more hogs, and sold another litter. That way, I saved enough money to fund part of my way through college and buy a used pickup truck for transportation and work.

Sister Broke the College Barrier

My parental value system included the mind-set that I could achieve anything if I worked hard enough. Farming was hard work. Knowing that education was important to my future, I applied that work ethic to my schooling. Fortunately, my parents reinforced it with all of us. My father struggled to make as much as $10,000 a year to support a wife and four children and deal with the contingencies required in farming. When I was preparing to enter high school, my older sister was accepted to college. No one in our family had been educated past high school until then. With loans, savings, and scholarships, my sister made her way to higher education and served as a terrific example for me. I wanted the same—not only to prove to myself but to prove to my parents I could achieve more than a meager subsistence on a very small farm.

To a certain extent, this way of life created inside a sense of what I could accomplish. I wanted more and was prepared to reach for it. I knew what it meant to "do what it takes." I aspired to raise my own family one day, yet with more financial security than I had known.

High School Days

High school in a one-horse town came with few group activities and no amenities. My school bus ride on mostly dirt roads took between 45 and 60 minutes to get to or from home and school. Basketball was our school's sole sport. I was a scrappy point guard who wasn't all that tall, and couldn't jump all that high or run all that fast. But I still played competitively—in everything. Among the 16 students in my graduating class, I competed feverishly with one other student for top grades. Named valedictorian, I was the only one of my classmates who was college-bound. I headed to the University of Arkansas with a sense I would do something *big*.

With my own savings, loans, a scholarship, earnings from raising hogs, a college work-study program, and the 20 bucks my father passed me whenever I came home, I funded my education. This educational foundation gave me an extraordinary sense of myself that I've used to my advantage every single day since.

College With Mentoring Along the Way

It didn't take long for me to realize my back-in-the-hills high school preparation for college was lightweight compared to my contemporaries. To be competitive, I had to work harder than they did. A drive to compete—to put myself equal to or better than the guys sitting around me—has always been there. Without stepping on anyone inside, I needed to prove that someone from my background could stand toe-to-toe with anybody out there.

My sister probably had the most influence in directing my career path. She earned her degree in accounting. I followed in her footsteps, not quite understanding what that meant. By my junior year in college, I had begun to think about interviewing for jobs. One professor in particular, the head of the accounting department, took an active interest in mentoring me. He said, "You want to work for one of the Big Eight accounting firms." Behind closed doors, I found out later he'd helped set up some of my interviews, including the one with Arthur Andersen.

✳ What was your career progression before joining Maidenform?
Early Years in Big Eight Accounting Firm

With a degree in accounting and an offer in hand from Arthur Andersen (AA), I began as an auditor in the company's 100-person Tulsa, Oklahoma, office—fairly small compared with other AA offices. I was considered a mid-market specialist. Most of its clients were oil and gas, manufacturing, printing, and publishing companies along with a few IT consulting firms.

Shortly after starting at AA, I married a wonderful woman who became an instrumental force in my career.

Throughout a full decade from 1980 to 1990, I advanced in AA's audit practice. At that time, Arthur Andersen was extremely well respected within the Big Eight for its training and development of people. The firm had its own training center outside of Chicago. Every three to six months, we received increasingly more advanced training and were put through a variety of situation simulations with a group of excellent mentors. Some of the partners in the firm took me under their wings and gave me guidance along the way. I not only learned the requirements for financial consistency, controls, and mechanisms, but in my 20s, I learned to manage projects through people. I also learned to conduct myself as a professional with those in positions well above my own.

As a result, my responsibility grew from a member of the audit staff to a senior accountant leading an audit team. Then I managed multiple audits and dealt directly with CFOs, CEOs, and board members of companies. Imagine me at age 27 sitting across the table from 60-year-old CEOs and their leadership teams engaged in high-level discussions about strategy or financial performance. The experience with Arthur Andersen taught me the behavior to inspire confidence and then feel confident myself, although in many respects, I felt inferior whenever I walked into one of those meetings.

An Early Test in Gumption

One particular experience will always stay with me. When I was a newly minted auditor, my boss sent me to see the general counsel of a long-standing oil and gas client to retrieve minutes from its board meetings. The general counsel, a real tiger, had been at this company for more than 30 years. Intimidatingly, she occupied a huge corner office.

I knocked on her office door. She didn't answer, so I opened it and walked in. On the far side of the room, she was bent over looking at an open bottom file drawer. I said, "Excuse me," and introduced myself. "Do you have a moment?" She looked at me and, as I met her halfway across the room, she walked up to me, stuck a letter opener in my chest against my shirt, shoved me all the way back to the office door, pushed me outside, and then shut the door. She never said a word.

I had to decide. Do I return in defeat and tell my boss I didn't accomplish my task? Or do I take her on? So, I knocked on the door again, opened it, and walked back in. She stood there laughing. I proved to her I had the gumption to stand up to her, which earned me a certain respect. My boss was testing my determination to compete, do what I had to do, and not fail. He knew exactly what this confrontation would be. He wanted to see if I gave up or persevered.

Successfully managing confrontations, I subsequently learned, was part of a manager's job. Establish a common ground and deal with it straight up.

Financial Accounting Standards Board (FASB) Fellowship

Ten years into my career with Arthur Andersen, the managing partner of the Tulsa office called me aside and asked, "Would you consider applying for a fellowship to work at the FASB?" This was the governing and standard-setting body for the accounting profession. After interviewing at AA's Chicago headquarters, I was chosen as AA's only representative from among 30,000 employees interviewed to earn this distinguished fellowship position. I went to FASB's Connecticut office for a grueling set of eight one-hour interviews. Some were one-on-one; others were with a group of financial technical people who knew the accounting rules cold. The only interview protocol was this: They could only ask me something technical if it was something I professed to know or experience.

The interviewers grilled me: "Have you ever been involved in this situation or that?" The minute I said "yes," we dove into the muddy details of highly technical accounting rules to see what I really knew. After that, I was one of three in the country selected for what was a two-year FASB fellowship. "Not bad for a country boy from Arkansas," I thought.

In this job, I mainly provided interpretive guidance to controllers, CFOs, audit committees, and public accounting firms on technical accounting rules. They focused on areas in which little, if any, literature existed on how to address a particular situation. Over the span of my fellowship, I focused on the accounting and tax treatment of stock compensation and how to apply stock pooling or purchase accounting rules for mergers and acquisitions (M&A).

Interpretation for a Giant Computer Industry Acquisition

The largest and highest profile situation I dealt with was AT&T's $7.5 billion acquisition of NCR. In 1991, this was the computer industry's largest-ever M&A transaction. AT&T approached FASB to determine how the acquisition might be best accomplished. At the time, the accounting rules stated that, under certain conditions, acquisitions could qualify for accounting treatment as a *pooling* of stock versus a *purchase*. Each option came with its own set of accounting rules.

Combined company earnings were generally higher under a pooling-of-interest scenario, which enabled AT&T to pay an additional $325 million for NCR. Of course, AT&T wanted to use the pooling rules. The Securities and Exchange Commission (SEC) objected and preferred AT&T to use purchase accounting rules. That meant the amortization of the cost of the NCR acquisition under cost accounting rules would have depressed AT&T's earnings for a 40-year amortization period.

FASB worked closely with a whole host of parties, including the SEC, NCR's and AT&T's financial staff, their public accounting firms, and their respective investment bankers The FASB would review the fact pattern and issue an interpretive ruling in the absence of firm black-and-white rules covering this particular set of circumstances.

I researched the rules and past practices, collaborated with key members of the organization, and presented my recommendations to FASB's panel. When the two companies eventually concluded negotiations and merged, pooling rules prevailed for AT&T. However, rules in a dynamic setting don't stay the same for long; FASB has since discontinued pooling accounting for acquisitions.

Provide Answers Quickly

In the early 1990s, FASB was governed by a seven-member board that operated under the Sunshine Act. All of their board meetings were public. When I started as one of six practice fellows, some of the board's projects had been around for years.

FASB added three fellows yearly, each with a two-year term. That way, we overlapped each other for a year. We often got together for lunch and laughed that we were establishing what we called GAAP (general accepted accounting principles) on any given day. In effect, we gave interpretive accounting guidance through our conversations with professionals who reached out to us for answers.

Our board members discussed some issues for 10 years and hadn't come up with answers. But we, the junior fellows, reviewed facts and dictated an interpretation that became accounting gospel within weeks. Whenever I've been on the spot to provide quick answers to questions, I've cited that experience. It trained me to consult the facts quickly so I could either provide an immediate interpretation or ask for more time. Taking in the circumstances at hand, I always followed through to provide the best answer I could. At times, I've been quick to point out that some questions simply don't have answers.

Thanks to my FASB experience, interpreting facts and connecting the dots of disparate information is a talent I've developed well.

Career Shift From Public Accounting to Operating Companies

With my two-year fellowship at FASB coming to a close, I faced a choice: I could return to AA's Tulsa office on a public accounting career path or apply what I'd learned to private industry. I enjoyed dealing with CFOs, controllers, senior staff, and various situations on what we called "the client side." A friend knew that PepsiCo was recruiting a financial executive to be part of its international expansion. Because I had no international experience at the time, I thought it would be a valuable assignment—one that would build on my knowledge and add to my experience.

In world events, the Berlin Wall had just come down. Both Pepsi and Coke were going head-to-head in "who can get there the fastest," which evolved into "who can get into China and other underdeveloped markets the fastest." I arranged a job interview and, in 1992, I received and accepted an offer as Pepsi's assistant international controller.

International Operations and Business Development in Consumer Products

The job turned out to be different than expected. I led due diligence teams to expand bottling and franchise operations in China, Eastern and Western Europe, and other areas in the Far East and South America. I served on a team that negotiated terms with the Chinese government. Within two years, Pepsi invested about $2 billion in either country start-ups or joint ventures, including 10 of the provinces within China.

Coming from a small remote farm in Arkansas, I had an exciting time learning firsthand how to do business and behave professionally in various cultures. Pepsi applied my solid financial, accounting, and technical skills to developing businesses around the globe. In dealing with startups, I made sure the right team was in place to operate the business efficiently and report results according to SEC and corporate standards. In every major country, we put an expatriate CFO in place for at least two years. That gave us time to develop local people who could step up to that responsibility.

My assignment turned out to be more of a line operational management responsibility than a financial one. I often acted as an operational consultant to country managers and their CFOs, developing me as a general manager and not solely as a financial executive.

General management and operational savvy are expected from CFOs today. They must understand the strategic, operational, and financial aspects of a business, putting the right team in place for the tasks at hand. They can't work in a vacuum; they have to function as a key player within a team.

Personal Circumstances Required an Employment Change

For two years, I traveled out of the country 80 percent of the time. Over 15 years, my personal life had changed. My parents had divorced and both remarried. My wife and I had three children, and she was doing most of the work raising our family. To be more than an absentee husband and father, something had to give. Just when I asked for a different position within Pepsi, my mother was diagnosed with debilitating early dementia and my stepfather was diagnosed with stage-four cancer. Pepsi promoted me to another international position with no change in 80-percent travel requirements. Within a week of my promotion, I gave my notice to return to the southwestern U.S., find employment, and personally tend to family needs.

Silverado: A Flyer in Specialty Foods

Upon returning to the southwest, I joined Silverado Foods, a small company in Tulsa, Oklahoma, that recently went public. I became the

CFO reporting to the founder and CEO. He had executed a roll-up strategy in which Silverado had acquired a variety of "hand-held" consumable foods (cookies, pound cakes, biscuits, and such). They reached the consumer via variety stores, delis, and specialty food stores.

I stepped into an administrative disaster. The business had poor integration among all of its acquired pieces, each with its own staff, culture, and manufacturing process. The sum of the parts equaled a negative cash flow, putting the company on the edge of bankruptcy to keep the business afloat. The CEO was loaning the business his own money and money borrowed from other family members. It seemed to me a strategic operational and cultural integration—along with process and financial discipline—could make an immediate difference.

I knew how to do that. I took a flyer at Silverado Foods.

Integration with the right people and skills

This wasn't a one-size-fits-all situation; it required hundreds of moving parts. We had to get the right people to do the right things that would advance the business. I needed flexibility to locate a skilled talent base. New hires had to add value to what had become a complex assortment of geographically dispersed small product lines.

I found the right people, and it didn't matter if they lived outside of Tulsa, Silverado's headquarters. The business had personnel scattered throughout the country, and it was publicly traded with a CEO who had never been inside a public company. If the founder resisted my coaching, I used members of the board to coach him. My actions supplemented the skills of a visionary yet insular founder who was reticent to leave his office.

The whole revitalization process proved to be taxing but fun. Within a few years, we built the business to about $50 million in revenue and achieved modest financial performance. But we got stabbed with a dagger that we should have realized was drawn.

The risk of an oversized account

Silverado had acquired a highly profitable, fast-growing, well-branded niche biscotti cookie business in San Francisco. The company produced a nicely packaged, tasty product called Nonni's that had gar-nered a substantial following. We expanded its distribution to include the big discounters, Sam's and Costco. Our revenue grew and grew until, within a couple of years, Sam's accounted for half of the product's business. That's when two of these customers delivered the ultimatum: Reduce your price to X (which was less than cost), or we'll find another vendor. We tried to negotiate but when we did, they quickly dumped us. Our business, which had built its infrastructure to scale for the volume Sam's and Costco needed, couldn't adapt quickly enough. In fact, it was hemorrhaging.

We had to move quickly. If not bankruptcy, then we needed either:

＊ Interim financing to allow time to recoup, or

＊ A buyer who could benefit from its pieces and parts.

A boutique banker in New York helped us sell some preferred stock, which provided enough cash to give us time to figure out some-thing different. The board of directors listened to the alternatives—with calculators in hand to measure risk and return—and opted to find a buyer for either the whole company or pieces of it. A private equity firm acquired the business and carved up the parts, keeping Nonni's. It became a strong seller in Starbucks for a long time after that.

Move to New York

During my time in Tulsa, my stepfather succumbed to his cancer and my mother's dementia worsened. She entered full-time nursing home care. For better or for worse, some rigidity had been taken out of my personal circumstances. With all of my business contacts in New York City and a career direction in consumer products, I decided to move there.

While job searching in New York, I visited the head of the boutique investment firm that had arranged Silverado's preferred stock sale. He was a youthful yet experienced man in his 70s. I thanked him for his help and mentioned I'd made a mistake in taking the Silverado job. He looked at me and said, "Let me explain something to you. I've been around the horn and seen a lot of things in life. Situations come up in the corporate world that benefit from having somebody who's been to war. You've been to war. Too many others have never been tested. You have, and you passed."

That helped me look at my failed Silverado endeavor as a significant win. I thought, "Perhaps I'll go to war again." I have since found that, more often than not, companies actively recruiting new senior talent had issues. They valued my "wartime" experience.

Reader's Digest: Changes in Demographics and Sweepstakes Regulations

When I started as senior vice president and controller in 1998, Reader's Digest had been an extremely profitable company. Half of its $2.5 billion in revenue came from outside the U.S. The international business continued to grow rapidly, while the U.S. business—with a younger customer demographic than the international business—had stagnated. The biggest segment of the business was the Books and Home Entertainment Division, comprised of books, audios, videos, and music titles. Reader's Digest bought rights over the years and, in 1998, owned more titles than anybody in the music business. Its new CEO from American Express—a hugely successful direct marketer—preceded me by several months. One of his first moves was to sell off an extensive art collection the founders had purchased over the years. The Sotheby's auction fetched $100 million for about a dozen pieces, including paintings by Monet.

I didn't sell art, but I made immediate contributions to the company by driving projects that consolidated operations and service centers to support its European business. The efforts saved considerable cost in a nominal amount of time.

Over the years, offering sweepstakes to stimulate consumers' purchase of books, magazines, and music through large cash prizes had produced gangbuster revenue for Reader's Digest. When I joined, the Reader's Digest sweepstakes was mainly a direct mail business generating a 5-percent to 6-percent response rate—three times more than the 1.5-percent to 2-percent industry norm.

The U.S. Congress had been debating the whole sweepstakes industry for years. In 1998, it mandated that any sweepstakes participant needn't buy *anything* to enter and win. Plus those who provided the sweepstakes were forced to not only disclose but also promote that fact. With the stroke of a pen, Reader's Digest response rates dropped like a stone to 1 percent. As a result, the company's revenue in the U.S. plunged by almost 50 percent in less than 12 months.

Simultaneously, the disruptive forces of digitization began to affect the publishing world. Young readers of *Reader's Digest* continued to drop off, and old readers continued to die off. The trends were clear. Some wars can be won, some can't, and some leave you wondering why you're fighting.

I opted out of fighting this war and joined Toys "R" Us—a company that had issues, too.

Toys "R" Us: $12 Billion Struggling Retailer

From the 1970s through the 1990s, Toys "R" Us was the category killer. By 2001 when I joined as senior vice president and controller, Toys "R" Us had its share of competitive issues, not as much from Amazon.com as from the likes of big discounters Walmart and Target.

Like Reader's Digest, the company had a new CEO, who came from toy boutique FAO Schwarz. The CEO had started six months before I arrived. A publicly traded company, this struggling retailer operated as three retail business units. More than half of its revenue was generated by the traditional Toys "R" Us, with one-third from a lighter-on-its feet and faster-growing Babies "R" Us. The third and much-smaller unit, Kids "R" Us, struggled for a market identity against a large number of competitors. The company had also developed a small online business for the emerging world of ecommerce. On top of it all, Toys "R" Us had just regrouped from a fiasco in which its fulfillment systems had malfunctioned, leaving it hard-pressed to actually ship anything during the previous holiday season.

As a senior member of the Toys "R" Us team, I was asked to streamline the operational component of the business. That was familiar territory: shared service centers to serve all retail groups and the international business. I knew I could make a difference quickly. My role was highly strategic as well as operational.

Directing a project team, I identified several areas of inefficiency. Inside of four months, we constructed a plan to take $450 million of redundant costs out of the business. However, the executive committee had difficulty approving the ax on some sacred cows. So half of the plan was executed, saving $225 million versus the whole $450 million. The status quo was simply too powerful a force to change overnight.

Strategic discussions centered on how to reposition the brand and deal with an array of competitors in both the brick-and-mortar and digital worlds. We experimented with a number of initiatives that included exclusive brands. Strategic consulting giant McKinsey chimed in. Everything worked a little better, but we found no big needle-mover. By 2003, the board was preparing to take the company private and began courting the private equity community for a buyer. I viewed that process and outcome as career limiting.

After being in the Toys "R" Us war zone, I had to set my own career growth path. My ambitions grew. I knew it was time to take the mantle as a CFO. After looking at a number of companies, I was then introduced to Maidenform.

✳ What was the situation before you entered the organization that led to its issues?

Maidenform has a long and fabled history. It was founded in 1922 by a Belarusian-born seamstress, her husband, and the owner of the New Jersey store where the seamstress worked. The three rebelled against the flat-chested designs of women's undergarments at the time. They designed and manufactured dresses and support undergarments, particularly bras, that accentuated the natural shape of a woman's figure, hence the name *Maidenform*.

World War II Conversion

To support the war effort in World War II, Maidenform converted its factory to make, from bra-like material, parachutes and carrier pigeon vests that paratroopers strapped to their chests. After landing in a war zone, paratroopers undid their pigeon bras, loaded the birds with coded messages, and sent the pigeons back to home base.

After the war, with the help of provocative advertising in the 1950s and 1960s, Maidenform aggressively promoted its bras and became a leading brand available from women's retail shops and major department stores. During that time, it expanded its manufacturing plant in New Jersey to handle the increasing volume. The company became known as a cradle-to-grave employer, with a large segment of its workforce like an extended family never working anywhere else. "Made in the U.S.A." became part of its branding and identity accented by the famous branding slogan "I dreamed I [doing some ordinary activity] in my Maidenform bra."

Bankruptcy, New Ownership, Slow Change, and a Second Threat

Throughout the 1980s and 1990s, its competitors embraced off-shore manufacturing to lower cost substantially. As discount retailers became a sizable consumer distribution channel, Maidenform failed to swiftly adapt. With high costs and lost market share, the company filed for bankruptcy in 1997, emerging from Chapter 11 proceedings in 1999.

During this time, a private equity firm had been purchasing Maidenform's bonds in the open financial market for pennies on the dollar. When the company came out of bankruptcy court, the bonds converted to common stock, which left the private equity firm as the company's owner. This new owner made changes to manufacturing and distribution, but the adjustments occurred too slowly to enable Maidenform to be cost-competitive. The company was in jeopardy of declaring bankruptcy a second time.

A Second Ownership Shift, New Issues, and New Management

Compounding the issues, Maidenform's auditors declared the company had material weaknesses in its financial processes. In accounting terms, that made a major black mark. With the founders and their hand-picked successors gone and new management installed, the manufacturing shifted offshore, at first to the Caribbean. Then, as the company began to make progress, the private equity owner sold 80 percent of its Maidenform stock to another private equity firm in 2004. That new owner took an aggressive stance toward updating Maidenform's methodology to compete in the 21st century.

With industry veteran Tom Ward appointed as CEO, Maidenform had to rebuild its management team. Tom began moving product manufacturing to top-tier Chinese contractors. In the meantime, he was searching for an operationally savvy CFO to take a seat on his executive staff.

✳ What attracted you to this situation when many would run away?

I was ready for a CFO's assignment. Since my time with Arthur Anderson and Pepsi, I had been through a number of difficult situations. This scenario looked bright compared to the situations I faced at Silverado, Reader's Digest, and Toys "R" Us. Yes, I had grown from all those assignments and wanted to grow more. I'm competitive by nature and felt up to the challenge. In addition, material weaknesses and Asian offshore manufacturing were financial and operational issues that were well within my experience base and skill set. Besides, the primary shareholder had made a multimillion-dollar investment and was committed to fix what ailed the business.

Under private equity ownership, generally two outcomes emerge if things work out: a company either gets acquired at a profit or it goes public. Given the situation, I thought we had a shot at taking Maidenform through an IPO. The bonus? I would expand my experience in that scenario.

So I interviewed with the new ownership, the new CEO, his head of sales, and his general counsel. They all had a pragmatic handle on the situation and seemed to have the chops to do what it took to change things. They sold me on their game plan:

* Speed Chinese offshore manufacturing to set competitive prices and increase profit margins,

✳ Sell Maidenform products through multiple channels, and

✳ Fix the material financial weaknesses.

In summary, they wanted what I brought to the table.

✳ How did you hatch the plan to address this situation?
Phase 1 of the ABCs: Hatch the Plan

> "The only way to make sense out of change is to plunge into it, move with it and join the dance."
>
> —Alan Watts

Two of the three components of that game plan were right up my alley. I needed to test the overall assumptions and construct my own game plan to accomplish my two pieces of the puzzle, the offshoring and repairing financial weaknesses.

A: Ask Questions and Listen; Then Ask for Help

My FASB training taught me to gather facts; my other experiences taught me due diligence. I applied both.

Through a series of meetings with insiders and outsiders, I tested the three points of the game plan. Where were the material weaknesses? Why? How could they best be tackled? What was needed tactically and operationally to successfully offshore production? Where were the sources of the highest-quality lowest-cost production? What was the pricing and gross margin impact of multiple channels of distribution? What was the best mix of distribution channels to yield the best gross margin for the entire business?

During my first week on the job, I set up a meeting with the public accounting firm's partner in charge of Maidenform's audit. I wanted to hear her view of material weaknesses and get her advice, so I asked, "What do we have to do to get rid of this material weakness?" She quickly answered, "Don't ask me what *we* need to do. It's what *you* need to do!" Okay, I knew that.

B: Base the Plan on What You Hear and See, or Don't Hear and See

Maidenform had been essentially a family-run business before its bankruptcy and new ownership. Although its accounting system was more sophisticated than a shoebox full of receipts, the company lacked processes, documentation, and disciplines that I'd grown to expect from a sizable business. In my first week on the job, the private equity owners asked me, "How long to get this ready to go public?" During my job interviews the previous month, they didn't appear to be in a hurry. But their view had changed, and they felt confident Tom's team was on a fast track to right the business. That created a sense of urgency.

Simultaneously, a change in legislation loomed, which added another dimension of complexity that was bigger than fixing material weaknesses. Much of the company's financial staff lacked public company background and experience. Because the Sarbanes-Oxley legislation was brand new, nobody on the accounting or operational staff had compliance experience. The array of controls, documentation, and communications processes that were needed to comply with both SEC requirements and the new legislation were far beyond Maidenform's current reach.

A piece of the company's production had already shifted to Caribbean manufacturers. Though that move did provide some cost advantage over New Jersey production, many competitors looked to Asia, mainly China, for the best return for the buck. Tom initiated that Chinese move, but still, Maidenform was far behind its competitors in achieving cost advantages. We needed a full-fledged Asian offshore effort—and fast.

Selling through multiple distribution channels made sense. The Maidenform brand, pricing, and margins, however, needed to be protected from slash-and-burn discounters. Meanwhile, Maidenform hadn't significantly tapped the international marketplace.

Tom and his sales crew understood the sales and marketing issues as well as the opportunities. They formulated a plan to address them.

C: Challenge the Sacred Cows or the Status Quo

When I joined Maidenform, it had never been a public company. Culturally, it was a family-owned business that, frankly, had been operated by the seat of its pants. Controls, processes, documentation, disclosure committees, and such were all new ground. The idea of establishing these protocols as part of day-to-day management practices seemed foreign to many. Their typical responses varied: *"This will slow us down!"* *"This is an obstacle to running our day-to-day business." "We're busy; we don't have time."* Thinking past the next month or the next quarter and planning two, three, even five years out was totally new for the organization as a whole, although not for the newly installed senior team.

We knew that the status quo had provided a comfort zone, especially since a large cross section of Maidenform's employees had been with the company for 20, 30, even 40 years. Not everybody was onboard with the plan to outsource manufacturing and particularly moving production to Asia. The culture was not only "Made in America, baby!"; it was "Made in New Jersey."

How fast could these old timers make a cultural shift—a shift that had to be made?

S: Share the Vision to Create a Collective energy

Before we shared the game plan with the entire company, we ensured that the four of us on the executive staff were completely behind it. We each had responsibility for executing a piece of that game plan. We understood that and supported one another. We could make some key hires, but we couldn't fire the whole company on day one to make the changes required to become a cost-efficient, public company. We agreed that we needed to sell and educate our staff while changing the culture to boot. So each member of the executive team met with key departmental lieutenants to outline the game plan.

The long-term goal was simple: We would become a successful public company. And for an IPO to succeed, our financial house had to be in order. That required earning a clean opinion from the public accounting firm on the next audit, with no material weaknesses. The audit was only five months away. Processes, controls, and documentation had to change to be compliant with SEC requirements and Sarbanes-Oxley legislation. The benefits to the brand and the access to capital made it worthwhile to struggle through the changes.

We set out to move full-tilt into Asian outsourced manufacturing, most likely in China. That was the only way to remain in business, period! That meant requiring and even augmenting many of the skills the company already had in design, quality, product specifications, warehousing, and logistical distribution. We planned to assault the marketplace from multiple channels, gain a larger international presence, and become a truly global brand. No, we wouldn't save our way to success; we had to grow. And that was exciting. What was not said but inferred was this: "Get on board or get out."

This game plan cascaded from departmental lieutenants to their staff. We met over and over again, with Tom presiding over all-company meetings and members of the executive staff conducting their own departmental meetings. We set up cross-functional meetings at the mid-manager level. We made sure the messaging of one meeting reinforced the messaging of other meetings, and each member of the executive team reinforced each other's messaging. That's how we presented the game plan, answered questions, and spoke with one voice.

✳ Once the plan was hatched, how did you align your team to kick off the plan?

Phase 2 of the ABCs: Kick Off the Game Plan

"Nobody has ever built a brand by imitating somebody else…."

—David Ogilvy

A: Act Boldly to Kick Off the Game Plan

To tackle the financial compliance requirements, I needed trustworthy people with the appropriate skill sets. I couldn't do it all by myself.

I went back to Toys "R" Us and hired the best, most experienced person there, and brought him in as my controller. We mapped out our strategy to tackle operational weaknesses and address compliance requirements. The controller kicked off an internal task force. We traded some members of the finance and operations staff for outside hires who had the experience and skills we lacked. We asked the auditor to provide real-time feedback along the way to help us overcome our deficiencies. We built an air of respect, communication, and trust with the auditor—qualities that had been lacking. In fact, that had led to their bad opinion and the citing of material weaknesses in the first place.

Compliance had an operational overtone; it wasn't solely financial. We staffed an experienced operational team in Hong Kong to ensure that contract manufacturers were in compliance with all the laws and regulations, including child labor issues, import restrictions, and shipping and warehousing requirements. They also performed quality audits. We watched in horror as other companies struggled with the public relations nightmares that stemmed from surprise audits of contract manufacturers who operated as sweatshops, employed 9-year-old children, and produced sub-standard goods. Fortunately, we had protected the brand.

B: Build on Strengths

Though several things were wrong with finance, administration, and operations, a number of things were right as well. Billings, collections, payables, and vendor selection and relations were well run and staffed with capable people.

Among the strengths was the quality and reputation of the more-than-82-year-old Maidenform brand. Embedded in the corporate culture was a reverence with which the brand was held. It stood for quality at a fair price. In fact, salespeople were always able to get their foot in the door when they led with our brand. Thus, protecting it had been built into the corporate DNA.

The Maidenform designers were among the best in the business. With fashion involving a fleeting, rapidly changing environment, designers had to be on top of all the trends. It some cases, they set the trends. "Quality at reasonable cost" translated into detailed product specifications, including the quality of material and stitching.

Still, Maidenform designers stayed true to the brand's traditional product positioning that had catapulted Maidenform to its original success—that is, to complement and amplify the natural shape of a woman's figure.

C: Control Through Visible Measurement

Given the game plan, we had only a few key levers to judge our progress. They were gross margin and product costs, to be sure, plus revenue by channel. We already had a handle on the material weakness issues and corrections were underway. When it came to regulatory compliance, however, we came up with a laundry list of 250 control items. With Sarbanes-Oxley legislation being so new, we had to figure it all out.

In early 2005, I attended a compliance conference to provide clarity on this issue. The controller at GE talked about his 50 key control items. *"Wait a minute,"* I thought. *"GE is much more complex than we are."* I went back to my financial team to rethink and prioritize, and we narrowed our list.

This process reminded me of a lesson learned from Pepsi's international CEO when he was asked at a meeting, "When you're flying around the world and visiting your various segments, how do you know if they're on track or not?" He replied, "It always just comes down to the team and what I call the *cold gut check*. I expect people who run businesses to have a *cold gut check* of it. That means if I walked off a plane without a binder, folder, or an assistant and I met with people, I could ask questions and tell if the people in charge had the *cold gut check* of the business."

Yes, it's important to use graphs and charts to view performance against goals, but so is talking to the right people and getting the *cold gut check*.

S: Streamline the Activity Schedule

Vision, mission, and elevator pitch

In fall 2004 when I joined Maidenform, it was already owned by private equity investors. They hired the right CEO. The board and executive team both subscribed to the overriding vision: We were out to right the Maidenform ship and create a global, profitable brand centered in a successful public company. It would offer a high-quality product line produced by outsourced manufacturing partners. And of course, its owners sought their return on investment.

Maidenform's mission—to provide fashionable quality that complemented a woman's figure to the mainstream market at reasonable prices—was well ingrained in the company. Instead of changing it, the new management team embraced and reinforced that mission.

In fact, we repeated the vision, mission, and game plan so often, in combination, that it became the de-facto elevator pitch: *a growing, publicly traded global brand of high-quality undergarments that complemented a woman's figure at mainstream prices available through a variety of retail outlets.*

Competitive positioning and targeting strategy

Maidenform's products were competitively positioned at the mid-range price point. At the time, that meant about $20 for a department store bra. The lower end was priced at $10 and the premium at $30 to $50. Maidenform's attention to fashion and quality were far superior to any competitive product in the mid-priced range. Cheaper products didn't approach its quality or fashion. Premium products existed, but Maidenform's value proposition attracted the mainstream marketplace.

The retail world had grown in complexity since Maidenform's post–World War II heyday. Department store sales of branded Maidenform products had certainly been its most profitable sales channel, but mass merchandisers took large chunks of market share throughout the 1980s and 1990s. They had to be part of the distribution mix.

Private label avenues were also targeted. That meant products customized for exclusive distribution by a chain could gather market share and protect the Maidenform brand from pricing encroachment. To convert overages in vendor inventory into cash, liquidation discounters became an important channel for the clothing and fashion industry overall. Added to the mix were 90 Maidenform outlet retail stores that featured Maidenform's entire product line in key locations. A small online component added an ecommerce dimension to this brick-and-mortar retail approach.

Primary goals (the BHAGs) to focus the energy

Achieving the vision—to right the ship, create a global, profitable brand centered in a successful public company that offered a high-quality product line produced by outsourced manufacturing partners—became the overarching driver of our goals. It encompassed our game plan.

In 2005, we sought to go public. We knew we had to correct material weaknesses and be compliant with all SEC rules and regulations in the 2004 audit for the IPO. We also had to accelerate our offshore manufacturing. That would enable our sales team to penetrate multiple distribution channels globally with cost-competitive, quality products that could generate reasonable profit margins. All of these elements tied together.

Critical success factors to prioritize the actions

Our team took a cross-functional approach to our planning and coordination. After all, we were mutually dependent on each other's functional areas of expertise. We knew we needed to be in synch to pull off our vision. Successful execution in correcting materials weakness and compliance was the purview of our cross-functional task team. Thankfully, people knew what was at stake and embraced their roles in putting together the puzzle.

Tom and I drove the push to manufacture increasingly more Maidenform products through offshore partners. We asked, "Could we increase the profit margin by 800 basis points?" With each basis point at one tenth of 1 percent, we looked to achieve a full eight-percentage-point increase in gross margins. Given where gross margins were—in the high-20s—we sought to increase the margins by one third, to the mid-30s. So we created a cross-functional team to drive that process.

As new sales channels opened, the product differentiation of private labels to protect the brand and its pricing point became critical. We weren't sure how this new approach would play out. We needed accurate forecasting of would-be sales by specific product through specific channels. That was critical to ensure timely product availability in sufficient quantity (but not too much quantity) as well as meet our revenue and margin goals.

Because protecting the brand was a huge piece of the cultural value system, research and development's revised product flow had to keep the products relevant and current with fashion trends. New product design and testing to ensure the quality of color and shape could stand up to multiple washings became critical to success on several fronts.

To monitor everything, we placed momentum indicators—for example, sales by channel, profit margin, product mix, forecast versus actual, quality and compliance checks—on a summary report. We would review the chart at frequent meetings held at the department, cross-functional team, and executive levels. We understood that transparency was an important part of accountability.

Yet, to be credible, our hopes and dreams had to be realistic, not pie in-the sky. At the end of the day, I had to add a cold *gut check* so that graphs, charts, and numbers included an element of human judgment. We all agreed: Achieving the vision was a tall order, but it was doable. We were committed.

Define and reinforce the culture

For all of the resistance to changing the status quo, the theme of pride around the Maidenform brand and its insistence on quality were gifts. We embraced that theme and the insistence to carry us past the initial resistance. With protecting the brand as the common denominator, conflict resolution came quite easily.

Once the executive staff made the case and touted the benefits for change, we didn't experience a tremendous amount of conflict. Rather, we spent our time integrating new people into the business. We also focused on teamwork to get people aligned on everything we wanted to accomplish. That meant no room for any competition between long timers and new people; we had work to do.

✳ With the game plan hatched and kicked off, what was your approach to execute?

Phase 3 of the ABCs: Execute the Plan

"War is a series of catastrophes that result in victory."

—Albert Pike

A: Assert Yourself at the Focal Point

Successful IPO

As it related to the material weaknesses and compliance issues, within a matter of months the task team presided over Maidenform gaining a clean accounting opinion on its 2004 audit. At the same time, we contracted with a Sarbanes-Oxley expert and put those procedures and documentation in place. We had prepared to become compliant as a public company; now we had to keep it that way. High impact—high stress! Our team really came through.

In summer 2005, we filed for an IPO and the company was taken public at $17 per share by a cadre of investment bankers. Wall Street bought our game plan. The trend lines reinforced that we were on our way to achieving it. That was nine months after the day I started working at Maidenform.

Expansion to specialty channels

The sales and marketing team had set out to execute its specialty channel plan by approaching Walmart and Target with the notion of a private brand especially for them. They liked it. Walmart's brand carried the "Sweet Nothings" label; Target's brand was "Self Expressions." Both products were a customized and differentiated version of Maidenform's product priced at about $10 retail.

Once Walmart and Target bought the private label idea and stocked their shelves, sales took off. Then the team took this private label idea to Victoria's Secret, with fancier customization and a higher price point than Walmart and Target. Victoria's Secret also stocked and sold Maidenform's customized shapewear branded "Flexees"—a new-age girdle. Sales took off.

The traditional bread and butter department stores such as Macy's, Dillard's, and JC Penney that carried the higher-margin Maidenform brand didn't miss a beat. Sales volume, pricing, and margins remained whole. Excess inventory was kept to a minimum. When we had to, we moved inventory through TJ Maxx and other liquidators.

In addition, the 90 Maidenform outlet stores provided about 20 percent of Maidenform's revenue, with the remaining 80 percent generated on a wholesale basis through the other channels. This mix was balanced enough to achieve our gross margin goals.

Move to second-tier manufacturers to expand capacity and lower cost

Our Hong Kong–based supply chain team became saturated in work. The team's process evolved and improved over time as they managed relationships and organized production forecasts, logistics, regulatory, and quality audits.

As unit volume increased and more U.S. production was offshored, the initial top-tier production contractors had reached capacity. As global outsourcing increased, other top-tier manufacturers located in Chinese coastal population centers became capacity-poor. The cost advantages began to plateau as the manufacturers exerted pressure to increase their prices. Oops! That would move the profit margin needle in the wrong direction.

So we expanded our Hong Kong team. This team looked inland for second-tier manufacturers that hadn't been first when global outsourcing expansion started. Constructing new supplier relationships put pressure on us. Detailed product specifications, training, quality and compliance auditing, additional referencing, and more layers of forecasting, production scheduling, shipping, and inventory ware-housing logistics and cash management added layers of complexity to an already-complex supply chain. With cross-functional teams aimed at achieving our BHAGs, we still pulled it off, decreased costs, and increased our margins.

✳ What obstacles did you encounter along the way? How did you deal with them?

Although I wouldn't use the term *obstacle,* a few tough operational issues faced us. We dealt with them head-on and, if we hadn't, they might have spelled trouble down the line. The issues included investor relations, supply chain overload, international expansion, slowing revenue growth, and stagnant stock.

Investor Relations' Void

There we were inside a brand-new publicly traded company. As we had budgeted before our IPO, I planned to add an investor relations professional to join the staff. The board pushed back by saying, "Don't spend the money. You've already increased staff. Investors want to speak to the CFO anyway." Although I had no public company CFO experience myself, I backed off. What did I know?

After the IPO, I found myself inundated with calls from both current and prospective shareholders and investment analysts. They had questions, and I couldn't simply ignore their calls. Within a matter of weeks, this became my full-time effort.

As an example, Tom came into my office and complained that I hadn't provided this or that. When he realized I was consumed by investor relations, he said, "Recruit the best investor relations professional you can find, and do it now. I'll deal with the board." I was all smiles.

Supply Chain Overload Led to Sales Force Conflicts

Tom and I worked hand and glove to oversee the increasingly complex supply chain. We both already had full-time jobs, but this became a second full-time effort. As we executed our plan, margins increased nicely, but I became concerned about excess inventory, the balance of product mix into the liquidation channel (the lowest margin), and our ability to achieve growing sales forecasts. We added controls through a purchase order system, which started with input that the sales team had solicited from customers. We tied the balanced style and season changes to manufacturing, procurement, shipping, and finally warehousing and inventory. Too much inventory led to too much lower margin business through the liquidation channel, so we had to be wary.

We formed a group we called the SKU Cops. (SKU stood for Stock Keeping Units.) The SKU Cops met weekly, examined the inventory on hand and trend line of past sales, and challenged the forecasts based on color and by style. Although rules were flexible, the general rule was that to add a new SKU, an old one—presumably the slowest-moving one—had to be removed. Did we miss sales? Did we miss opportunities? Maybe we did. On the flip side, we also managed overall profit margins and reduced the requirement for huge markdowns of excess inventory through our liquidation channels.

International Expansion

As we grew our international business from scratch, some stress to our whole process occurred. We created controls and processes to serve these new customers although we had no historical trend data to help anyone predict or forecast. Because it was a new growth opportunity to expand the top line, we took a pilot approach to nibble a little bit rather than making a big gamble. We debated this at a few executive staff sessions. Tom showed his support not only in looking at the opportunity but also in putting boundaries around the risk as we delved into something new. We struck a balance.

Slowing Revenue Growth and Stagnant Stock

After a few years, the $300 million Maidenform revenue had grown by one third to $400 million. Not bad, but our growth had slowed. As a result, the stock price had stagnated. Initial growth occurred as the company reclaimed and then added market share. But growth was topping off, and the overall market in our mid-range market segment wasn't increasing fast enough to please Wall Street.

The luxury market segment, however, abounded with new, higher price-point products and increased growth over the mid-range segment. We asked tough questions. Should we participate in that market segment? If so, how would we do it?

Bringing a mid-range product line to the premium segment didn't make sense to us. It didn't protect the brand. So we proposed to supplement our core brand (Maidenform) by selectively acquiring a premium brand that could benefit from Maidenform's infrastructure and save costs. We brought that strategy to the board and highlighted a few prospective acquisition candidates. The board's assessment? Too risky and too costly. We had to find another way.

B: Borrow From Alliances and Partnerships

In every corner of Maidenform, the company struck some form of alliance or partnership to augment its own resources. This was done to realize the vision, execute the game plan, and achieve the goals we'd set at the outset.

Outsourced manufacturing was certainly a borrowed resource. We initially hired Chinese contractors who had the knowledge and contacts to find and manage those outsourcers. A good deal of the supply chain, therefore, originated from borrowed resources. These reasons enabled the company to achieve lower costs, more competitive price-points, and higher gross profit margins faster and more efficiently than it could if left to its own devices.

Our sales channels were essentially borrowed resources with less than 20 percent of revenue coming from company-owned stores. The remainder came from others' store shelves—traditional department stores, mass merchandisers, private label arrangements, or inventory liquidators.

Without the benefit of in-house knowledge or resources to accomplish regulatory compliance, we hired third-party experts to work closely with our task force to educate us. At the same time, we had to build Sarbanes-Oxley compliance into our financial and operational practices. The IPO might have resulted in SEC violations had we not borrowed that expertise.

C: Communicate Progress and Results to Get/Stay on Track

It was critical for us to have alignment at the top. The four of us on the executive staff coalesced on the details of our game plan before we communicated anything to the rest of our team. It was important that the right people to execute the strategy absolutely knew what they were asked to do and why they were asked to do it. They had unwavering support from the senior leadership team to do it.

Similarly, it was critical the senior leadership team had the same unwavering support from its board of directors. We communicated with the directors like crazy to gain their alignment from the start.

The executive staff ensured multiple touch points throughout the organization to communicate progress versus plans, milestones achieved, and more. We did so within the functional departments and cross functionally as well. Company meetings, departmental meetings, and cross-functional team meetings happened frequently. We set up two-way communication paths, not all up-to-down communication. And we provided plenty of room for down-to-up dialogue as well; we had to listen, too. I'd like to think our leadership style was empowering. Although we didn't micromanage, we were ready to redirect an approach if something faltered along the way.

Though the organization knew how to communicate internally—and its marketing communications knew how to communicate its message to the market in general—Maidenform was still a newly public company. Much of the rank and file had no experience in a public setting, so we trained our people on what they could or could not say or do. We had to remain compliant with rules and regulations as a public company.

Management was as accountable to public shareholders as it was the board of directors, which required a focused communications effort. We plugged our marketing communications and a new investor relations function into one another for consistent messaging. That put the left hand and the right hand consistently in synch with one another. Both marketing and investor messages made their way to the company's Website and digital media as well as through the traditional media.

S: Spread the Rewards of Wealth and Recognition When Things Go Your Way

We constructed two general ways to reward our staff. The first was financial, with team and individual goals carrying bonus opportunities. Accomplished targets captured an annual financial prize. At certain levels, members of the staff were granted stock options, both at the time of hire and annually thereafter. As the price of the stock increased and stock options vested, we had opportunities for financial gain. Presumably, as shareholders get rewarded with a higher-priced stock, so does the individual.

Second, we recognized success by promoting ambitious employees to increased positions of responsibility to advance their career as they achieved their goals. We also worked to develop people to handle additional duties and challenges. And we recognized both groups and individuals for their feats that contributed to our game plan. Once in a while, people who didn't perform or couldn't be coached to improve were asked to leave.

✳ What was the end result of the execution?

The team converted a bankrupt brand with outdated business practices and serious deficiencies to form a successful, global public company. We fully realized our vision and hit every goal we had set for ourselves.

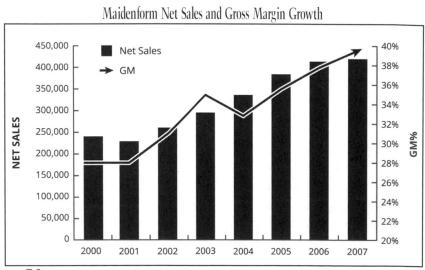

Maidenform Net Sales and Gross Margin Growth

Image 7.2.

As a public company, Maidenform received only positive audit reports from its public accounting firm, and it maintained compliance with all regulatory requirements. Manufacturing was fully outsourced to Chinese partners overseen by a senior supply chain executive added to the staff. The company increased its gross profits by a full 1,000 basis points versus the 800 to which it originally aspired. That turned out to be a full 10 percentage points higher than planned, increasing profit margins by nearly 45 percent—no small feat.

With Maidenform products selling in more than 8,000 stores nationwide, the brand has been stocked and sold off the shelves of Debenhaus and House of Fraser in Europe and Takashimaya in Asia. Over a four-year period (from 2005 to 2008), revenue grew by a third to $400 million. Maidenform achieved a 40-percent market share in its segment. Its designers received countless awards for style and quality for a mid-market price-point—the hallmark of its brand identity remaining unblemished. After this success, Tom retired, with the company's leading sales executive succeeding him as CEO.

International expansion, while achieved, only accounted for 10 percent of Maidenform's overall revenue. The board of directors never approved the acquisition strategy to gain a brand that would penetrate the faster growing luxury market segment. During the financial crisis, the price of Maidenform's stock plunged (as many companies' stock did) from $17 per share to $7 per share. As the world economy recovered, though, so did Maidenform. Then in 2013, HanesBrands acquired Maidenform for more than $23 per share—nearly a 40-percent increase from its earlier IPO price.

✳ What's your reflection as you look back?

So many things connect in life. I have no doubt the head of University of Arkansas's accounting department influenced my joining Arthur Andersen. I never would have gone to the Financial Accounting Standard's Board without working for such a firm as Arthur Andersen. There's no way PepsiCo would have hired me without the Arthur Andersen and FASB background. I grew through experiences with firms that suffered from major issues. Without that "wartime" badge, Maidenform might not have considered me up to the task for my first CFO role.

It goes on and on. One decision or one event in life leads to something else. That's my best advice for anyone starting out: Just go out and do something. Be prepared for a fun journey with twists and turns. You'll find your path. And it sure helped me that I had a supportive spouse along the way.

If I could do some things over, I'd have made certain decisions more quickly. Not that my results had necessarily suffered, but I'm more experienced now and would move faster. In addition, I'd love to have taken the firm to the next level and executed on the multiple brand strategy by acquiring a premium product offering. Overall, I had fun with a terrific cast of people, and I'll always treasure the experience.

As for Maidenform, the brand now occupies a prominent place inside a global firm. HanesBrands has the muscle and the market presence to help it realize additional potential by being featured on more international store shelves. In addition, HanesBrands owns sister products with both low-end and luxury positioning. With its company-owned offshore manufacturing capacity, costs could be further reduced, thus yielding an even more competitive and profitable brand.

Maidenform's remaining staff can realize additional opportunities to advance their careers in this platform.

✳ How did this experience help you advance?

I certainly grew personally while serving on the executive team as one of the key leaders of a company. Maidenform took a risk on me. And I took a risk. Succeeding wasn't a cake walk for me or the company, but I'm now an experienced CFO with an IPO under my belt. I've emerged from another "wartime" experience with distinction, which has enhanced my credentials to be considered for other CFO roles.

In 2008, I joined Ace Hardware as CFO. This large, complex $15 billion company with a 100-year-old history and wonderful people considered going public. But when its board voted to stay private, it was time for me to make a move on my own terms.

I returned to a "wartime" role as CFO with Radio Shack. Its CFO had just been promoted to CEO and the company was on the back end of a turnaround. It looked like things had turned. The business positioned itself to benefit from the mobile computing revolution, with major cellular carriers such as Sprint, AT&T, and Verizon being its largest suppliers.

Six months after I got there, though, these carriers essentially changed their pricing structure and subsidy payments. That cut Radio Shack's margins significantly. I thought, *"Oh, this again!"* Radio Shack's dagger came from overly relying on a couple of vendors instead of a couple of customers for success. Overnight, product margins went from 40 to 20 percent on half of Radio Shack's revenue. The math simply didn't work.

The board and the CEO parted company, and the board sought a new CEO with a retail merchandising background. I agreed to stay on as Radio Shack's interim CEO to provide time to find a new person. While there, I was introduced to Planet Fitness. Once Radio Shack selected its CEO, I joined Planet Fitness in 2013 as executive vice president and CFO.

Planet Fitness (PF) enjoys a recurring revenue stream driven by an entrepreneurial team that's building the PF brand. The company is positioned as a health club for the masses. With about 50 company-owned locations and nearing 1,000 franchisees, the company has been executing a major expansion initiative. Because Planet Fitness is private equity–sponsored, a liquidity event is likely to happen down the line. That usually means an IPO or an acquisition. At PF, I'm having a blast with a whole host of tremendously talented people. I'm putting my acquired skills to use to manage rapid growth and keep my organization out of an unneeded war. If, for some reason, a war would be thrust upon us, I have the experience to deal with it straight up and come out the other end standing up.

I'm also exploring sitting on a corporate board or two, either public or privately financed. The corporations could be doing just fine or facing issues. I know I can offer a diverse set of experiences that would add value.

Kevin L. Rakin:
Restarting a Failed Business at Advanced BioHealing

"The first step toward success is taken when you refuse to be a captive of the environment in which you first find yourself."

—Mark Caine

Image 8.1: Kevin L. Rakin. Photo copyright Kevin L. Rakin. Used with permission.

✳ **How did you get to be the person you are? What's your story?**

Let me take you back to growing up in the 1960s and 1970s in South Africa, a small country at the bottom of the world. My South African childhood took place in a very protected and closed kind of environment. I had a calm, nurturing family life. We always thought everything was bigger and better outside South Africa. In addition, of course, we had huge sociological problems in the heyday of apartheid and the black struggle for freedom. Nelson Mandela was in prison.

I grew up in a Jewish community, which was comparatively liberal among the white minority. The family immigrated to South Africa around 1900. The Holocaust that took place in Europe in the 1940s was recent history. So when I was growing up, it was discomforting that we weren't living in a country where we felt pride in a system in which we believed.

On the other hand, day-to-day living was pretty idyllic. Cape Town is a beautiful coastal part of the country. The region had always been politically and socially liberal. It hadn't seen the same kind of strife as Johannesburg in the north, which had the mining industry and therefore attracted more of the labor. Cape Town was a center for tourism, wine-growing, and insurance.

Family of Entrepreneurs and Small Business Owners

My father was a pharmacist with two retail stores. He worked with his father-in-law, my grandfather, who was also a pharmacist. From the age of 12, I worked at my father's pharmacy a few miles from our house. I learned the business from the ground up on Saturdays and summer vacations. His stores were the British style of pharmacy that had, among other things, a camera department. I remember the excitement I felt at age 13, showing customers our cameras and making a sale.

Everything was close to home. I had no need to travel, not even to go to college. I attended the University of Cape Town. In the South African system, if you went to your local university, you stayed at home. Why would you pay to live in a dormitory?

My first time out of South Africa came at the end of my first year at the university when I was 18. My father and I traveled to Frankfurt, Germany, where we attended a major international photographic exhibition. It was eye-opening to see such a huge display and understand the world of Japanese photo equipment during this time of change for the industry. The process of developing negatives was changing from using a centralized Kodak-style lab to using retail shops that offered the service themselves. We looked at different machines and talked to Japanese suppliers. My father bought a one-hour photographic machine. It started a whole new world for me.

Next, I pursued an undergraduate business degree. In South Africa, one went into business by becoming a chartered accountant. In 1981, I graduated from college with that accounting training.

Anxiety of a Failed State

My family had two recurring topics of conversation at the dinner table: We either discussed the pharmacy business or the uncertainty in South Africa. Where were we going to live someday? As Jewish white South Africans, we didn't believe there was a long-term future for us. Before Mandela was released from prison in 1991, people were leaving and emigration was common. South Africa didn't have a true democracy until 1995. Apartheid dramatically affected our society. A famous Jewish politician, Helen Suzman, was the only liberal member of South Africa's Parliament who always talked about Mandela, justice, and fairness. Many protesters cried out that apartheid was not right and there should be more equality.

At the same time, I think Jews felt like they were the proverbial canaries in the coal mine. They wanted to never again get stuck in a country that could collapse. Jews only came to South Africa in 1880–1900, mostly from Lithuania. But in the 1960s and 1970s, they were leaving in droves. At its peak around 1960, the Jewish community was about 120,000 people. It dropped by 40 percent over the next 20 years. Jews who left South Africa began living on the East Coast or West Coast of the United States; in Canada, Australia, Israel, and England; and all over Europe.

In my home and in our community, we always discussed where we were going to live one day. Where would our parents go?

✳ What was your career progression before joining Advanced BioHealing?

Public Accounting and a Ticket to the United States

I initially worked for the Big Eight accounting firm Arthur Young. It later became Ernst & Young after its merger with another Big Eight accounting firm, Ernst & Ernst. This merger made Ernst & Young one of the world's largest public accounting firms. It was certainly among the largest in Cape Town.

I learned the basics of business by doing sales in my father's pharmacy. Specifically, I learned that more needs to come into a business every day than goes out. Otherwise, you don't take a paycheck home, your family doesn't live, and the business doesn't prosper.

From there, I studied accounts, taxes, and economics inside multinational businesses. I worked on big company audits and small audits, too. In South Africa, by law, every business had to have an audit. So I'd go from a shoebox of receipts to Mobil Oil's sophisticated accounting system.

After three years, Arthur Young offered me a transfer to the United States to work in its Hartford, Connecticut, office. I jumped at the opportunity, volunteering for an assignment in its up-and-coming Entrepreneurial Services Group (ESG). I didn't think of myself as an entrepreneur. But based on my experience with my family, I was interested in how businesses were shaped.

So there I was, all of 25 years old and very excited to be in the United States. I came with the view it could be my long-term home. What a contrast! I had always been in a cloistered South African environment. Even when I got the job at Arthur Young and moved out of my parents' home, my new home was only seven miles from my childhood home. It was still in the same town.

In South Africa, we grew up in the British system. To say the focus was on manners and politeness would be an understatement. If you said you're going to do something, you'd better do it. When I first came to the United States, I was surprised. From the South African perspective, the American people have an attitude like "We're going to accomplish the impossible. We're doing this. Everything's great." Then if they only get 80 percent of the way there, they pat themselves on the back (although they did get to the moon). But we were taught "You didn't do what you said you were going to do." I've probably become more American in that regard. I see the difference when I go back and talk with my South African friends. We grew up in a more conservative culture, one less focused on sales, marketing, and self-advancement.

I was fortunate that Arthur Young gave its young managers more responsibility than most. Hartford was a small office, and I got a lot of responsibility quickly. That included exposure to its Mergers and Acquisitions Group and my first memorable exposure to biotech. I worked on an audit for a fledgling biotech company that planned to go public. With no revenue or profit, this firm raised tens of millions of dollars on the basis of its vision. It was ultimately valued at $3 million (according to a PhD on staff).

Whole New Track to Pursue

Totally fascinated, this made me ask questions. How does venture capital work? How do you put a business plan together? Where does that venture capital come from in the first place, and how are those people smart enough to know where to put that money?

I started to see the entrepreneurial world through a biotech perspective. In those large public accounting firms, one aspires to become a partner. That was the golden ticket. I used to think, *"Could I be a partner one day?"* Then I realized there was another track: *"Could I become a chief financial officer (CFO)?"*

Fortunately, I got that opportunity five years after coming to the United States. I was assigned to the audit of a consulting firm being acquired by a large European parent to expand its global reach. Would I be the CFO? As a piece of the offer, the decision-makers agreed I could also start a financial consulting practice. This gave me general management, international, and CFO experience that I could leverage. I wanted to be a global businessperson.

At this point, I joined one of my biotech consulting clients as CFO. This little company in New Haven, Connecticut, was my first experience of biotech meeting high finance. As one of the first Yale University spinoffs, it developed reagents and consumables used in early-stage genetic research. It had gone through all its venture capital. A big-name healthcare consulting firm that had invested in the company had run into problems of its own and suspended financing. The biotech company would be shut down.

I came in to help the CEO concoct a plan. We created a restart to acquire the assets. Then we attracted $150,000 of venture capital from Connecticut Innovations, a state-run funding source intended to stimulate job growth. Because the shareholders planned to shut it down anyway, we essentially bought the company for a dollar. At age 29, I suddenly owned 20 percent of a biotech company with $1 million of revenue. The CEO owned 30 percent, the head scientist owned 25 percent, and we gave the employees the remaining 25 percent. At the current expense rate, we had five months of cash. We cut back on our costs, focused on products that sold well, and negotiated credit terms with our suppliers.

Interestingly, I was the only one in the company who didn't have a PhD. By then, though, I was armed with an Executive MBA from Columbia. Our first instinct was to clean up the company, buy time, and flip it to an acquirer who wanted the revenue. That didn't work. So we opted to try to build a business. One of our Yale PhDs received a patent involving gene sequencing. We licensed the technology to two firms for $300,000, which paid for another year. During that time, we built the business from $1 million to $3 million in revenue.

In the meantime, I befriended a young Yale MD/PhD and helped him attract $10 million in venture capital to launch another company. This company correlated genetics with medication to determine what worked best for a unique individual. We actually constructed the idea on the back of a napkin at a pizza restaurant. This was the burgeoning new field of pharmacogenomics or personalized medicine. We merged my company and the new one, naming our creation Genaissance Pharmaceuticals. We slowly sold off the reagents business. That cash became Genaissance's seed capital.

Next, we targeted and pitched Jürgen Drews, who had been a legendary head of research and development at Roche. He said, "Of course, personalized medicine! It's the future! I would love to be your chairman. I'm just stepping down from Roche." Suddenly, we had a rock star head of research and development as our chairman. We attracted $8 million of capital from a small Swiss fund, and we got going.

A Huge Vision

We were two kids, really—only 33 and 34 years old. We had developed a huge vision we had no idea how we would realize: We would capture genetic variations, and then figure out a way to integrate that into drug development. This would become the panacea for the future development of new drugs.

After a couple of years, we saw we needed to scale our business. It suddenly came into focus that the genome project was delivering new insights, and personalized medicine would be big—really big. In going out to raise $20 million in venture capital, we attracted three big names. We actually raised $60 million just before the bubble burst in 2000. Our timing was perfect.

Then we went straight from that into an IPO, which raised $100 million that August. Our initial success was mind-boggling. We had a vision, some early-stage science, and a term sheet from Johnson & Johnson saying it would pay us $5 million per year for our database. And it wasn't even a signed deal yet. We had no revenue. The market cap for the company, when it went public, was $350 million. That increased to $750 million before everything collapsed in 2001.

We thought we were the smartest guys in the world. Of course, we weren't.

As I look back at that decade, it taught me how to put the vision together, raise venture capital, do complex deals, and go public. However, I still hadn't figured out how to actually make a business out of the science.

What Next?

When the bubble burst in 2001, the chickens came home to roost. I was smart enough to realize we had to downsize and change direction. For a public company, the rules change and we had to, as well. I had a dispute with my partner over this point, so we went to the board and asked its members to arbitrate our disagreement. My partner preferred to continue unabated. I preferred to downsize by 35 percent, sell a few services to bring in revenue, use our public stock as currency to acquire smaller businesses, and then build. The board approved my path, and I took over as CEO.

In 2001, the company completed a couple of small acquisitions and sold some service revenues. We launched a diagnostic test and bought a DNA testing business out of bankruptcy. Then we licensed a drug from Merck KGaA to couple with our genetic markers. All in all, we developed a strategy and plan, and we started building.

But by 2004, I realized pharmacogenomics was taking too long to become an established industry. In 2005, we merged with another public company controlled by a billionaire with the money to take the vision all the way forward. Genaissance shareholders got 40 percent of the deal. I was proud of that solution; it gained us a leader who had resources and shared our vision. I stayed on for a few months to help with transition. By the end of 2005, I'd had 10 years of post-MBA experience with all the biotech experience possible. I was 45 years old.

That's when one of Genaissance's venture capital investors, Canaan Partners, asked me to join the company as an executive in residence (EIR). EIRs evaluate the flow of deals, work with companies in the portfolio, give advice, and potentially join one of the companies in a full-time executive role. This made me take a step back. Vision is great, and PhDs are great, but again I asked questions: *How long does it take for the science to become something? How do we couple that with capital, which is expensive and deserves its return? To respect that capital, how do we create a focused vision complete with risk we can manage and business goals we can achieve?*

My Big Biotech "A-ha" Moment

The biggest biotech "a-ha" moment for me came out of the previous five years. The only way it made sense was to start at what I call the end of the beginning. Sure, starting at the beginning was exciting when I was young. But I couldn't connect the dots to make commercialization happen fast enough for the capital needs of either venture capitalists or Wall Street.

In addition, it didn't play to my skill sets of shaping businesses and doing deals. Instead, why not find something that had already gone through the messiness of the entire research and development process, even to the point of collapse or bankruptcy? After all, bright people with a fresh new business plan and a focus can get started without much investment capital. Why not start when the science and the product are already developed? After that, I could figure out the competitive positioning.

That was my big "a-ha" moment.

✳ What was the situation before you entered Advanced BioHealing that led to its issues?

As a venture capital firm, Canaan obviously had cash and wanted to put it to work. In early 2006, it had invested $5 million as part of an $8 million syndicate in an early-stage company called Advanced BioHealing (ABH). As its brand new healthcare EIR, I was asked to give my take on the company. Canaan liked the product—a cellular-based artificial skin used for severe burn patients—but company leaders were unsure of the capability of the MD running the business.

Too Small, Too Long, Too Bad

I initially advised them to pull money out. In my view, the product was much too early in its life cycle. Food and Drug Administration (FDA) approval looked to be a longer and more difficult process than anticipated. The FDA had sent ABH a letter asking serious questions about the trial design for testing the product. The CEO was a vascular surgeon with no experience building a business.

About that time, I traveled to a medical burns conference in Las Vegas. My takeaways were that other products for that application had failed, and even with the best product in the world, the market for serious buyers was too small. We couldn't build a business on it.

Opportunistic Acquisition

Canaan's leaders weren't happy. They said, "Jeez, we just put in five million dollars. Do we just walk away? Do we do something else?" I believe in serendipity in life. Right at that time, Canaan received an e-mail from an investment banker who was marketing an advanced wound care business owned by an international healthcare giant. The business was based outside of San Diego, so I went to Southern California with a small team to take a look.

This business owned an FDA-approved product called Dermagraft for diabetic foot ulcers. We walked through a complex manufacturing plant and saw people drinking coffee in "clean" rooms because operations had been totally shut down—I mean, *totally* shut down. The business had made progress with insurance and Medicare reimbursement but couldn't figure out how to price the product. It had sold $25 million of Dermagraft in 2005, earning an 18-percent gross margin. But for our company to get involved, we needed a 75- to 80-percent gross profit.

In addition, Dermagraft was sold through a commodity-based wound care sales force that offered the parent company's entire array of products to nurses and hospital administrators. I realized the only way to effectively commercialize this product was through a separate, specialized business unit. A report from McKinsey research recommended a similar plan. But it appeared the parent company didn't have the stomach to invest the suggested $50 million and recruit another management team.

In fact, the banker told us the parent company wanted Dermagraft off the books for 2006. After receiving the McKinsey report in October 2005, it chose to shut the business down and take the loss. Immediately surgeons using Dermagraft complained that a life-saving product was being taken off the market. So the parent company decided to have the banker sell the business instead. The banker attracted a number of lookers who only saw a broken business. Big companies generally don't buy broken businesses.

✳ What attracted you to this situation when many would run away?

The situation was perfect for my team, my skill set, and a venture capital lead and restart. Here was an FDA-approved product that gave us an opportunity to take a fresh look at the market and focus on developing the commercial strategy. It would be independent of the baggage of how the business had evolved. So in 2006, Canaan sponsored ABH to acquire all the Dermagraft assets for $2 million and assume the rent for the manufacturing facility. As interim CEO, I drove the process.

✳ How did you hatch the plan to address this situation?
Phase 1 of the ABCs: Hatch the Plan

> "Discouragement and failure are the two surest
> stepping stones to success."
>
> —Dale Carnegie

Canaan gave me 60 days to analyze and put together a business plan. This was a little backward. One would think a plan comes before committing to funding. However, this was a comparatively small additional investment. Canaan viewed it as saving the $5 million it had already sunk into the venture.

A: Ask Questions and Listen; Then Ask for Help

First, my team questioned the skeleton crew still on staff in southern California. We listened to the people. They had such a passion for their product! That crew brought in a surgeon who told us how he had used Dermagraft. He outlined his success in treating diabetic foot ulcers with the product. Here was a company that had been shut down but still had paying customers, a product serving a genuine need, and real revenue.

After gaining the insiders' view, we looked outside. We went to a diabetic foot ulcer conference, talked to several doctors, and invited a few into a focus group. Then my team reached out to a number of wound experts on both the product and the application, flooding them with questions. *Too often, people skip over this research, thinking they already know what's best. We did not.*

B: Base the Plan on What You Hear and See, or Don't Hear and See

I realized the parent company had been selling Dermagraft as a commodity, not a specialty product. While I thought that was all wrong, it had still garnered $25 million in revenue. The information from both the insiders and the doctors supported the view that we needed to have a product specialist to speak to a wound care specialist.

A diabetic foot ulcer patient faces a significant risk of losing a limb through amputation. Our company had an FDA-approved product, backed up with clinical data, to meet that serious need. And the market was sizeable—a $500 million market, by our calculations. I knew there must be a way to make this work, if only we could connect with the doctors and customers who needed our product.

We learned there were 1,500 wound centers in the United States, and 400 of them comprised 80 percent of the market. The owners were considered the thought leaders in the industry. The more we dug into it, the more we said, "Let's become the world leader in a regenerative medicine product for diabetic foot ulcers."

Within two months, we put together a plan that called for raising $30 million. Talk about contentious board meetings! The legendary professor at Harvard who had developed the original Advanced BioHealing product had developed a new technology as an alternative to Dermagraft. He screamed at us on the phone—and he was a gentleman, a truly wonderful human being. Still, he screamed as forcefully as a polite man can, "How can you possibly take 30 million dollars and put it into a failed product that's old technology when I have a state-of-the-art next-generation product?" Unfortunately, older technology that's already FDA-approved is worth more than next-generation science that will take several years to approve and go commercial.

I realized the market didn't care whether or not a next-generation alternative to our product existed. Dermagraft had to be shipped frozen and used within a few hours after being thawed; the new technology the professor had developed could be used off the shelf. But physicians using it didn't care about that feature. Their nurses would thaw Dermagraft, and the doctors would use it. The logistics had all been figured out, including dry ice, validated coolers, and FedEx shipments.

I consider this a classic case of not talking to customers. People can sit in an office or lab and think about all these wonderful next-generation products. *But you have to ask buyers in the marketplace if they care.*

In 2006, we had much to do. We had to restart manufacturing, which was no mean feat. We had to rehire people and build a sales team and a management team. We needed a cogent business plan and an effort to raise additional capital. That's what we did, which culminated in receiving $30 million in financing.

With that in place, I left my EIR role and signed on as ABH's full time CEO in early 2007.

C: Challenge the Sacred Cows or the Status Quo

The product's selling price was a huge unresolved issue, with Dermagraft previously priced at $600 per application. This was a regenerative medicine, a living cell biologic, with some of the most complex science possible. The McKinsey report stated that no more than $999 could be charged, but no magic formula existed for that price. Yet, the only way the model worked to realize the required 75- to 80-percent gross profit was with a $1,250 selling price. The prevailing attitude seemed to be Dermagraft wouldn't sell if we priced it higher than $999.

But that was based upon asking doctors. Why ask doctors? They don't pay for the product; the insurance community does. So we got that $1,250 price into the existing insurance reimbursement system by comparing it to the cost of amputation. The insurance community could see that $1,250 for Dermagraft was a paltry expense by comparison. That was one fortunate breakthrough.

S: Share the Vision to Create a Collective Energy

As mentioned, our business plan included a vision to obtain $30 million in financing. I needed to rally our people around a plan to do that. But I had no people. I had to put a team together. Who's going to fund a business with no team? My style of servant leadership is definitely about the team. So I put together a team that came from three places.

First, some of them were previously employed at Dermagraft, including the head of manufacturing and the head of reimbursement. I had to build mutual trust with these people: to have them trust me, and to develop my own trust in them. As we were building the team, our head of manufacturing had to have her say in the composition of team members. After asking them to give me all their trust, I couldn't take the ex-employees and say, "Here's your team." Clearly, the heads had to be part of the decision-making.

The 120 people working in Southern California were mostly manufacturing, shipping, and research staff members. We brought back about 40 or 50 of them—all workplace buddies who had gone to other companies. The parent company had dismissed them in November 2005. We started bringing people back slowly, over six months, beginning in mid-2006. They were highly trained, proficiently skilled, and working somewhere else. But they believed in Dermagraft. They just wanted to see a plan that made sense. The plan that would attract and inspire them was captured in the promise of $30 million in financing to enable a focused business unit. We also expressed it by using something simple and unique: a ballpoint pen (to be explained later).

The second group of people worked with me at Genaissance. This included the head of human resources and the marketing leader.

The third group consisted of fresh recruits, including the vice president of sales. I deeply felt we needed a professional sales leader. I still remember the head of manufacturing saying to me, "Show me a sales leader who can make this happen, because I've not seen one yet." She heartily endorsed my leading sales management candidate who had come from the healthcare industry. A driven, buttoned-down guy, the new sales manager presented himself well, and he could sell. He was hungry but not a big company stiff. He grew up poor in Louisiana yet managed to get a college education. Could he build a staff of specialists to pull off their piece of the game plan? It turned out we made a great decision.

My new leadership team outlined a four-point game plan:

* First, maximize the U.S. Dermagraft franchise.

* Second, diversify the revenue stream instead of relying solely on one product.

* Third, take the product outside the U.S.

* Fourth, seek new applications for Dermagraft.

Then we handed all of our employees ballpoint pens with the four points of the game plan on it. Each time someone pushed the button on the ball point pen button, one point of the game plan appeared on a side panel.

Later, we initiated a survey about culture and what our people thought the four points of the game plan were. Only 10 percent of the people in the company could remember all four even though they had a pen. So we summarized it down to three points by consolidating "seek new applications" into "maximize the Dermagraft franchise." From there, we remade the pens to feature a three-point instead of a four-point game plan. When we re-surveyed, 40 percent of our employees could recite all three points. We kept repeating the three-point game plan at every employee meeting and in every monthly newsletter. It really galvanized people.

When people understand their role in a game plan, they are super engaged. In a sense, it also made our job easier. Many people had seen this company be reduced to five employees and get shut down. Whether they were new hires or previous employees who had come back, they all knew the history of the near-collapse of this business. They were all part of the new game plan to put ABH and Dermagraft on the map.

That common mission energized and directed everyone from the rank and file to the leadership team.

Image 8.2: Photo of pen "Share the Vision."

✳ Once the plan was hatched, how did you align your team to kick off the plan?

Phase 2 of the ABCs: Kick Off the Game Plan

"When a gifted team dedicates itself to unselfish trust and combines instinct with boldness and effort, it is ready to climb."

—Pant Anjali

A: Act Boldly to Kick Off the Game Plan

It was basically all or nothing. We couldn't do this halfway. To ramp up manufacturing, we had to have an integrated business. We weren't relying on a distributor or any partner. We needed to set reimbursement and pricing ourselves. Marketing and sales needed talented staff who were executing according to a strategy. We had everything in place, and I had the business plan and a slick slide show to attract capital.

The biggest risk was kicking off this under-funded organization with a $10 million to $15 million annual consumption of cash, called the cash burn. I had the board's confidence that I'd line up the financing before the money ran out. I simply couldn't wait for the financing to bring on the people, start training, and ramp up manufacturing, sales, and marketing. Having no organization to execute a game plan surely would not attract capital. We raised the $30 million on that basis—after the fact. Whew! It worked out.

B: Build on Strengths

We had an FDA-approved product that worked wonders. Not many organizations have the opportunity to focus on a product, one they control, with such positive clinical data. Dermagraft was a biologic with huge scientific and regulatory barriers to market entry. But the market seemed to want it. We didn't intend to execute market awareness and sales force development halfheartedly. With everyone signed up and the capital in place to go full tilt, the product was our huge strength—pure and simple. We built everything around it. That made the biggest difference.

Diabetic foot ulcers made up one of the few big markets the large healthcare firms hadn't tackled successfully. We found virgin territory, and we took advantage of it.

C: Control Through Visible Measurement

You should be able to track your business on one sheet of paper. Each week at our management meeting, we would track a few key metrics. Could we produce the product efficiently? After all, Dermagraft was a complex cellular-based artificial skin. The production process required equally complex bioprocessing manufacturing, so we had to have production metrics.

But our biggest metric in 2007 was sales productivity. How many accounts? How many orders per week? What was the average salesperson's productivity? Once we saw that productivity happening, we had a model around which we could plan. We then calculated our capacity based on how many salespeople we could hire, train, and get up to speed each quarter.

We realized the productivity we needed by late 2007. When their first two quarters of revenue was projected to four quarters (the run rate), our salespeople would be producing $1 million per territory. That's a highly productive number. We had scaled the manufacturing and conquered the missing piece, the commercial model.

S: Streamline the Activity Schedule

Vision, mission, and elevator pitch

We crafted our vision and mission statements early on. They were straightforward and centered on Dermagraft not as a wound care product but as a highly innovative regenerative medicine.

I always wanted our people to believe they were providing the most complex science at the most value possible to patients. It involves taking living cells and growing them, putting them on a Vicryl mesh, passing quality control, shipping them, and putting them on a patient. It's among the most complex science out there.

However, I never wanted us to be a wound care company. That just doesn't have a sophisticated connotation. I was clear our primary long-term vision was to build the leading regenerative medicine company to benefit patients. Repairing and regenerating human tissue was the next big opportunity in healthcare. Under that umbrella, ABH was the only independent company with real revenue and a fully integrated product. We embedded that vision in all ABH's marketing materials, press releases, and plastered it all over our elevator pitch.

Competitive positioning and targeting strategy

We thought we had better technology than our primary competitor, but the whole competitive strategy involved attracting doctors away from passive therapy to these active therapies. Our best approach was to act boldly where we saw virgin territory. The approximately 60 account clients held by our competitors thought ABH had an inferior product. Instead of going after them, we hit the empty spaces of least resistance. Our biggest competitors, then, would be apathy and ignorance.

Wound care was just starting to emerge as a specialty. We went to diabetic medical conferences as the big man on campus. This specific targeting crystallized our message to the doctors of the 400 or so wound centers. Fortunately, they treated enough patients to significantly move the needle on sales once they adopted Dermagraft and increased its use in earlier therapy. Those thought leaders begat other followers.

Primary goals (the BHAGS) to focus the energy

Our overarching goal was to realize the vision of becoming the perceived market leader in regenerative medicine. We obviously needed to grow revenue, achieve positive cash flow, and gain mind share in the market. Working toward the three-point game plan got us closer to those goals. It gave us direction and focused our activities on what mattered most to achieve them.

Critical success factors to prioritize the actions

We launched our game plan and made visible the basic goals, revenue metrics, and production metrics we deemed critical to gain momentum, profitability, and leadership. To provide some framework, I gave everyone who joined the company a copy of Jim Collins' book *Good to Great* and wrote on the inside flap, "Welcome to our company."

One principle I loved to say was this: "Get the right people on the bus and the wrong people off the bus." Anytime someone would whine about someone else being a problem, our company practice was to say, "Get the right people on the bus and get the wrong people off." Frankly, it was more important to get the wrong people off.

We also talked about the flywheel principle—that by just doing Dermagraft over and over, producing it, and selling it, how could we not be successful? I also subscribed to this principle: "Face the brutal facts." Whatever the facts are—good, bad, or ugly—face them. I hammered at those three principles, especially during company meetings.

Critical to me was putting the right team together and building a strong culture. I started with five castaways from a failed attempt and abandoned by its big company owner. Building our teams, putting the resources behind them, and establishing the right work culture made all the difference.

Define and reinforce the culture

Because we were geographically all over the place, we put a good deal of focus on teambuilding. We had a disparate group who didn't know one another, so we conducted weekly meetings and video conferencing calls so we all could at least see one another. We met face-to-face as frequently as possible, picking Chicago as a midpoint. We got the team together at least every other week. Our teambuilding exercises included a cooking day. We sat in a kitchen, chopped, talked with the chef, and then had dinner together. One of the guys whined about it at first but ended up loving it.

I went out of my way to show those in the commercial team they were the foundation to success. I personally interviewed our first salespeople. I attended the first sales meeting to show them they would become a significant piece—perhaps even the solution—in our growth plan.

We valued openness, transparency, integrity, and working with people we really wanted to accompany us. When giving out employee of the month awards, we reinforced a specific cultural behavior we wanted to ingrain. We strived to keep alive the passion everyone had at the beginning.

Here's an example that fits perfectly. At one point, wildfires burned all around San Diego. Roads were blocked and the plant had no electricity for five days. The emergency power generator could keep us running for a day or two, but we were running low on fuel. Any loss of power would have destroyed inventory that needed to be kept in the freezer.

While the fire raged, a member of our manufacturing team drove around barricaded roads to get extra fuel for the generator. Also, a shipping teammate boxed up the orders for the day and drove past those same barricades to the UPS store. It had cancelled pickups and deliveries until the fire was under control.

Without the efforts of these teammates, we might have lost millions of dollars of inventory and failed to service our customers. Who else would have driven around those flames? It was dramatic. Cultures get shaped by extra efforts such as these.

From this disparate group, we built a culture of trust, camaraderie, spirit, and accountability that served us well as we built the business. We behaved as a real team and had fun in the process. Nothing builds morale like the success of overcoming adversity.

✳ With the game plan hatched and kicked off, what was your approach to execute?

Phase 3 of the ABCs: Execute the Plan

> "You may not realize it when it happens, but a kick in
> the teeth may be the best thing in the world for you."
>
> —Walt Disney

A: Assert Yourself at the Focal Point

We intended to tear up the wound care marketing positioning and make Dermagraft the standard of care for diabetic foot ulcers. We know that more than 100,000 diabetic foot ulcer patients have their lower limbs amputated every year. It's not because they don't seek therapy; it's generally because the doctor doesn't go in early with aggressive therapy.

To counteract that, we came up with a branded ruler that said "Four and Fifty." Our message was crystal clear: "Treat the patient however you like, doctor. But if after four weeks the wound isn't down by 50 percent, the literature says you've got to go in aggressively. Here's Dermagraft. It's proven." That became the core of our marketing strategy.

We had taken the early-stage science that had stumbled, and we made something of it. I like to joke that, in 25 years, this was the first business plan I've ever exceeded. In biotech and life sciences, it's tough to raise the money unless you put a somewhat-ambitious plan together. Investors always say, "It'll take twice as long, and they'll be lucky if they achieve half the result." ABH's first-year revenue plan was $20 million, which started from a standstill. We hit that target, and it was twice what our investors expected we could do.

Driven sales team

Our forecast was driven by how many salespeople we had in the field once we had proven the sales productivity model. We were extremely disciplined about how we expanded. As the game plan worked, we added more sophisticated training to quickly bring new salespeople up to speed. We continually refined our marketing message. We put the HR machinery to work. We hired support staff to coordinate sales activities and free up our sales force's time to sell.

Regarding sales, we looked at activity within specific accounts to help us divide our sales territories. Maximizing our sales by better managing how we divided sales territories became a commercially centered focus of our business. As we generated the right levels of revenue, we added five salespeople every quarter. Then, we doubled our training capacity to 10 salespeople a quarter.

We were especially ruthless about identifying qualities that would make our salespeople successful in this field. They constantly underwent retraining. The best ones thought of their new territories as a franchise—their own business. If a salesperson wasn't productive within the first six months, we quickly put that person on warning. The worst of all worlds was a good regional manager spending time with the worst salesperson instead of the best. The more we brought people through our training classes, the more we had the ability to put winning people into territories.

Over four years, we grew revenue from the initial $20 million in 2007 to $147 million by 2010. We were on track for a more-than-$200 million fifth year in 2011. Our average salesperson was producing $1.5 million a year. Why complain? But we did.

Progress on our goals

We were on track with goal number one: maximizing Dermagraft revenue in the United States. Dermagraft was an exceptional product and was doing well. But achieving the other two points of the three-point game plan had become problematic. ABII still relied on one product in one geographical region. Regenerative medicine was still a nascent area. The risk of diluting shareholder value rather than enhancing it was real. We had hoped to acquire a product or two to diversify the revenue, but we weren't finding desirable products available.

We believed we could double Dermagraft's market opportunity by gaining FDA approval for its use to treat venous leg ulcers. We could double it again by expanding beyond the U.S. border, but this proved difficult for us. We didn't have full regulatory approval in Europe, so we had to run a new trial. Talk about expensive! We looked at Japan, which required a new trial to gain approval as well. Surmising the best way to globalize was through this venous leg ulcer trial, we allocated research and development expenses for that trial. We estimated the whole ticket—start to finish—at $25 million over two years or so.

Growth on fire

All in all, however, our growth was on fire. The board and investors supported exploring a sale to cash out. We hired a banker to introduce the company with potential buyers including private equity firms, wound care companies, orthopedic cell-based companies, Global 100 healthcare companies, and conglomerates with a healthcare interest.

By the first quarter of 2010, after the banker attracted significant interest, the board agreed to run a formal process. By mid-year, we received a purchase bid from a Fortune 100 company. It looked like a possible $500 million payday, plus an extra $50 million if the venous leg ulcer trial in Europe succeeded.

✳ What obstacles did you encounter along the way? How did you deal with them?

Next, we went through due diligence with the potential buyer. The buyer flew out a team to our Southern California plant. Everything looked great. The ABH board, the investor group, and all our senior executives were eyeing a 10-fold return. I'd gone with my family to South Africa the first week of August, feeling exuberant that the buyer's board had approved the acquisition. They were just wrapping up the paperwork with the deal set to close in three weeks. The last thing we needed was a manufacturing glitch.

The Glitch That Spoiled the Deal

That first week of August was the second week of experiencing a severe manufacturing glitch. I had to inform the buyer about it. Glitches had happened before and we resolved them quickly. This glitch, however, went on for six weeks and caused production yields to drop from their normal rate of 70 percent down to 40 percent or even 30 percent.

I remember our conference in the second week of August so well. The buyer said, "We just want to hold off for a month to see that everything's fine." Yields started to come back, although we couldn't identify the root cause of the decrease. Then the acquisition was put on hold. Feeling uncomfortable not understanding why our yields had decreased, the buyer asked to see yields for the next three months. It could happen again at any time was the fear.

We hired an acclaimed bioprocessing manufacturing consultant and threw everything at the problem. Our head of manufacturing was tearing her hair out. Her dream of $500 million with wings on it was flying out the window. We felt terrible. We enhanced training, provided more stringent operating procedures, and vastly increased our quality assurance staff.

Yields improved, rising back to the 60- to 80-percent range, but they still suffered from too much fluctuation. Not even this dream team consultant could pinpoint a definitive cause, even though what we did to remedy the situation worked. Those in the bioprocessing manufacturing business understood that dramatic yield variation happens on occasion. It's a complex biologic process. But our potential buyer had no experience in biologics. These events shook the buyer's trust.

By the end of 2010, the buyer was still saying, "We don't know. We'll wait." That's when both management and the board, with consultation from the banker, decided to control our own destiny and seek an IPO. If this buyer came forward, that was fine. If it didn't, at least we controlled an IPO.

We filed the IPO documents in February 2011.

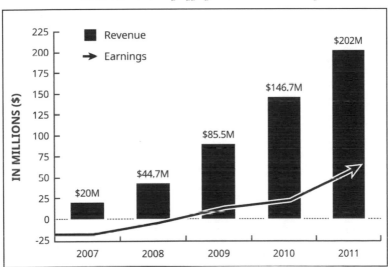

Image 8.3.

B: Borrow From Alliances and Partnerships

Grabbing that expert manufacturing consultant to help us with our yield glitch was our best example of borrowing from the expertise of others to help us through a tough situation. Outside of that, we didn't construct partnerships or alliances well. Our regenerative medicines business was unique. An operational alliance with another manufacturer didn't seem to fit. International distributors needed a product with regulatory approval, but ABH didn't have it. We attempted alliances with big outfits that had the muscle to license and distribute, but the approval process took time and money. We simply couldn't pull it off.

C: Communicate Progress and Results to Get/Stay on Track

We grew from a staff of five people to 500. As a proponent of over-communication, I liked walking around and talking to people wherever I was, but as we grew I couldn't do this informally. We held monthly meetings with slide shows in the Southern California plant and included everybody in the field who phoned in. Our agenda was simple. Where did we stand on achieving our goals? What were our momentum indicators? Were we on or off track? We either gave high fives of praise or acknowledged where we needed to improve.

We also posted success story videos on our Website. At some of our meetings, we brought in patients. (There's nothing like hearing success stories firsthand.) We told the story of Lisa, a kindergarten teacher in a wheelchair. When her doctor had discussed amputating her foot, she asked, "How am I going to move around my classroom like that?" The doctor said, "Well, we can try one last thing. There was a rep in here with Dermagraft." This diabetic woman *walked* onstage just after we debuted this newly posted video at a company meeting. She talked about her kindergarten kids, how she could go to the gym, and how Dermagraft gave her another life. People had tears in their eyes. Her story kept the passion burning.

I insisted our board of directors attend these meetings. There's nothing worse, in my view, than board members who never see the employees, and employees who never see their board members. We often had employee luncheons with them in which both groups listened and told war stories. These sessions energized all of us.

We circulated monthly employee newsletters in which we publicized team and individual awards specific to our goal achievement. The newsletters also outlined problem areas. Our message was clear: "We appreciate what everybody does."

As we got a bit bigger, we conducted more and more off-site sessions with both our senior managers and the people being groomed for advancement. Central staff and all our salespeople attended our sales award presentations.

Our marketing team drove the outside communications. With a public relations firm, ABH embraced social media for both internal and external communication. Digital media to the medical community became an ever-growing piece of our marketing communications mix. Presentations at a variety of healthcare conferences made a big impression on our ultimate target audience. We always sought to take the podium as the regenerative medicines spokesperson and thought leader. While we belonged to a trade association, we essentially invented our own regenerative medicine trade association. It served as our communications vehicle within the industry. Plus the whole process of seeking a public stock offering via an IPO raised ABH's visibility not only to the financial community but to the healthcare industry at large.

S: Share the Rewards of Wealth and Recognition When Things Go Your Way

Recognition, recognition, always recognition! Employee of the month, manufacturing team, research and development team, sales team—you name it. We liked to celebrate our successes and the people who enabled those successes. We kept our goals visible.

I'm a big believer that everybody needs to be a stockholder, even if you're a janitor and you've only got stock options for 100 shares. With 20 percent of our stock in the hands of employees, about two dozen of our people made more than $500,000 through their stock options. Everyone had a stake in ABH. For instance, an HR assistant who was a single mother was able to buy a house when she never thought she could!

What a great country. I told my team we were the luckiest people in the world. There's no other place in the world I can imagine obtaining a $30 million investment for a failed product when a large company couldn't succeed. We said, "Trust us! We'll make a success of that."

✳ What was the end result of the execution?

Not every company gets to build itself from nothing to a nicely profitable $200 million revenue run rate inside of five years and file for an IPO. I had recruited a talented, experienced CFO to help me in that process. I should have done that earlier; he made my job easy.

We walked on a dual track: Either complete the IPO or sell the company. We wrote the IPO documents and talked to potential buyers at the same time. The IPO pricing range valued ABH at approximately $600 million. That mid-point of the pricing range set the valuation bar.

From IPO to Acquisition Bait

Among the companies interested in acquiring ABH was Shire, a global healthcare giant with major interests in specialty pharmaceuticals. We fit the bill as a means to capture a regenerative medicine franchise. The week before a planned three-week IPO roadshow, one of the ABH board members called an executive contact at Shire to stimulate interest in the IPO. The board member impressed upon the executive that Shire might lose out as a buyer. As a result, Shire planned to fly in a team for a serious look. Any meeting would be with me alone. But we were getting ready for the roadshow, and we weren't changing our time line. Given the IPO process, Shire had three weeks to respond.

The stars all aligned. Because my time had been freed up from writing the IPO documents, I focused on our message and meeting every key objection. I took my team's best points and put them into sales language. Eight people from Shire showed up, and I basically gave them the IPO roadshow. I could see their eyes get wide.

Two days later, Shire called. The company wanted to acquire ABH but needed another week of due diligence. I said, "There's no way. We're starting the roadshow." The only concession we gave them was to shift the roadshow kickoff from a Monday to a Tuesday. That meant we gave them one day to evaluate the company for potential acquisition.

I informed the team, then went with the investment bankers for the IPO roadshow on Tuesday. During that time, the heads of manufacturing and commercial managed the due diligence process with Shire.

I later learned that someone from Shire contacted an ABH investor to get a sense of what price Shire might need to offer to gain ABH's board approval for its acquisition in place of the IPO. Without answering the question directly, a comment was made about how a Boeing 757 was a fine aircraft that could take any flyer where he wanted to go. Shire came through with a $750 million cash offer to acquire ABH 24 hours before the IPO priced. *That was 25 percent above the mid-point of the IPO pricing range.*

Guess what? The ABH board approved its acquisition by Shire.

✳ What's your reflection as you look back?

On a business level, it definitely reinforces for me the thoughtful plan to raise money, assemble and lead a compatible team of people, and drive value in a land of opportunity called the United States of America. My early thought was to get this mess called ABH cleaned up, get Dermagraft back on the market, and raise $30 million. Then, I hoped, we could find someone to buy it for $100 million and make three times the money. Who knew that we'd fetch 13 times the money?

On a personal level, I learned I've got to be true to my values and my family. I've seen too many people make a little bit of money and alter their personal lives by playing the big shot. Money doesn't buy happiness. It helps, but it's not what drives it. It's just smarter to be true to yourself.

✳ How did the experience help you advance?

Americans think bigger, bolder, and brasher than most. They aren't afraid to have a vision. I've incorporated that into my own style. I've put plans together, raised capital, executed, and built a team and a business. I have gained a hopeful and quiet confidence. I will strive never to lose humility, because we all know how much can go wrong and how tough the world really is. I'll be true to what I believe is right, follow my instincts, argue my position, and work through the opportunities and business plans in which I believe.

Thanks to the credentials and personal wealth I earned at Advanced BioHealing, I've been able to found an investment firm: HighCape Partners. Its vision is to finance and build scalable commercial health-care companies that already have regulatory approval for their product and are on the cusp of having a real business. Other ABHs are out there.

HighCape aims to find, fund, and advise these companies on how to build a tightly focused group and transform commercial-stage companies into sustainable businesses. Along with personal funds, my partners and I have raised tens of millions of dollars to fund our investments.

I learned another important lesson at ABH: It's not about me or my vision; it's about the quality of the whole team. My partners in this newly formed business include ABH investors and its marketing exec, chief science officer, chief medical officer, and human resources executive. HighCape can bring terrific human capital to a situation and make a difference. Should I need them, the former venture capital investors in Advanced BioHealing would also be investors in my new business. They know the stakes, the rewards for success, and the quality of the investment team.

9

Dr. David M. Barrett:
Recovering From a Botched Merger and Cash Crunch at the Lahey Clinic

"The right of commanding is no longer an advantage transmitted by nature. Like an inheritance, it is the fruit of labors, the price of courage."

—Voltaire

✳ How did you get to be the person you are? What's your story?

My value system emerged from my parents' background. They survived the austerity of a meager Depression-era farm environment in west-central Michigan. My mother's farm dates back to the turn of the 18th century. She was one of seven children raised by her parents and grandparents. They farmed 80 acres that never harvested a sustainable

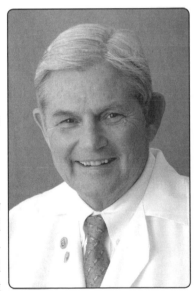

Image 9.1: Dr. David M. Barrett. Photo copyright David M. Barrett. Used with permission.

cash crop. They lived off the land. All seven children were educated and lived an adult life at a much different level than their parents. My father's farm was only three miles from my mother's. This only son learned how to manage a farm. Although it wasn't very lucrative, it was his. That's how people there lived.

My mother and father initially struggled as newlyweds. They both left their farm environment and moved to Detroit, Michigan, where I was born. My mechanically adept father was employed as a tool and die maker while my college-educated mother taught school. Not liking Detroit's city atmosphere, they subsequently moved to Grand Rapids, Michigan. My father developed a product called Die-Draulic that used hydraulic pressure and a series of valves to support dies and provide even pressure when the press stamped out a piece of metal. He had several patents granted and ultimately became a successful business owner with proprietary products.

Average Student, Gifted Athlete, and Med School Graduate

In high school, I was a "good enough" B and C student. But I was an A athlete. A running back in football, I became team captain. In track, I was captain and a middle distance record holder. I had never looked at myself as having leadership qualities. Whenever I'd win or achieve something, I was the most surprised guy in the world.

Athletics gave me stature in high school and a team environment to exercise my competitive spirit. I was taught life lessons including that I don't always win. I can compete, lose, and improve. Failure lies not in falling down but in not getting back up.

For me, going to college was an afterthought. With parental guidance and my football coach's influence, I went to Albion College, a small, Methodist, liberal arts school in southern Michigan. There, I played football, became team captain, and was surprised by my recognition as All-Conference, Methodist All-American. Once again, I was a low-average student, at least during my first two years.

While in high school, I had worked in my father's business and seemed to be groomed to take over his successful private company. But when I was in college and the unions had made several runs at his company, my father announced, "You've got to do something on your own. This is a rat race. I'm going to sell the company." Once he did, he lived a comfortable life.

I look back at how insecure I felt at that time—and how imperfect I saw myself. But I heard my parents say, "You can do what you want. Don't worry. Things will be fine." They provided a positive influence that ultimately dictated how I dealt with any challenge. But right then and there, I realized I needed to chart my own course in life.

During my last two years at Albion, I befriended a couple of class-mates who inspired me in their own right. As academic achievers, they dragged me into being a better student. I visited one of my friends at his home in Detroit and met his neighbor, Dr. Jim Fryfogle, an Albion alumnus who ran a research laboratory in his backyard. He was researching the prevention of blood clotting in synthetic and vascular grafts and prosthetic devices.

That first exposure at age 20 kindled my fascination with science applied to medicine. It's where the idea of medicine as my career originated. All of a sudden, grades became important to me and medical school would be in my future. Also in my future was a young lady I had met when making a collection for delivering the *Grand Rapids Herald*. I was 12 years old and this cute girl was only nine. We've been in each other's lives ever since.

My father's mechanical and entrepreneurial spirit, my mother's goodness, their survivalist farm roots, my sense of athletic competitiveness and teamwork, my new wife's support—all of this, plus Dr. Fryfogle's mentorship and dedication to his patients, came together. These qualities have driven me for the rest of my life.

Wayne State University's med school became my next source of insecurity and fear of failure that earlier had plagued me. It gave way to a growing self-confidence once I passed my first biochemistry test. It's biochemistry that separates the graduates from those who flunk out of med school. I not only passed it, I finished med school and was named Intern of the Year at Detroit General Hospital. Who? Me?

It came about after Dr. Fryfogle had introduced me to the Mayo Clinic in Rochester, Minnesota, where he had previously trained. Though I had never heard of the Mayo Clinic, I applied, got accepted (to my surprise), and entered its surgical residency program in 1969.

A Life-Changer: Flight Surgeon in Vietnam

In high demand during the Vietnam War, doctors were being drafted left and right. Through a program called the Berry Plan, a doctor in training could defer his military obligation to finish his residency before induction. After my internship, I spent one year in general surgery and identified urology as my specialty. Like many, I lost my deferment as I changed specialties and received my "greetings." Uncle Sam gave me three choices: Army, Navy, or Air Force. I had learned how to fly an airplane while in high school, so I said, "Well, give me the Air Force."

After basic training, I actually had a couple of choices. I could have been assigned somewhere as a Class D surgeon, with no control over my location, like Germany (appealing) or the Aleutian Islands (not so appealing) or who knows where. Because I was a pilot, I could choose to be a flight surgeon, which made sense.

Off I went to the School of Aerospace Medicine at Brooks Air Base in San Antonio, Texas, where I met people in the Apollo space program. With the U.S. landing a manned spacecraft on the moon in 1969, aerospace medicine had become a big deal.

Part of my curriculum included compression chamber training, so I thought that a compression-chamber-trained recruit wouldn't get sent to a jungle war zone. The Air Force had other ideas. Within the year, I was assigned to a fairly secure beachside basecamp in the South China Sea called Cam Rahn Bay, Vietnam. Because it already had six flight surgeons on staff, I was an unneeded seventh. The U.S. Air Force quickly reassigned me to fill a temporary opening in Thailand where F-4 Phantom jets and other fighter aircraft were based.

For a month or so, I flew about two dozen missions north of the DMZ (demilitarized zone) en route to Hanoi in the backseat of the F-4s. When I returned to Cam Rahn Bay, I was assigned as flight surgeon to an outfit called the 20th Special Operations Group at an Air Force hospital. This group was comprised of Special Forces Air Force gunships and twin pipe Hueys, which spent most of the time in nasty places with plenty of action. So much for relaxing on the beach.

Until that time, the Air Force had been educational. I never felt unsafe, even though flying in the Phantoms we dodged surface-to-air missiles. All of a sudden, though, my very existence came into jeopardy.

Most of our crazy missions took place in the tri-border area (Vietnam, Cambodia, and Laos). We inserted Special Operations teams, provided air cover for them, and pulled them out when things got hot. A few times I stayed on the ground with them. I did things I had no intention of doing as a war zone physician who spent little time in a hospital environment. Mostly I applied tourniquets and administered a lot of analgesia in the form of morphine.

Facing my own mortality by being shot at and firing back was quite contrary to why I was sent there: to save lives. I can't talk about this experience without getting emotional. There was no room for anybody who didn't participate as a combatant. Until you've had a mortar shell go off 20 feet from you, you have no idea of the dizziness and the hearing loss.

What did I take away from this assignment? The fact that most people who experience combat do what they do because of the guy next to them and because of their leaders. If leaders can't hold the line, everything disintegrates. Combat is controlled chaos—sometimes *uncontrolled* chaos—with a lot of panic and fear. It certainly brought out a side of human emotion I didn't know that I or others possessed. Keeping control when things were going to hell in a handbasket became critical to me later on as a surgeon. When things quickly spiral out of control during a surgical procedure, you have to maintain your composure and do what you can for the patient and those around you.

In every major decision I faced, I thought back to the courage required to get through a hard time. It's so easy to fall apart. As Sir Winston Churchill once said, "Courage is rightly esteemed the first of human qualities...because it is the quality which guarantees all others." The experience reinforced deep inside my own courage to make decisions, pursue given concepts, and have my own convictions. And believe in myself.

✳ What was your career progression before joining the Lahey Clinic?

Separation from my wife and young son during my Vietnam experience put the most important things in my life into perspective. When I returned from the war zone in Southeast Asia and concluded my military obligation, I picked up where I left off at the Mayo Clinic. I'd had two years of surgical training under my belt at that point, plus three additional years of training in my specialty, urology. It was time to go out in the world and practice medicine.

Then, as a father of three, I looked at my options. Would I go into private practice? Go back to Grand Rapids? Go to the western U.S. and pursue my interest in the outdoors as well as practice medicine? As it turned out, I was offered the opportunity of a lifetime: to join the medical staff at the Mayo Clinic. No contest! You simply don't get asked to be on the Mayo Clinic staff; you have to be vetted and re-vetted. Shocked and honored to be invited, I felt thrilled to accept.

A Long and Fruitful Career at the Mayo Clinic

To me, there's no medical institution in the world like the Mayo Clinic. My Mayo experiences ingrained in me a culture to deliver outstanding healthcare with an unparalleled concern for the patient. I spent 27 years advancing my career at this exceptional place and always kept an eye on why I went into the field. The specialty of urology provided a unique opportunity to care for patients of all ages and both sexes. The combination of medical and surgical genitourinary condition suited my intellectual and technical skills perfectly. In my mind, this was the ideal platform to put "the needs of the patient first."

During my surgical practice, I read, wrote, lectured, and became recognized by my medical peers as an academician and authority in urological surgery. With several milestones achieved, I woke up and found I had worked toward an appointment as professor in the School of Medicine at the Mayo Clinic. Before long, I was appointed chair of the department of urology—a surprise to me because at the same time I was elected to Mayo Clinic's board of governors, the operational body that ran the place. Two years after that, I was appointed a trustee for the Mayo Foundation, and then ultimately named vice chair of the board of governors. Everything came together beautifully.

In addition, I was one of several people in line as an internal candidate for being the next CEO of the Mayo Clinic. I didn't get the job but it sparked an unfulfilled ambition. Then I received a call from a CEO search committee in 1999. I was given an opportunity to interview for the CEO's job at the Lahey Clinic in the Boston area. The Lahey Clinic was a notable medical institution patterned after the Mayo Clinic. Although not as large as the Mayo Clinic, it was well regarded and touted for its delivery of high-quality healthcare. However, it faced serious trouble due to a failed merger.

I received an offer to become its CEO.

✳ What was the situation before you entered the organization that led to its issues?

To paraphrase the Website (*www.lahey.org*), when Dr. Frank Lahey founded a group practice in 1923 and gave it his own name, it was an unconventional step in the world of medicine. His plan to create a clinic in which many specialties would coexist was a source of debate. His innovative group-care model—medical specialists cooperating to provide comprehensive patient care—was at first viewed with skepticism. But Lahey held firmly to his belief that the best outcomes are produced by teams of physicians who share their expertise. Only a decade later, newspaper headlines were describing this pioneering clinic as the "World-Famous Lahey Clinic."

Group Practice: At the Forefront of Medicine

By the 1930s and 1940s, the Lahey Clinic had become known worldwide for its phenomenal surgical outcomes, its state-of-the-art treatment of thyroid, gastrointestinal, and gall bladder disorders, and the growing importance of anesthesiology for successful surgery. The reputation it has for innovative technology, pioneer medical treatment, and leading-edge research was built on Dr. Lahey's belief that group practice should be a center for research and learning. From the beginning, the clinic offered its residents and fellows a chance to polish their skills under the careful supervision of some of the nation's leading physicians.

To groom new talent in interns and med students, the clinic allied with Tufts Medical School. A teaching hospital requires cutting-edge technology, which the Lahey Clinic consistently made available. Examples include becoming the proud owner of an X-ray machine in 1925, a state-of-the-art Model O heart-lung machine in 1969, and a whole-body ACTA scanner in 1975.

In the early 1970s, the Lahey Clinic had offices located in several Boston neighborhoods. It became evident that it would operate more smoothly if all the specialties were under one roof. By 1980, in its new central Burlington Medical Center, the Lahey Clinic had expanded to include services offered by more than 30 departments. Many of them had begun with a single physician who worked to promote his or her specialty.

Coasting and a Botched Merger Created a Crisis

Some observers noted that the Lahey Clinic coasted throughout the 1980s and 1990s. Its growth had always been organic. Did its leaders grow complacent or dysfunctional? Was there a sense of entitlement? I don't know. They appeared to ride the wave and ceased any meaningful investment in marketing themselves. The Boston healthcare scene was hotly competitive. Massachusetts General, Beth Israel, Brigham and Women's, Children's, and several other high-profile healthcare providers did active fundraising in this landscape.

On the front end of the heady economic times termed "the bubble" in 1997, the Lahey Clinic succumbed to "merger-mania" to accelerate its reach. It merged with the Dartmouth-Hitchcock Medical Center in New Hampshire, but the merger had failed within a short time. The failure seemed due to a complete lack of compatibility. The two administrations clashed and fought over leadership and authority. Dartmouth-Hitchcock managed the medical school, with its managers seemingly more interested in maintaining their professorial environment than in the patient-care routine. It was a clash of cultures.

The two merger partners separated very publicly. It appeared the Lahey Clinic was rudderless, wandering around not knowing what to do and in financial straits. With fewer than 30 days of cash on hand, it was losing money. Its systems and procedures, or lack thereof, were a disaster, and an attempt to implement new computer software failed. That meant the clinic had lost its ability to bill and collect payments from patients and the insurance industry that served them. Crisis time.

✳ What attracted you to this situation when many would run away?

I saw an opportunity to turn around a clinic that needed my kind of expertise. All of the things I'd learned about the best practices of crisp healthcare delivery, while focusing on the patient and not losing sight of the staff needs, came naturally to me. To fix it, I needed to have somebody say, "Okay, guys. Let's get together." Plus from knowing the business of healthcare up one side and down the other, I knew what it would take to make it financially viable.

Besides, I wanted to be the CEO of a leading healthcare provider. Philosophically, I'm a great believer of UCLA's winning basketball coach's attitude toward teamwork. John Wooden's book *Coach Wooden's Pyramid of Success: Building Blocks for a Better Life* influenced both my managerial and leadership approach. Wooden believed that to build a pyramid, every brick had to be considered equally as important as all of the others. As the new CEO in 1999, I was ready to build and felt confident I could make a lasting difference.

✳ How did you hatch the plan to address this situation?
Phase 1 of the ABCs: Hatch the Plan

"It's what you learn after you know it that counts."

—John Wooden

A: Ask Questions and Listen; Then Ask for Help

As the new CEO, I walked around and followed members of the staff. I immersed myself in that institution and its people. We met and we talked. I went in the field where they worked. I sat down with them at their desks. I looked at how they did everything: how they sharpened their pencils, how they turned on the computer, what fingers they used to hit the keys. I mean, I looked at every process I possibly could to thoroughly understand what was making the Lahey Clinic the way it was. And I consciously used Wooden's *Pyramid of Success* approach as I walked around, asked my questions, and listened. Every day, I came to work and turned over another stone underneath existing stones—or found snakes under them. Always something!

B: Base a Plan on What You Hear and See, or Don't Hear and See

As I lifted these stones and examined what was under them, a handful of issues immediately surfaced. To me, they were glaring.

First and foremost, Lahey Clinic's billing and scheduling program had been adopted for the combined organization from Dartmouth-Hitchcock's system. Its implementation as an information technology (IT) project had been taken live without proper testing. The incompatibility within its infrastructure had shut down all of the Lahey Clinic's IT billing and scheduling systems for three full months. No wonder there had been so little cash on hand.

Second, I observed that the people within the organization, both high and low, had lost belief in themselves. They didn't know how *good* they were. In fact, they'd read in the newspapers how *bad* they were due to the aborted merger with Dartmouth-Hitchcock. Nobody had brought them together. Therefore, in the aftermath, they were behaving as wayward individuals instead of a cohesive team. Several key administrators and physicians had threatened to leave.

My third, fourth, and fifth observations were closely aligned: marketing, fundraising, and growth. Marketing efforts had been neglected and fundraising had set its sights too low at $5 million. We needed to think bigger—say $200 million—to keep pace with the growth demands on healthcare providers in general. We needed to attract outstanding nurses and doctors.

C: Challenge the Sacred Cows or the Status Quo

Prior to the Sunshine Act (officially termed the Physician Financial Transparency Act), a good deal of witch-hunting was underway in the healthcare field. (Author's note: Passed in 2010 as part of the Affordable Care Act, this act requires federal healthcare programs to report certain payments and items of value given to physicians by manufacturers of drugs, medical devices, and biologicals that participate in U.S. teaching hospitals. The Centers for Medicare & Medicaid Services (CMS), charged with implementing the Sunshine Act, has called it the Open Payments Program. As part of this program, manufacturers are required to submit reports on payment, transfer, and ownership information.) Walking in the door of the Lahey Clinic as CEO before the passage of the Sunshine Act, I learned a witch-hunt had already been underway.

Specifically, the U.S. Attorney's Office in Boston had targeted the Lahey Clinic in an investigation. Allegedly, one of its leaders had an arrangement or relationship with a drug company that violated federal law. I immediately looked into this and launched an investigation of my own. I also engaged outside legal counsel in this analysis. I was absolutely convinced—and every fact I gathered aligned with it—that dealings were on the up and up. Nothing illegal had been underway; no relationship would taint the individual or the Lahey Clinic. As the CEO, I had dual responsibilities: one to the individual and one to the organization. Officially, I reported to the Lahey Clinic's board of trustees. But sometimes the interest of the institution and the interest of an individual diverge. Do we abandon faith in an individual at a time like this?

No way! Had there actually been a problem? There wasn't!

After determining that, I had a few sharp moments with the chair of our board of trustees about ethical, fiscal, and managerial responsibility— and where that responsibility lay. I wanted other board members to be aware of our conflict, but the chair would have none of it. Eventually, we reached a consensus about process. The rest of the board supported me. And due to this conflict, we ultimately created a stronger board— one that gave me the authority to move on with my planned turnaround for the Lahey Clinic.

One of the successes I've been privileged to enjoy over the years has been the relationships with people to whom I've reported. I've been successful in terms of being respectful, legal, and morally and ethically correct. That has gone all the way into managing, litigation, and individual personnel issues.

S: Share the Vision to Create a Collective Energy

Shortly after I arrived and completed my fact-finding, I spoke to the entire staff conversationally, without notes. I told them they were part of this incredible organization, the Lahey Clinic, where some of the loftiest things anyone can do in this world were performed. I acknowledged that the situation had been disorganized, and then I outlined the road to collective recovery that would make everyone proud again within the year.

First and foremost, I committed that we'd work together to fix the dysfunctional infrastructure. That way, the organization could put forth the best practices to collect fees for care in a fully compliant manner. With that big issue fixed, we would reshape a culture that restored pride in the organization and in their profession—one that rewarded teamwork. We would recapture recognition within the healthcare community as a true winner; we would effectively compete for increased funding; and ultimately we would grow once again.

As a leader, I didn't want to pull the pins out from under anyone. That meant no scolding, no shaking of heads, no handwringing. I wouldn't allow a negative attitude. From then on, I could see a kind of faith in people's eyes. "My gosh, he believes in me!"

✳ Once the plan was hatched, how did you align your team to kick off the plan?

Phase 2 of the ABCs: Kick Off the Game Plan

"Surround yourself with the best people you can find, delegate authority, and don't interfere as long as the policy you've decided upon is being carried out."

—Ronald Reagan

A: Act Boldly to Kick Off the Game Plan

We immediately formed the Billing Enhancement Group (BEG) to focus on properly documenting every single patient encounter in the medical records. It required assigning a legal and appropriate code on each encounter. With that in place, we collected the money owed, plain and simple. Prior to BEG, patients had been seen, but the new system hadn't properly documented the visits. You can't collect money that way. We returned to the legacy system, the old thing that had previously worked but required a lot of manual activity. We hired additional people to pull it off.

Everyone had specific responsibilities, and the whole organization participated. I also continued my medical practice, doing surgery one day a week to ensure I still understood what it's like in the trenches.

Initially, our entire game plan rode on the success of BEG. But much more was required. Reputation and recognition awards didn't go to those on the edge of bankruptcy. Staff members wouldn't suddenly believe in themselves. Banks didn't extend credit lines. Donors didn't line up to commit expansion capital to weak players. Without a bold, successful thrust, other pieces of the game plan would fall flat.

B: Build on Strengths

In spite of the public failure, the Lahey Clinic's brand remained strong, with the powerful legacy of Frank Lahey being similar to the Mayo brothers'. The clinic was a vertically integrated group practice, a multi-specialty organization with salary-based employees—something unique in Boston. Although Lahey's merger failure was so public, our dysfunction was mainly internal. The damaged goods had to be rebuilt, but the underbelly of the Lahey footprint was solid. It provided a strong foundation to launch our game plan and achieve something special.

C: Control Through Visible Measurement

Obviously, we had to look hard at our cash reserve each day. The number of days of cash on hand was highly visible during the BEG program. We measured how many days it took to get a bill out the door, and we reviewed the dollars per transaction to assess the productive efficiency of our resources.

The metrics of managing a hospital are, in some respects, similar to that of managing a hotel. To add patients, or guests, you need more capacity, which spills over to the size and configuration of the physical facility. But whereas hotels study occupancy rates, in hospitals the percentage of occupancy doesn't make a big difference as long as the average length of stay is short. Medicare or other insurance will only reimburse so much.

For people coming into the hospital with congestive heart failure, for example, insurance policies have limits to cover that hospitalization. We can make money if the stay is three days; we take it in the shorts if it's for 10 days because we have to eat the cost of the extra days. That metric helps balance the quality of healthcare with the financial wherewithal to pay for that quality of healthcare.

Quality metrics are measured nationally as well as independently. The metrics define if a facility is a Magnet hospital, which is an important nursing quality award from a nationwide joint commission that accredits hospitals. It's like having a Food and Drug Administration (FDA) review. Having quality metrics were important to the Lahey Clinic on two fronts: 1) to support the "patient-first" mind-set, and 2) to enhance our brand.

S: Streamline the Activity Schedule
Vision, mission, and elevator pitch

A vision statement and mission statement are often "boilerplate" language. Lahey had them—comprised of all of the right words. But nobody believed those words. So early on, we tweaked the boilerplate inclusively and injected passion from within our ranks.

Our driving vision was to be recognized as one of the world's premier healthcare organizations that provided superior care leading to the best possible outcome for every patient. That vision provided a framework for our mission to exceed our patients' high expectations for service, advance medicine through research and education, and promote health and wellness in partnership with the diverse communities we served. It also dictated the way we cared for our patients—with compassion, openness, respect, caring, teamwork, excellence, and commitment to give our personal best. We incorporated the vision and mission into an elevator pitch that took less than a minute that highlighted our differentiation, the group practice of healthcare providers under one roof, giving superior care through their collective engagement on the patient.

Competitive positioning and targeting strategy

Our positioning and targeting had two audiences: 1) the community to which Lahey provided healthcare services, and 2) the donors targeted for fundraising initiatives. Lahey's competitive positioning and differentiation were important to both audiences.

We examined our strengths compared with competing healthcare providers. Lahey offered an integrated group practice with salaried physicians—a differentiation that was a big deal. We made healthcare decisions based on individual patient needs, not on the requirement to glean more funds for the doctors or their institutions. Competitive hospitals in the area all had doctors who were in private practice. Lahey's group approach created the collective wisdom to enable superior patient care.

Lahey's de facto tagline had become "Everything under one roof." Its logo featured three pillars with Practice in the middle, flanked by Education and Research.

We intentionally positioned the organization as atypical, not just another Boston academic healthcare center. The expert in a given field and current in education and research resided here. If a patient needed care from another specialist, it was available under one roof. We made our systems seamless. Once a patient had registered, only one medical record was required to provide a continuity of patient information flowing through the system. That was true even before electronic medical records came into use.

Our would-be donors were willing patients and well-heeled individuals. We knew Boston-area institutional donors had too many causes all vying for funding. We couldn't tap into a cadre of foundations without project or research strings attached.

Primary goals (the BHAGs) to focus the energy

Our primary goals mapped around a five-point game plan.

Always first was fixing the infrastructure to bill and collect cash; it had been badly broken, which we prepared to fix in stages so we could keep the doors open. Plus the organization was losing money. That wasn't sustainable.

I challenged the organization to achieve positive margins, targeting 3 percent to 5 percent instead of 0 percent or less. I also sought to increase by more than three times the cash on hand so it would approach 100 days of cash versus fewer than 30 days. This had a rating agency overtone as well—that is, it was hard to capture an acceptable rating from any agency with our precarious financials. In turn, that affected donor funding and credit worthiness. The third early goal targeted organizational recognition awards to both restore pride within the ranks and add credentials to Lahey's fundraising initiatives, which entailed some marketing.

Critical success factors to prioritize the actions

We would not have existed if we had not turned the financial picture around. Bankruptcy might have been on the horizon. The Sisters of St. Francis in Rochester, Minnesota, ran a large Catholic hospital when I lived there. The head sister talked about the care and well-being of every patient, but always added, "No money, no mission." The Billing Enhancement Group (BEG) was the most intensely active group of people in my early days there. If that initiative didn't succeed, nothing else mattered. Culturally, everyone had to buy into the teamwork aspect of such an all-important initiative; no one could work in a vacuum. The right hand and the left hand needed to be in synch to operate efficiently and eliminate redundancies.

Marketing activities that enabled community and industry recognition spilled over to fundraising metrics, which in turn spilled over to growth opportunities for expanding our facilities. These were all critical to achieving the primary goals. We made these metrics highly visible throughout the organization.

Define and reinforce the culture

The culture in healthcare breeds on itself. It centers on what's perceived to be the proper treatment of the patient. I'd been affected by my Mayo Clinic experience where the only consideration was focused on the patient. In fact, every decision made in healthcare is easily addressed by first thinking about the patient. If we were building a new parking ramp (and we did), we'd first ask, "Where will the patients park?" In a patient-centric culture, patients park near the front door and doctors park toward the rear.

To install and reinforce the right culture, I needed the right people in their positions and give them the authority to execute. Most of the people I've dealt with had been accomplished and talented in their own right. I let them do things their way, as long as they adhered to best practices and worked on prioritized goals. I largely executed the plan through the staff and tried to bring out the best in each and every one of them.

When we couldn't change people's behavior or contribution to do what was needed from a team standpoint, we changed the personnel. That becomes necessary when skill sets don't match the requirements. Generally, the staff at the Lahey Clinic was a compatible group that worked together for the betterment of the organization—and did so with passionate commitment.

✳ With the game plan hatched and kicked off, what was your approach to execute?

Phase 3 of the ABCs: Execute the Plan

> "There are few, if any, jobs in which ability alone
> is sufficient. Needed also are loyalty, sincerity,
> enthusiasm and team play."
>
> —William B. Given, Jr.

A: Assert Yourself at the Focal Point

The BEG program that engulfed much of the organization's early focus and activities had given us an early win. We quickly dismantled the system used by Dartmouth-Hitchcock, initially reverting to an older, more manual way to bill and collect. Ultimately, the system's upgrade was cost-effective and productive. Most important, it worked. Within several months, cash on hand had more than tripled. We no longer had our backs to the wall.

Cash consequences

Rating agencies were happier to look at the Lahey Clinic with its cash resources. With some marketing initiatives, Lahey received early accreditation and recognition. Banks were more willing to extend lines of credit to a recognized player who had visible cash resources. Had it not been for an extraordinary effort that encompassed the entire organization, those early successes might never have materialized.

The initial early goals seemed well in hand. The cash crisis had abated. The staff had worked as a team. Recognition rewarded the inside staff and paved the way for some increased fundraising.

Funding facility upgrades to enable growth

Our facilities were either dated or antiquated and had to be brought up to grade, with the last facility upgrade two decades previously. We needed new operating rooms, a new cancer center, and a new intensive care unit to stay current and relevant. The organization had previously geared itself toward a $5 million fundraising campaign; it had never raised more than $15 million from a small, cultivated circle of donors. We needed a more aggressive approach so we could think in terms of $200 to $250 million.

With a newly recruited development executive, we launched the clinic's first major expansion initiative since moving to its current centralized facility 20 years before. Nearly 60 percent of the funding came from 12 different donors, with the lead gift at $50 million and several $10 million gifts. With a shared vision, consistent messaging, some recognition awards, and visible achievement metrics, a growth initiative that once looked impossible had become real.

✳ What obstacles did you encounter along the way? How did you deal with them?

Obstacles aren't surprising; they're always there. We just put them in proper perspective, applied resources, brought in the right people, and focused. We had overcome billing, cultural, reputation, and fund-raising issues to grow once again. With standardized systems and procedures, less redundancy, and a cultural alignment, we also integrated some acquisitions.

By 2010, the Lahey Clinic was on track to go from a $1 billion organization to a $4 billion company and glean economies of scale. I used my Mayo Clinic template and modified it to fit the circumstance. A combination of organic growth and merger/acquisition would be needed in the future.

Who Cared About Parking?

What threw me most was finding the $35 million in funding to build a needed parking facility. Nobody cared. When we met with our funding sources, their responses were "A cancer treatment center? Sure! But a parking lot? I don't think so!" And even though banks had extended our credit lines and we had a positive agency rating, the banks had imposed certain debt-to-cash covenants that limited how much we could borrow.

Yet when we did the math, the return on the investment (ROI) on a parking facility had been meaningful. Even by charging $5 to park, the ROI made a compelling case for a tax-free municipal bond. We had to get this project off the ground and announce the fundraising and expansion projects early. They were all part of the image-building that went along with our marketing.

Because a hospital bond approach had worked so well for the parking garage, we took that approach once again to build Lahey Clinic North in Peabody, Massachusetts. Patients, staff, and the community at large loved to see its construction; they viewed it as a positive move for the institution.

B: Borrow From Alliances and Partnerships

Any major institution like the Lahey Clinic is a city under one roof, with a number of specialties and different types of professional people. This includes administrative support, janitorial services, food and beverage, and security people, to name a few. We outsourced in the areas that supported our delivery of healthcare where we didn't have the expertise. That increased our efficiency, decreased our inventory, and made better use of our cash.

Specific to providing healthcare, Lahey didn't have a large practice in pediatrics, although we had pediatric coverage in our emergency room. We stood in the shadows of Boston Children's Hospital and Massachusetts General, touting world-class pediatric practices. So we struck alliances with and spun off our pediatrics to these pediatric referral partners. It came down to doing the right thing for the patient.

C: Communicate Progress and Results to Get/Stay on Track

I had both an inside and an outside job. My role required that I communicate to the healthcare community, to the vendors, to my people, and to the community at large.

On the inside, I held regular management meetings and kept track of the momentum indicators. I had special one-on-one meetings as needed. My day started at 6 a.m. and I always made myself available. Various departments held weekly or biweekly meetings. As we grew and got to be multi-centric over the miles in three states, we used Skype or other electronic means as a tool. We held varying town meetings, especially in the beginning of my tenure. I also went to various outposts either right before work, during the lunch hour, or just afterward. Whatever was convenient, that's what we did. Any issue could be surfaced. If anyone felt inhibited, I encouraged him or her to send me a note and I'd deal with it.

The board of governors met once every two weeks. The board of trustees met every quarter, with occasional calls between meetings. The execution of the game plan, the metrics to measure our progress, and any issues we encountered found a place front and center on the agenda.

Compare that to when I began in 1999 at the Lahey Clinic, which had no one responsible for communications. I created a department and hired a capable staff to use all of the media—both traditional offline media and emerging online and social media channels—to consistently deliver our messaging and progress toward goals. We also viewed a comprehensive Website as a communications vehicle that was personalized or used for broad audiences.

Our communications group published a monthly health letter featuring information about what was going on around the organization. It communicated with local media about various education and research projects, putting the Lahey Clinic repetitively in the news. The department also coordinated with the philanthropy staff and enabled regular donor communications. We knew every patient might also be a potential donor.

The protocol we established for communications, both internal and external, was to use "we" as our primary pronoun. If someone used "I" instead of "we," we jumped all over him or her. The team message got transferred quickly and effectively.

S: Spread the Reward of Wealth and Recognition When Things Go Your Way

The team signed up to complete our goals. A payout was implicit because the goals were built around the concept that if the organization's performance improved, more compensation would be available. We were not only taking care of our product line but also the people who built the quality of our offerings.

As everything came together, we used praise and recognition to appreciate our employees who brought the Lahey Clinic out of its doldrums. That appreciation and support from the top, including the board of governors and the trustees, helped achieve the quality that I sought.

✳ What was the end result of the execution?
Financial Stability

What I thought would be a five-year assignment lasted 11-plus years. Everyone in the organization took credit for what we accomplished.

The Lahey Clinic went from having $30 million in the bank in 1999 when I started to about $500 million when I retired in 2011. Billings jumped threefold. The Lahey Clinic earned an A bond rating and was recognized as one of the healthcare leaders in New England.

The Lahey Clinic Cash and Billings Performance

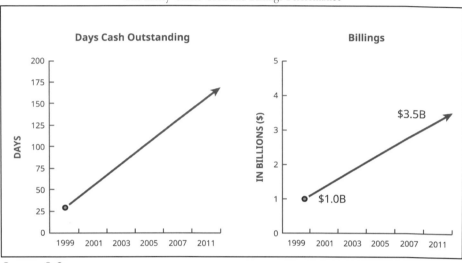

Image 9.2.

Recognition

The Lahey Clinic has been consistently named in "America's Best Hospitals" issue of *U.S. News & World Report,* and Lahey physicians have been consistently ranked "tops" in their fields. The Lahey Clinic was fully accredited and given Magnet hospital recognition by the Joint Commission. It received praise for breast center treatment from the Commission on Cancer of the American College of Surgeons' National Accreditation Program. It was recognized in the American Stroke Association's stroke goal performance achievement, and the clinic received the Health Resources and Services Administration's Silver Medal of Honor for success in increasing organ donation rates. It was also named in the Top 100 Integrated Health Networks in the United States. Although the Lahey Clinic had been under-recognized for a couple of decades, it enjoyed more than a decade of earned recognition.

Between the additional cash and the recognition, rating agencies gave the clinic high scores. That made the brand all the more creditworthy to attract expansion capital and donor support. Our pride was restored.

Growth

I was able to see my last two expansion undertakings completed. The Future of Medicine Initiative was accomplished in 2007 with the development of the Landsman Heart & Vascular Center and the Sophia Gordon Cancer Center. The Lahey Clinic Medical Center, North Shore, facility and clinical services expansion helped ensure that Boston's North Shore and surrounding communities received the finest care for years to come.

In addition, space for procedural and diagnostic testing was scheduled to be added. This included a dedicated surgery and procedure center and an expansion of radiology services. All of these efforts will ensure patients receive top-notch diagnostic care and treatment close to home.

Reputation

The clinic is now known as Lahey Hospital & Medical Center, a physician-led nonprofit teaching hospital of Tufts University School of Medicine. *U.S. News & World Report,* in its list of "America's Best Hospitals" also recognized Lahey for excellence in my specialty, urology. Lahey hosts several residency programs including internal medicine, general surgery, diagnostic radiology, neurology, neurosurgery, otolaryngology, urology, plastic and reconstructive surgery, and dermatology. Lahey's staff holds professorships at Tufts University School of Medicine, Harvard Medical School, and Boston University School of Medicine.

In addition, Lahey hosts extensive fellowship training in cardiology and interventional cardiology, gastroenterology, interventional pulmonology, bariatric, hand surgery, sleep medicine, and stroke. Nearly 719,000 outpatients and 18,000 inpatients were treated at Lahey Hospital & Medical Center in 2013, the highest number in its history.

Lahey's billings surpassed 3.5 times (3.5x) what they were when I started as CEO in 1999.

✳ What's your reflection as you look back?

Opportunity

What a wonderful opportunity I had to make a difference. I've appreciated the self-satisfaction of having had that opportunity. I'm still struck by the fact I got that job. That's just my flaw.

Would I do it again? I'd do it again. Would I make changes? Of course! I would have built a bigger building or raised more funding. And I'll probably die feeling incomplete, because I don't think I've ever done anything as perfectly as I should have. But that's the way it is.

Interestingly, back at the Mayo Clinic, the person appointed CEO lasted about 24 months. Some said I missed the opportunity. But at that fork in the road, I gained an exceptional opportunity that I otherwise might have missed.

Teamwork

We did this together. This turnabout couldn't have been accomplished by any one person. Certain individuals (and I've told them this) executed superbly in their areas of responsibility. They reflected the best of the institution and were highly visible to the outside world. I don't get a kick out of standing with a crown on my head. The crown belongs to the team.

Culture

I'm most pleased about aligning the culture with the needs of the patient coming first. The healthcare world has changed a good deal. People entering the profession today are trained to be experts, tuned into technology and highly efficient. Do they have a mind-set of working 9 to 5? Does it matter to them if the needs of the patient come first?

I know I had to be totally immersed in the care of my patient. If I didn't think about my patients after leaving them in the operating room, who would? I still believe that young medical professionals need to make a lifetime commitment to medicine and avoid the nine-to-five mentality.

Changing Time Commitments to Have a Personal Life

Throughout my career, I was privileged to have a stable home life filled with love and support. That helped me execute my career well. I spent much more time on the job than today's professionals do. Young physicians and healthcare professionals, male and female, work their nine-hour shifts and then somebody else takes over. This started when shift workers staffed emergency rooms. Emergency docs work on eight- to 10-hour shifts. So do hospitalists. Internists may be working on shifts, and ophthalmologists, and so forth. It used to be we'd get there early and left when the work was done. It's different now, but the needs of the patient do come first.

Privilege

At both Mayo and Lahey, we've cared for presidents and leaders of countries and patients from every continent. I've seen their cultural differences, but when it came to medical care, they all appreciated being treated properly and compassionately. There is no equal to healthcare in the United States.

The biggest privilege I've enjoyed is joining the healthcare profession with the example and guidance of Dr. Jim Fryfogle. It was from his teachings I learned that patients came first. They still do.

✳ How did the experience help you advance?

For having been an uninterested student, I've grown a good deal. But with the Lahey Clinic experience, I parlayed my knowledge of business and healthcare into other businesses. Thanks in no small part to the credentials that the Lahey experience gave me, I currently serve as a member of the board of directors for five different companies, both publicly traded and privately held. They range from healthcare products and services to investments. I find these interesting companies self-satisfying and stimulating.

Serving on the faculty at Dartmouth College Geisel School of Medicine, I'm involved with residents, interns, and medical students. My days of pursuing academic research are probably behind me, but I've had the privilege of learning a lot about the limitations of medical research. Given my Lahey Clinic exposure to continued research and the additional expertise gained in my field, urology, I hold a patent on a totally implantable artificial bladder. It has been implanted in laboratory animals but not yet in humans. What an exciting opportunity to improve the lives of so many who face bladder removal due to cancer, thus avoiding future renal and voiding dysfunction.

The opportunities before me to make a difference are limitless. What an exciting time!

10

Shawn K. Osborne:
Overcoming Misalignment and Defection at TechAmerica

"The future is not set. There is no fate but what we make for ourselves."

—Irish proverb

✳ How did you get to be the person you are? What's your story?

As a working class, second-generation Irish kid born in a little town all of one mile square in upstate New York, I saw my father for the last time on a summer's day in 1973. We were in a Long Island Holiday Inn. He had prepaid for a hotel room that would cover a two-week stay and house my mother, my 12-year-old sister, my 5-year-old brother, and me. At 13 years old, I was the oldest.

Image 10.1: Shawn K. Osborne. Photo copyright Shawn K. Osborne. Used with permission.

Then he left. This hard-drinking, womanizing Kirby vacuum cleaner salesman and 3M copy machine salesman had moved us from various New York towns to Memphis, Tennessee, and back again. I had attended four different schools. The bickering between my parents stopped when my father left and divorced my mother. Or did *she* divorce *him?* Anyway, he simply disappeared. There was no further contact, and he provided no financial support.

Early Sense of Responsibility

Until then, my mother had been a highly committed, under-educated stay-at-home mom. At that point, she piled us into her Oldsmobile with all of our worldly possessions. We stayed with one of her friends along the western Connecticut–New York state border until she found a secretarial job and a place for us to live in a town with a decent school system.

We struggled. Food stamps helped. She never pressed me. But being the oldest, I felt a big responsibility to be the man of the house. I was compelled to work after school to make my financial contribution. I balanced restaurant dishwashing jobs with my high school classes and athletics schedule (soccer and hockey). I made a point of eating a good dinner at work before going home to complete my homework.

School was important to me. My peer group was comprised of good kids who, like I did, looked forward to building their future. The State University of New York (SUNY) system provided ample financial aid packages for students needing help. I qualified, received a scholarship, and studied computer science. Then my mother, a smoker, was diagnosed with lung cancer. It eventually spread to her brain.

With a computer science degree in hand, I left school and returned home to care for my dying mother for the last years of her life. I was appointed the legal guardian of my younger brother, who was in middle school. By then, my sister had entered the SUNY system with an aid package. My computer science training helped me quickly find employment to support us.

Having felt a tremendous amount of responsibility, I did what I needed to do. Having watched my mother work hard and barely get anywhere, I quickly scoped out that gaining an education would help me. Driven and tenacious, I wanted to be the best I could be.

Even though negative events occurred, I have positive memories of my childhood. The constant change and adversity taught me to roll with the punches, put my head down, and forge forward. In my life since then, I haven't shied away from adversity. I've always found the work ethic to figure out how to plow through it.

Mistake Quickly Corrected

It was a challenge to balance my early career needs in my 20s with supervising a teenage brother in high school. I needed help, so I asked my paternal grandparents to move in with us for a bit. While I worked late or traveled, they could provide supervision. Great idea, bad execution! Unfortunately, my grandparents were more dysfunctional than I ever knew. They needed even more supervision than my little brother. So I did what I had to do and conducted a difficult conversation. I essentially fired my grandparents and drove them back to their home in upstate New York.

Over the years, I've made mistakes—like the one with my grandparents. Anyone who makes decisions makes mistakes on occasion. I've used that example to reinforce the concept that, once a mistake is recognized, I'd better correct it—pronto! The consequences of letting it ride can be worse than the pain to fix the error.

✳ What was your career progression before joining TechAmerica?

My first post-college job was with the maker of Hostess Twinkies and Wonder Bread: Continental Baking Company, owned at the time by mega-conglomerate ITT. I worked for a couple of years as a computer operator. Then I moved to Nestlé as a communications analyst who ran the modem pools. There, I gained four years of technical hands-on experience working with mainframe computers and communication systems. About that time, I married my high school sweetheart.

Sales and Sales Management

On the tennis courts in the late 1980s, I was introduced to a small public technology company's CEO, an A-level tennis player. After playing together and getting to know one another, he told me I had a natural sales capability. He then invited me to interview with his vice president of sales for a position with his firm. I interviewed well and accepted the resulting job offer. In that job, I sold technical tools—hardware used by telephone company field engineers.

The vice president of sales ensured I was well trained on product line features, benefits, competitive advantages, and relationship selling that would establish trust. He taught me to conduct business with a firm handshake before putting arrangements in writing. In that environment, I moved from junior salesman to top salesman, then from junior sales manager to senior sales manager. Because he provided no management training at the outset, I thought sales management meant helping a sales rep close a deal. I later witnessed more capable sales managers in action. That's when I realized the good managers provided their teams with tools, knowledge, and encouragement to do a great job versus doing the job for them. Over time, I not only learned how to sell, market, and manage; I also picked up leadership skills.

Apparently, I had developed a reputation within the telecommunications industry. A communications software firm sought me out and offered me the position of vice president of sales with responsibility for its global revenue operations. This company was twice the size of my previous company, privately held, and nicely profitable. It provided signaling software that enabled enhanced features including wireless communication. During this time, I honed my skills and added global experience through both subsidiaries and third-party agents. Much of the firm's staff had been technically trained, so the members looked to me to provide the non-technical leadership. What I didn't know I learned on the fly.

How did I learn leadership? I developed an uncanny knack to look in the mirror, realistically assess situations, spot mistakes, and take corrective action quickly. As part of my developing leadership style, I shared my successes and failures, both teaching and learning from them. In effect, I became my own worst critic.

First-Time CEO and Entrepreneur

Along the way, I met private equity and merchant banking groups that exposed me to a small, troubled startup wireless data company that was well ahead of its time. The company manufactured wireless point-of-sale terminals for what is today known as cloud computing. Through the cloud, the terminals could interface with banking systems to process transactions. The company's early management team had run the boat ashore and wasn't effectively commercializing the product. By the mid-1990s, I was appointed CEO, which meant running the entire operation.

In this role, I can't say I knew what to do, but I felt confident I could make a difference. People's livelihoods depended on my ability to hire and organize, create realistic budgets and forecasts, and lead them in delivering our products and services. By way of stock options, I became a part owner in the firm, not simply an employee. In effect, this gave me the opportunity to live the American entrepreneurial dream.

The business grew from no revenue and no customers to become a genuine commercial organization that had testimonial customers, several million dollars of revenue, and a future. The private equity owners then merged the business with another company they owned. They rewarded me, and I moved on with this wonderful learning experience of operational and financial discipline behind me.

Next CEO Assignment

Something must have worked, because my network introduced me to my next CEO assignment. For the next 14 years, I built a business that led to a hugely successful IPO, and then I patched it back together after everything blew up. What an experience!

Ulticom was owned by a parent company, Comverse, which was publicly traded at the time. The opportunity at the time entailed my transitioning a $4 million service business to software products by commercializing its signaling software intellectual property. The burgeoning wireless networks market provided fertile ground for major growth. "If you can make this a big success, take the business public," Comverse said to me.

Within a few short years, I recruited and led a team to do exactly that. The strategy we constructed and executed built the company into a highly profitable, global $60 million market leader. It went public as the fourth-best-performing technology IPO and the ninth-best-performing IPO overall in 2000. Between its initial public and secondary stock offerings, Ulticom raised $200 million of cash. Right place, right time!

We had built this business on three pillars: quality programs, information systems to manage the growth, and talent. With a world-class leadership team both during the upswing and the downturn, the company facilitated those shifts with less than 5-percent unforced turnover—well below the industry norm.

But our success didn't last forever. Two hugely disruptive events occurred in slow motion. First, the company was strong enough to deal with the burst of the Internet bubble in 2000. But in 2002, combined with the post–September 11 recession, company revenue dropped nearly in half to $30 million almost overnight. Not realizing how bad the downturn would be, we downsized our business to accommodate the forecasted drop. But we had to lay people off *again* when we saw we had underestimated the magnitude of the fragile economy on our revenue. Mistake noted: *No matter how bad you think it is, it can get worse. You better have a plan.*

The second layoff was more disruptive to organizational stability and morale than the first. It would have been better to have quickly taken more drastic action earlier on. As time went on, the team walked a tightrope to balance operations with reality, and it succeeded in regrouping after both downsizings. We gradually rebuilt our revenue to $60 million once again before it reached a plateau. With the company off its high-flying growth track, its strong leadership team made all the difference in regrouping with discipline and delivering consistent results.

Scandal and Flight

Then we received a second unexpected blow. Just when we thought we had stabilized, Ulticom's majority owner got caught in a stock option back-dating scandal. The news of his behavior played out in every major newspaper and business journal like a bad B-rated movie. While the Securities and Exchange Commission (SEC) conducted its investigations, Comverse's CEO fled to Namibia. Of course, the business experienced a tailspin. Needing to raise cash, its leaders first issued Ulticom's cash as a dividend to themselves, then sold their controlling stake in Ulticom to private equity interests. The SEC investigated Ulticom, too, because it had been so closely related to a guilty party. When the investigation concluded, the SEC issued Ulticom a clean bill of health.

This adversity provided me with yet another tremendous learning experience. Comverse held the majority of my board seats. There were other board members who represented minority shareholders. I'd never been in a board situation where there had been so much conflict. As the CEO of a public company, I had fiduciary responsibility to all shareholders, not just the majority holder. This whole situation clearly tested my leadership skills. I communicated like crazy to customers, shareholders, and employees. It was a privilege to see them stand behind the company as a testament to the integrity and ethics of the leadership team. As Ulticom transitioned from private to public (with a majority shareholder) to private once again (with a different majority shareholder), it was a win-win for everybody.

It was also time for me to go.

I took a year off and thought about what to do next with my life. How lucky was I to have that time! I played golf, but I had few hobbies outside of work. While spending time with my family, I quickly realized how much I *liked* work and *wanted* to work, but I craved a different kind of arrangement. Again, I looked in the mirror and asked if I was good or simply lucky. I concluded that I wanted to challenge myself in a nonprofit setting working on a cause that makes a difference to people.

✳ What was the situation before you entered the organization that led to its issues?

TechAmerica positioned itself at the time as the largest nonprofit trade association representing U.S. businesses that provide technology products and services. Its stated mission was to advance the business of technology from grassroots to global and to champion the technology industry as the key driver of productivity growth and job creation. Its dues-paying company members benefitted from TechAmerica's policy and advocacy work at both state and federal levels. It lobbied on public policy issues of importance to the industry. Members also benefitted from TechAmerica's networking and information activities that fostered knowledge and business development among member companies.

Formed by Merging #1 and #2

In the aftermath of the burst of the technology bubble, the industry had experienced a rise of merger and acquisition activity as it further matured and consolidated. There were simply too many technology businesses with overlapping products and services competing for a finite amount of business. There were also too many technology trade associations with overlapping charters competing for finite dues and related fees. TechAmerica had been created by combining the largest technology industry trade association, the AeA (formerly known as the American Electronics Association), with the number-two technology industry trade association, the Information Technology Association of America (ITAA). ITAA had recently acquired two small industry trade associations. AeA members were primarily termed "commercial sector," meaning their businesses focused on private business. By comparison, ITAA members were primarily termed "public sector," meaning their business focused on the government or the federal market. Of course, some of the largest companies had business units aimed at both.

The combination was completed at the height of the 2008–2010 financial crisis in January 2009, just as the Obama administration was taking office. Both associations found it challenging to retain their members, dues, and service revenue in the midst of a financial downturn. The combination of these associations had the potential to give the newly formed TechAmerica a stronger voice on Capitol Hill while lowering the overall cost of providing industry membership services.

Before the two merged, the AeA had the larger membership with more field offices, revenue, and expense than ITAA. But it was cash poor and struggling to maintain a breakeven financial performance. ITAA was cash rich with several million dollars in reserve, making it relatively more financially stable.

At the outset of the merger, TechAmerica tallied 1,500 member companies that spanned across the technology industry—hardware, software, and services. Its members included both publicly traded and privately held firms whose stages ranged from pre-revenue startups to industry titans. It operated in 18 offices across the country, with international offices in Brussels and Beijing.

Its large members tended to value TechAmerica's policy and advocacy work. By comparison, the small members valued the business networking and information services that fostered their own business development. Membership dues varied by company size, with 80 percent of the membership made up of smaller firms, though 80 percent of the dues revenue came from the larger members.

Misalignment and Financial Stress

Against the backdrop of the biggest financial meltdown since the Great Depression, the merger between AeA and ITAA was completed. Neither association's board of directors had the vision nor wanted to go through a potential fight to install one leader. Instead, the boards created joint leadership with AeA's CEO named CEO for TechAmerica, responsible for overall performance, and ITAA's CEO named TechAmerica's president, responsible for policy and advocacy (lobbying). TechAmerica formed a governance board, but all the other boards and special interest groups within each association continued to function and meet as they did before.

As the Great Recession of 2008–2009 raged, TechAmerica's slightly decreased expenses continued to exceed its ever-decreasing revenues. The first two years of poor financial performance depleted 60 percent of its cash reserves. The CEO resigned, leaving the president in charge to deplete another 20 percent of its cash. If it had one more year like the previous few, TechAmerica would be bankrupt. The organization experienced low morale and high turnover. The merger, which looked terrific in concept, was a failure in execution. The lack of integration to realize the synergies, a cultural misalignment between the two merger partners, and a two-pronged board structure all added to the stress.

TechAmerica's governance board finally agreed to make a move. It hired an executive search firm to find a new CEO. That search firm contacted me. It liked my background and experience, and it outlined the TechAmerica situation. For the first time since my early professional employment, I interviewed for a position in a competitive process in which I wasn't contacted directly by the hiring organization.

✳ What attracted you to this situation when many would run away?

While CEO of Ulticom, I had become active in a trade association representing the telecom industry. After several years of involvement, I had been appointed its chairman. That gave me a sense of trade association activity and its governance via a volunteer board comprised of trade association members.

TechAmerica presented a leadership challenge outside of my comfort zone. I saw this situation as a huge growth opportunity. I wanted something different. So I got behind the notion of giving back to the technology industry that had given me so much opportunity. The idea of leading people to accomplish the mission of enabling an industry to add jobs and value for Americans excited me.

I certainly knew how to build a team. I had confidence and drive. I thought I could make a positive difference doing what I knew I could do. I'd been very decisive, faced adversity both personally and professionally, and never sat on the fence. If I made mistakes, I adjusted and corrected. Although I had never been the most talented athlete, I was the most tenacious. I could run and skate, and though I wasn't as fast as some, I succeeded because of my drive to win.

So I walked into this opportunity head first, challenged myself, and confronted what I thought could be turned into a winning situation.

✳ How did you hatch the plan to address this situation?
Phase 1 of the ABCs: Hatch the Plan

> "Close scrutiny will show that most crises situations are opportunities to either advance, or stay where you are."
>
> —Maxwell Maltz

A: Ask Questions and Listen; Then Ask for Help

I approached this as a crisis situation. Bankruptcy would be looming if we didn't find answers and take action quickly. First, I assembled a small crisis team comprised of the CFO, the general counsel, and the VP of sales. I asked for its collective analysis of our financial situation, competitive positioning, and the macro trends that affected the industry and the association.

I then divided my time in half between TechAmerica members and our employees. I would contact key people to help me figure out what to do. They included representative stakeholders—members of the board of directors and major dues-paying members. I asked which services they most valued. When I met with employees, I asked their opinions about strategy and operational problems to gain both a historical view and a future view. And there was no shortage of history. Both groups struggled more with the future than they did with the past.

I also tested the whole concept of two pillars that described the most important services we offered: public policy and advocacy (PP&A), and business networking and intelligence (BN&I). Some of my questions were organizational. Why were we structured with 18 different business units? I wanted to understand if they knew the financial situation of the organization. I listened to a good deal of griping about the budgeting process, human resources, compensation, recruiting, and the like. I just took notes without being judgmental.

B: Base the Plan on What You Hear and See, or Don't Hear and See

TechAmerica was divided into silos both within its membership and its employee base. People still spoke of the AeA and the ITAA separately. I didn't hear TechAmerica mentioned except in lament of the way things used to be. Their views differed based on a person's particular area of interest. Members felt like they were owners who had "sweat equity" in the association. They valued whatever was most important to them. For example, some valued an event whereas others valued the educational program. Yet others valued the government program, or the policy and advocacy program, or the networking for business development initiatives.

Outside of special events, TechAmerica's one reliable revenue stream appeared to be dues, dues, and more dues. But with the financial crisis, membership renewals had declined as budgets and discretionary spending stretched thinner and thinner. Legacy revenue sources from the old AeA had matured and could no longer be guaranteed. Those sources had previously funded the field offices and regional events the smaller member companies valued most.

Their biggest pocket of past revenue came from what they termed "The Classic," an investor relations event that went back 35 years. In the days when there were just four U.S. investment bankers focused on technology companies, only the biggest or fastest-growing players gained an investor audience or received analyst coverage.

The AeA filled that gap with an event that had only been open to member companies. Publicly listed firms joined the association to gain access. Investors flocked to see what was new and improved. The Classic was so successful, the AeA opened a second investor relations event for smaller companies only. Both events yielded the two largest annual revenue sources for the association.

Over time, those four investment bankers were acquired and subsequently splintered. A plethora of boutique firms took their place, each with its own investor relations event. After the burst of the bubble, the advent of Sarbanes-Oxley regulations, and the proliferation of merger and acquisition activity, the number of firms listed on the NASDAQ Stock Market alone declined by 40 percent—from 5,000 to 3,000. Those two biggest sources of revenue had matured and were marginally viable.

Another past AeA revenue stream had been royalties from the sale of group-discounted affinity programs such as healthcare insurance and car rental. New insurance regulations, more insurance and car rental competition, and a change in insurance regulations marginalized both the big group discounts and the association's third-largest revenue stream. No wonder the AeA had been financially stretched: It was offering the same services for much less revenue. That whole financial dysfunction had been inherited by TechAmerica.

I found an association trying to be everything to everybody, without quantifying the addressable market. The math didn't work by pouring resources into areas with narrow return prospects.

C: Challenge the Sacred Cows or the Status Quo

It had become clear to me that the addressable market had to be the mid-sized to large companies that provided 80 percent of the revenue, even though, in sheer numbers, the majority of the members were actually smaller companies. The bigger players didn't value a regional presence. Instead, they valued government procurement and lobbying programs at the state and federal levels. Smaller companies valued the regional offices and the business development and networking events, which they had hosted. The services that paid for themselves were tailored to the players who paid the bills. The past extraneous revenue that funded the services valued by the smaller companies had matured and tapered off. I sought to uncover quick and easy revenue replacements. I didn't find them!

The field offices were a long-standing legacy in the commercial sector, but they were no longer financially viable. Many local or regional special technology interest competitors had crept into the trade association scene over several years, adding competition for local events that had diluted field office revenue potential. Some smaller companies—especially those on a rapid growth track, we hypothesized—would see the value in TechAmerica's offering. Those that were small (and likely to remain so) might not. Therefore, they would defect to a local organization.

The reality of our financial situation required TechAmerica to offer a unique value proposition in a very crowded, competitive landscape of trade associations geared to special segments. We had to spot a segment that had value as well as a segment large enough to produce an organization that was financially viable. Survive first and thrive second! Providing a value proposition for the smaller firms through those field offices did neither.

S: Share the Vision to Create a Collective Energy

After joining TechAmerica in March 2012, I came to a June board meeting with a game plan I had vetted for buy-in both inside the association and with thought leaders on the outside. TechAmerica needed immediate restructuring. It was determined the field offices were to be closed. Though we might find a franchise partner to carry on the regional work, TechAmerica didn't have the cash to carry the offices for the time it might take to structure a program.

The member value proposition centered on two primary pillars that gave TechAmerica a longer-term potential: lobbying, termed public policy and advocacy (PP&A), and business networking and intelligence (BN&I). The plan called for BN&I programs that played to industry trends of traveling regionally. They would provide a platform for local interface in the absence of the closed field offices.

As part of the vetting and presentation process, we constructed a financial pro-forma that forecasted modest attrition with mid- to large-sized company membership. We expected a large percentage of the smaller firms to drop their membership and seek local organizations to take our place. This was a contentious measure, especially for those board members from smaller enterprises. But at the end of the day, no one had a better plan. The change was approved by a large majority, but the vote wasn't unanimous.

✳ Once the plan was hatched, how did you align your team to kick off the plan?

Phase 2 of the ABCs: Kick Off the Plan

"A single twig breaks, but a bushel of twigs is strong."

—Tecumseh

A: Act Boldly to Kick Off the Game Plan

In organizing ourselves around that game plan, we acknowledged we had too many silos. We had a VP of this silo and a VP of that silo. I created an organizational structure that facilitated the plan with clear lines of responsibility. This resulted in a far more functional organization comprised of finance, legal, sales, marketing, public policy and advocacy, and business networking and intelligence. They served our two membership constituencies: public sector and commercial sector. No longer AeA or ITAA, we talked about TechAmerica. We had one revenue number. One organization, one game plan!

Cash forecasts dictated we had no time to pussyfoot around. The varying field offices had to go, despite a long-standing energy to keep them.

B: Build on Strengths

A SWOT (Strengths, Weaknesses, Opportunities, and Threats) analysis conducted in the first month of my coming in confirmed three of TechAmerica's strengths. It also brought to light a fourth strength that quite surprised me.

Given their decades as the number-one and number-two technology trade associations, I anticipated finding clear strengths in these two pillars: public policy and advocacy, and business networking and intelligence. In addition, the cadre of member companies, which included the top 300 who's who of technology, certainly brought credibility to the association—a third strength.

The surprise came with the TechAmerica brand equity, both on Capitol Hill and Main Street. Though the integration of the AeA and the ITAA had failed dismally, the marketing and public relations machinery to promote the newly named combination created positive brand recognition—our fourth strength. When we walked in the door—whether it was at the White House, Congress, or a potential member company in any corner of the country—the name TechAmerica was recognized with positive regard. We had been our own worst critics.

We'd found four strengths upon which we could lay the foundation for rebuilding a stable organization that could add value to its membership as well as to our society. I was thrilled!

C: Control Through Visible Measurement

Cash, cash forecasts, and cash contingency forecasts were numbers one, two, and three on my hit parade to measure daily. They all depended on revenue and collections. New memberships and renewal memberships were big drivers of cash forecasts. Outside of memberships, the forecasted revenue from events—including award banquets and seminars—played a significant role.

Given all the employee dissatisfaction and the instability of the recent past, we also looked heavily at employee retention—especially of those employees we targeted as "keepers" on the A-Team to help execute the plan. Stability was needed both on the financial side and the human side. Because each was critical to our future, I wanted to see visible measurement of both.

S: Streamline the Activity Schedule

Vision, mission, and elevator pitch

The vision for our organization was ONE! TechAmerica was ONE organization, with ONE game plan and ONE team. Membership interests varied from public sector to commercial sector. Service offerings came from two pillars, PP&A and BN&I, but they were delivered by ONE association named "TechAmerica." We just didn't have room for "AeA" or "ITAA" in our vocabulary. The grass roots component of the marketing material was tempered to reflect the fact that field offices were going to go. We recast all of our words to reflect a renewed focus of ONE organization delivering specific value to the industry it served.

Competitive positioning and targeting strategy

Next, we positioned TechAmerica as the go-to trade association that addressed the needs of larger, mid-sized, and some smaller technology companies. It was the only association that could deliver PP&A and BN&I on federal, state, and (through active offices in Brussels and Beijing) international levels.

The sales team constructed two target lists: those members whose retention mattered to TechAmerica's future, and those who fit the profile as prospective members who could benefit the most from the defined value proposition.

When I was a new sales rep, my manager never provided collateral to document the company's value proposition. Disagreeing with that,

I subscribed to a different school. TechAmerica's value proposition and testimonial successes were put into collateral marketing materials. And we trained our staff to ensure consistent messaging of our selling points—with collateral to assist in that messaging.

Primary goals (the BHAGs) to focus the energy

Our goal wasn't only survival. The primary goal was to achieve the vision of ONE organization that had to achieve financial stability. Membership—and thus revenue—not only needed to stabilize; it needed to grow.

Critical success factors to prioritize the actions

I held a variety of meetings to align everybody on working toward the vision and three primary goals: one organization, financial stability, and revenue growth. The reorganization would eliminate the silos. To focus on what mattered most, we constructed an incentive program around the achievement of both organizational and individual goals for which varying department heads were responsible. Those goals typically consisted of revenue, operating income, membership, and membership satisfaction. I wanted these goals to be highly visible, clearly defined, and universally owned with no ambiguity. Incentives would help create the alignment we needed.

Define and reinforce the culture

The personality of an organization divided into silos creates little accountability for doing what's best for the organization. I had hoped the reorganization and the incentive programs—all aligned to the achievement of very specific, shared goals—would lead to a culture of accountability.

A culture of accountability had to begin with the right people in the right positions to execute. When I had been planning and meeting with the staff, I had been assessing available skills to accomplish what we deemed critical. Some people were properly skilled for their position while others played second base when they were skilled to play third base.

I brought in players from the outside, including a CFO who could fix a badly patched-together financial system, to give us the visibility and controls critical to our success.

✳ With the game plan hatched and kicked off, what was your approach to execute?

Phase 3 of the ABCs: Execute the Plan

> "A real man smiles in trouble, gathers strength from disaster and grows brave by reflection."
>
> —Thomas Paine

A: Assert Yourself at the Focal Point

The restructuring

The chairs from various regional offices had previously comprised a piece of TechAmerica's board. Some of the chairs had actually approved the initiative at our June board meeting. I took responsibility for personally meeting and communicating with each one of them when we restructured the field offices. It required my direct involvement and support as opposed to my dispassionate delegation. Some very good people were let go. The restructuring, although easy to explain, was hard to do. Still, I was convinced it was the right thing.

Personal selling

As the leader of the organization, I had been on the street with the sales team and those responsible for delivering our core products and services the minute we pushed the execution button. I led from the front.

In addition, I met with executives of our top member companies to outline TechAmerica's positioning, value proposition, and benefits to its members. Almost universally, major members stated they had never been visited by their trade association's CEO. They clearly appreciated the time I spent. Nothing can replace the power of a senior player telling his story to another senior player, especially during a time of such significant change. We had a powerful story to tell, a strong brand, leading members, and valuable services. The message was clear: Look at the new TechAmerica!

Early stability

We experienced a predictable decline in membership from the smaller companies, although we retained a number of those firms on a growth path to become larger. The value proposition resonated. We attempted co-sponsoring The Classic and the micro-cap investor relations events, but eventually opted to discontinue them. We retained the members we wanted and recruited new members into the association. Revenue stabilized. Breakeven achieved! In fact, we actually overachieved that year's revenue forecast and built a bit of a cash reserve, although a very little bit.

Yes, we were profitable with positive cash flow and free from debt. Morale had improved. Turnover had abated. The board was seemingly of one mind. But we were not home free by a long shot. We had no appreciable cash reserves nor did we have resources to invest in programs or hire additional employees to enhance our systems and remain competitive. I'd witnessed that dilemma before in the technology industry. Companies with the best products but without adequate financial resources either never got traction or failed to gain meaningful market penetration.

The board and I agreed. We needed a partner.

✳ What obstacles did you encounter along the way? How did you deal with them?

In the highly competitive technology industry, companies large and small actively practiced guerrilla warfare as a matter of strategy. They play rough, but at least they use tactics that are legal.

Solicited defection and alleged theft

TechAmerica rounded the corner of profitability, becoming debt-free and more stable. Time to find a suitable partner. But then we got hit with a tsunami that created another layer of uncertainty within the organization. All the team members who ran one of our most popular services—the government procurement team—defected *en masse* to the competitive association—one that focused on the top 50 tech firms in the commercial sector only. This competitor offered certain members on the public sector team a big signing bonus and a gargantuan increase in salary. That defection gave our competitor the staff to expand to public sector companies. Their pitch was simple: "Don't pay dues to two organizations offering the same service. Drop TechAmerica and stay with the staff who gave you great value." Doing something legal was one thing but ethical was another.

TechAmerica's executive committee reviewed the facts. It felt violated. It appeared the defecting team had sabotaged TechAmerica's systems upon exiting, stealing intellectual property and proprietary material. Guerrilla warfare incorporated solicitation and defection but *not* blatant sabotage and theft.

So TechAmerica filed a $5 million lawsuit, both against the competing association and the individuals who joined them. Within DC where most trade associations were headquartered, the defection and lawsuit became a big media event. Members took sides: either the side of the defecting staff or TechAmerica's side. It was a mess.

Adversity required swift action. Inside the first week, we filled those roles with internal people and didn't skip a beat to deliver services to our members. Like when we restructured the organization, I either met face-to-face or through teleconferences with leading members and employees to outline the board's assessment of what happened—and our swift response. Within a couple of months, we hired a well-regarded replacement for the head of the defecting group as well as replacement staff. We were back on track. Some would say we even upgraded. But the damage had been done.

The destabilizing impact

In prior times, the largest technology companies placed members of their executive staff on boards of varying trade associations. For example, a senior executive or CEO on Capitol Hill could be a powerful advocate for industry-friendly public policy. Over time, as the companies continued to grow, those senior executives replaced themselves on various boards with government affairs specialists. Those specialists held the big company board seats at both TechAmerica and the competing association.

In the view of a half dozen of these big company representatives, TechAmerica had taken the initiative to use their dues money to fund a lawsuit rather than fund public policy initiatives. The big players we'd worked so hard to retain during the restructuring chose not to renew their TechAmerica membership. They dropped out! All of a sudden, we had a revenue deficit of a few million dollars and very small cash reserves. The initiative to find a suitable partner was no longer a nice thing to explore; it was a necessity.

B: Borrow From Alliances and Partnerships

Event partners

We did what we could afford to do and invested in our core competencies. We actively outsourced areas we knew did not give us a competitive advantage. We focused our resources to fund new member recruitment or value proposition delivery to current members. When it came to selling sponsorships or seats to an event—or even managing the event itself—we found partners and paid them a success fee. Through our partnerships, we pulled off two events in which we gained visibility and revenue. They were the Technology and Government Dinner in DC and the Medal of Achievement in Silicon Valley.

Systems partner

TechAmerica had previously invested a significant amount of money in an information system that didn't work. Our next step was to outsource the entire system, including payroll and benefits, to a cloud-based provider.

Financial partner

The savings added up, but they were not enough. The focus gained from outsourcing added to our efficiency, but it filled little more than a dent in the enlarged deficit from the second wave of disruption and defection.

In the aftermath of the defection of the government procurement team, the lawsuit, and the resulting attrition of several large dues payers, I brought several potential partners to the negotiating table. We signed a letter of intent with what we thought was the best of the lot, but I kept our options open if things failed to come together. Their due diligence created hesitation and pause. Would the membership defections abate or continue? What would be the effect on revenue? Could they afford to assume the liabilities, the biggest of which was a large rental obligation for TechAmerica's Pennsylvania Avenue headquarters in DC? And what about settling that outstanding lawsuit?

As the clock ticked on the expiration of that letter of intent, it became increasingly obvious we needed a backup plan.

C: Communicate Progress and Results to Get/Stay on Track

Throughout the process of getting TechAmerica on solid footing, I actively communicated to three constituencies: employees, members, and the marketplace in general. Communicating to the organization's employee base was at the top of my list. Through this dishevelment, both attracting and retaining the talent base required over-communication. My frequent staff meetings kept the primary goals and our progress highly visible. We conducted all-employee conference calls frequently. In the meantime, I spent more time outside the office than in, keeping a steady flow of information on our successes and challenges quite visible.

Over-communication helped curtail the previous turnover. Although I couldn't be totally transparent regarding our partnering initiatives, I did attempt to address the ugly reality. I let people know that work was going on behind the scenes to address the defection that had caused our cash shortfall. Thankfully, our key talent base remained intact through that nightmarish situation.

Running TechAmerica was my first nonprofit experience. The dues-paying members needed to understand all the ins and outs of activity. Viewing themselves as owners, they wanted detail. This was tricky.

I'd led a company through a crisis without airing all the dirty details to my customers and shareholders. I did it by being honest and direct. Through personal meetings, social media, written newsletters, and public relations press releases, we conveyed our messages without breaching any propriety.

I knew how to communicate to a corporate board comprised of investors and independent directors. When I outlined a trouble spot, I hadn't worried that they'd all leave. But this was a nonprofit situation in which the most passionate, committed customers comprised my all-volunteer board of directors—a group that needed handholding. Once again, I was honest and direct. I told them the house was on fire, discussed how to put the fire out, and then explained why they should remain a member.

With all the turmoil and disruption, keeping the flow of communications going to the internal and external stakeholders evolved into a full-time job. Our public relations effort pushed a steady flow of news into the marketplace. We addressed restructuring, repositioning, and public policy initiatives. We gave visibility to varying business networking functions and market intelligence. I'm sure this effort contributed to our achieving some stability and returning to modest growth.

When the public sector employee defection occurred, however, the DC media had a field day. After TechAmerica filed suit, reporters went into high gear. It sure looked like the adversarial association had leaked half-truths of information to tabloid journalists about TechAmerica's demise. Our adversary got the better of me in its use of the media. As a result, I was constantly on the defensive, addressing false truths that had been printed. Perception became the ultimate reality. In my previous jobs, the facts had ruled; financial reports of how the company performed each quarter were highly visible. But this was a case of which side had the best spin. A mistake to learn from: I should have ensured we quickly and proactively reached out to the media when bad news was on the loose.

S: Share the Rewards of Wealth and Recognition When Things Go Your Way

In my corporate experience, I had stock options to provide financial rewards to various staff members. But TechAmerica was a nonprofit with no stock options. Still, our mission to advance public policy for the good of the technology industry was highly motivational for the employees of TechAmerica. Whenever we had a win, we shared it throughout our entire organization, celebrating little victories as well as big ones. Every employee played a part in every success.

Outside of providing a competitive compensation package, we used recognition to reward people for accomplishing critical success factors that led to a semblance of stability, new members, and breakeven cash flow. As a piece of our regular organizational communications, we recognized those people whose accomplishments drove us closer to achieving our goals. They were heralded at board meetings as well. We had built into our culture of accountability the recognition of those who made a difference.

✳ What was the end result of the execution?

A prospective partner that signed a letter of intent ended up backing out. Too much risk! It appeared this partner intended to completely disband TechAmerica's commercial sector and integrate the public sector operations into its own. Many of our members would have lost their voices had this scenario concluded. But here we stood—with a broken deal. And we had wasted two precious months.

Three activities coalesced almost simultaneously: First, we courted what ended up being the perfect partner for the circumstances. Second, our CFO and general counsel negotiated their way out of our large remaining lease obligations for the Pennsylvania Avenue headquarters. The deal they cut with the landlord to let us off the hook included paying him some of the proceeds from the lawsuit if we ever collected anything. And third, the adversarial trade association we had sued settled out of court, without admitting guilt.

Thankfully, the second and third activities diffused the risk of partnering with TechAmerica. We went back and forth with both the landlord and our adversary to bring them to the table with something we could sign. Plus we needed to accomplish all of this without leaking information about nearing a partnership.

My first meeting with the Computer Technology Industry Association (CompTIA) turned out to be highly synergistic. A larger organization than TechAmerica with little overlap, it was founded in

1982 with a focus to create open dialogue between IT vendors and partners. Its membership was comprised of mostly the smaller companies that TechAmerica had lost when it closed its regional offices. CompTIA recognized the organization's four strengths: PP&A, BN&I, the membership, and the TechAmerica brand.

With one letter of intent just expired, I signed another one with CompTIA. Of course, the due diligence brought to light the two TechAmerica risk issues: lease obligations and an unresolved lawsuit. We resolved the lawsuit while discussing the prospects of combining.

Relationships matter. CompTIA's CEO and I struck a chord in our relationship. We worked with our respective teams and constructed an integration plan right from the beginning to avoid TechAmerica's earlier integration failure. We defined and understood the finite details of the integrated organizational chart, integrated board composition, integrated services, and messaging to employees, members, and the marketplace. The merger between CompTIA and TechAmerica could be a poster child for how combinations succeed.

TechAmerica Membership and Retention

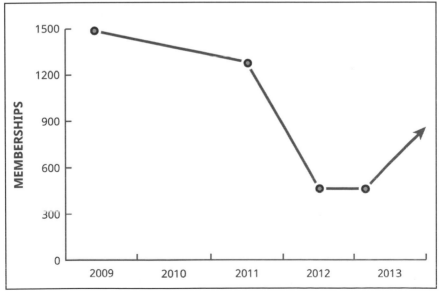

Image 10.2.

Today, TechAmerica is powered by CompTIA and has the resources to fulfill its mission. Its board is comprised of member-company operating executives, not internal lobbyists. Today, TechAmerica remains a powerful voice for the technology industry, is financially and organizationally stable, and is growing its membership.

Given where the organization was two years before I started, we'll call that a great outcome.

✳ What's your reflection as you look back?

Leading TechAmerica was a wonderful learning experience that challenged my leadership skills tremendously. I'll look back on those two years as having achieved the original vision: ONE stable organization in the face of fire. I feel stronger and more confident in my abilities to drive a team to success and make the right decisions—the big ones, anyway. Yes, I made some mistakes, but I learned to correct them quickly.

People make all the difference. I had the full support of a seasoned executive committee on TechAmerica's board that coached me every step of the way. Others might have run and hid when facing so much distress, but not this committee!

I can't say enough about the courage and tenacity of TechAmerica's management team and staff who had my back as they executed with me to bring TechAmerica out of its hole. My success is theirs.

My last reflection is the bubble in DC. When I first arrived there, I couldn't believe anybody would write an article about me. Several did, and most of them said, "Why is a businessman running a trade association?" I discovered the rules in DC were just different from elsewhere. I had come from a place that valued *what* you know. In DC, I observed the DC society valued *who* you know. Schmoozing and backslapping with the politically powerful was new ground for me. Perception was reality. The truth didn't always prevail.

It seemed hard to get things done in DC. I attended meetings in which we talked (and even agreed) about positive changes to immigration, taxation, or privacy that would make a difference. The next day, nothing happened. I wasn't used to that. If I had met with the CEO of another company and we had talked about ways to make positive change, we worked together to set activities in motion the next day. That didn't happen.

During my time there, I met some outstanding politicians. I remember walking away from a few meetings saying, "Wow. They really do want to make a difference." But I met far too many on an ego trip or just riding the wave. I struggled with the DC world more than I ever thought I would. I know I'm not cut out to be either a lobbyist or a politician.

✳ How did the experience help you advance?

In this nonprofit environment that was different for me, I grew as a leader. I influenced, motivated, set direction, and dealt with a volunteer board comprised of my shareholders and largest customers. I had to adjust my management and leadership style to be far more inclusive than in the private sector. I thought I had been an effective communicator before, but I became a much better communicator during the TechAmerica assignment.

Today, I'm better able to lead an organization that has a volunteer board and a staff with a mission mentality. I found one that has ignited the fire of passion within me: the Network for Teaching Entrepreneurship (NFTE). Its mission is dead center with who I am: to expose young people from economically challenged circumstances to the power of entrepreneurship to capture the American dream like I did.

I'm excited to embark on the next chapter in my career as NFTE's CEO. I hope to bring entrepreneurship to students who can experience the upward mobility that my own enabled me to achieve.

Ann Weaver Hart:
Offsetting Stagnation at the University of Arizona

"You must take personal responsibility. You cannot change the circumstances, the seasons or the wind, but you can change yourself. That is something you have charge of."

—Jim Rohn

Image 11.1: Ann Weaver Hart. Photo by Balfour Walker Photography.

✳ **How did you get to be the person you are? What's your story?**

My early years were firmly planted in the Baby Boom aftermath of World War II. My father returned from duty as an Army Air Corps pilot in Europe, married his wartime sweetheart, and resumed his college studies on the GI Bill. Their marriage took place the same week as her college graduation and birthday. My parents immediately began having a family, looking toward the future with anticipation.

In my Salt Lake City family of five children, my oldest sibling was 2 1/2 years old when she came down with Type 1 diabetes. I was the second oldest and only 1 year old when my big sister became deathly ill. The other three kids came later. Much of my childhood was shaped by the restrictions on our family dictated by my sister's dietary and behavioral requirements. An intelligent, assertive girl, she was quite resentful about being diabetic.

Early Responsibility

My parents asked me to be responsible for my older sister as if I were the firstborn. I became well trained in the symptoms of diabetic and insulin shock. (At the time, balancing insulin control was medically more difficult than today.) Because my parents didn't want to offend my sister, I had to keep their request a secret for fear of embarrassing her. Responsibility was simply part of my life. I understood that her life required extra attention, so I didn't mind, although my younger siblings had a hard time adjusting to the special attention required to keep her alive. But I never felt my parents' attention was a sign of favoritism for one child; my responsibility to her was simply a given.

Family Stress

Outside of this responsibility, my life involved no serious trauma until I turned 17 years old. That's when my father's family business went bankrupt. Sadly, my parents were unable to talk about it. His family had developed the only successful system for raising beavers in captivity. It involved a moving water system that replicated the beavers' denning environment and the development of special food. No one has domesticated beavers since.

But as wearing furs became less fashionable, the fur industry became economically unviable, especially while an early 1960s recession dragged on. The cost of raising beavers didn't balance with the demand for beaver fur.

In the midst of this financial stress, the Securities Exchange Commission (SEC) sued my father's business as a test case for violating the Securities Act. The SEC had originally targeted the cattle industry for how it sold livestock, with the seller retaining possession. The buyer simply invested but never took possession of the security. The SEC decided that livestock was a security. Similarly, the SEC rationalized that beaver, too, was a security.

Although he'd earned an MS degree in physics, my father had never worked in his field. As the oldest son, he had entered his family's fur business when his father had a heart attack. Unfortunately, he never achieved his career goals and dealt with heart disease himself at an early age.

Early Marriage

The bankrupt business, the lawsuit, the heart disease, a sick sister, and a lamenting father all added stress in our family. But this stress didn't stop young love; in fact, it encouraged it. I married my boyfriend, Randy, when I was 19 and he was 20.

Randy and I wanted to move out and be on our own, not because of any family disagreements but because we shared a strong need to be independent. Having both completed one year of university, we worked and went to college at the same time. We supported ourselves financially, paid our own tuition with scholarships, applied for and received financial aid, and took out student loans to fill the gaps. Within four years, we had both graduated from the University of Utah.

My mother raised me to believe it was important to become educated so I could be a better mother. My family approved of school, I loved school, and I did well. It was one of the places I felt truly at home and accomplished. But it never occurred to me I would do anything except work while Randy attended law school, and then I'd become a full-time parent.

✳ What was your career progression before joining the University of Arizona?

My career unfolded in stages. It wasn't particularly well planned until later in my life.

Teacher, Stay-at-Home Mom, PhD Student, and Principal

My mother had taught me the social expectations of the day—that is, my job was to be a stay-at-home mom. I should get a teaching certificate in case anything ever happened to my husband and I needed to support myself. "After all," she said, "you'd have the summers off with your children." This was considered insurance for the future.

In the 1970s in Utah, many of my contemporaries—some of whom were National Merit Scholars—succumbed to the social pressure and dropped out of college the minute they married. Many had a rocky time later in life, but I was fortunate my parents had encouraged me to finish my college education.

While Randy attended law school, I taught middle school. Then I focused on motherhood as we had four daughters comfortably spread over nine years. Still, I grew restless as a suburban mom who attended PTA meetings, went to church, and made my kids look beautiful on Sunday morning. We lived in a Salt Lake suburb that had a county library with a bookmobile that visited suburban neighborhoods. For a few hours every two weeks, that bookmobile stopped two doors from our house. I took advantage of its offering to satisfy my growing need for knowledge of the outside world. Voraciously I read the full multi-volume set of Will and Ariel Durant's *History of the World* and the new release of Richard Hofstadter's *Anti-Intellectualism in American History*. These weren't light reads, but I'll never forget how I felt. At that time, I decided to pursue goals that would affect the rest of my life.

Shortly after, I attended a weekly night history class as a non-matriculate student at the University of Utah. Since then, I've never looked back. Randy was a young attorney, we had four children, and he couldn't afford to send me to graduate school. So I returned to teaching to pay my way and became interested in school leadership. I earned an MA in history with a secondary administrative certificate in the state of Utah. Then I studied for my PhD in organizational theory and leadership in the educational leadership department with courses in business.

While finishing my PhD, I became a junior high school principal—an outrageous position for a woman at that time. Located at the foot of Brigham Young University in the shadow of the Mormon Church, the school required an hour's commute from my home. I felt so proud of my achievement—until I heard my parents' and in-laws' reaction to my first leadership position. They said, "Well, I guess your father can raise your children." (My father had been caring for my youngest child during the day.)

Randy and I both had changed during the time we'd been married. We'd grown up together. We were committed to remain together and be flexible as our lives looked different than we had anticipated. With Randy's support and with that of our daughters, I positioned myself to reach beyond any early aspirations or society's expectations. In my suburban house, our bedroom doubled as my academic center while I studied for my comprehensive exams to earn my PhD. I actually hung a sign on the bedroom door that said, "You have a father. Ask him!" When our youngest daughter made noises at the door, her bigger sisters shushed her and pulled her away. Their support during this time and later has been a huge part of my life.

Advancing in Higher Education

As a strong scholar who had taken to research and writing, I was offered a faculty position (the first woman) by my alma mater, the University of Utah. In academia, it was unusual for an aspiring research university to hire its own graduates. No one wanted to be accused of intellectual inbreeding that might hinder an independent academic agenda. It was a cautious move that they well realized. I didn't expect the offer, and deciding to accept the position was extremely difficult. I had to take a major pay cut and completely rethink my career.

Taking this opportunity presented a huge turning point. I felt at home in higher education. And I discovered I was a good independent researcher. Especially because I'd been hired by my alma mater, I made a special effort to do my very best independent work. My publications were mostly by a single author, and I chose research methodology that didn't require teams.

As an older assistant professor with four kids, I plugged away through those early stages of promotion and tenure work. With significant family responsibilities and a new career, I learned to compartmentalize my life well. We all had our stress points as all marriage and family relationships experience. We hit a few boulders in the road, but we all emerged from the process.

Appointments to the University of Utah leadership posts followed my professorship. I was promoted to assistant dean in the College of Education, then the first woman dean of the Graduate School in the University of Utah's entire history. I was a candidate to be its provost—academic vice president—when the University of Utah's new president took me aside. He said, "Ann, you graduated from here. You've built your whole career here. You're qualified to be a provost, but I'm not going to appoint you. You have to get out of here. Leave the University of Utah."

At the time, I was a bit shocked and offended. But by telling me to go, he furthered my career. I had to be able to learn and work in a variety of places; I had to perform outside of the environment where I had been trained.

Vice President in Southern California

At about the same time, a few prominent people in my professional circle of academic and business leaders encouraged me to position myself for a college or university presidency. One of them said, "You're not getting any younger." My girls had grown to become strong, independent women. That allowed Randy and me to be open to other dimensions and locations in which to live. I accepted an appointment as provost and academic vice president of Claremont Graduate University, a small private member of the Claremont consortium in Southern California.

University President in Northern New England

Four years later, I accepted the opportunity to become president of the University of New Hampshire (UNH), a medium-sized land-grant university. This move from Southern California to northern New England was the biggest cultural shift in our careers. That's where I learned to understand the land-grant mission. It captured my imagination.

UNH had issues: turnover in the presidency, conflict between the board of trustees and the faculty, growing financial pressures, and changing traditions about how they conducted themselves on and off campus. There, I put my organizational theory studies to work. Faculty members had openly told me they had supported an internal candidate; they were unhappy the chancellor had appointed me. They weren't hostile, but they sent warnings. Their very active union had been jaded by difficult past relationships with the administration, and the state legislature had decreased its financial support for the land-grant mission.

At the time, the biggest social challenge at UNH was fan violence following athletic events—a strong, growing trend throughout the Northeast. University students rioted whether their school won or lost. Sometimes, riots were stimulated by whatever happened to the popular professional team in their region. The year before I was hired, for example, the New England Patriots won the Super Bowl for the first time. After the game, guys from fraternity houses piled their old furniture in the middle of an intersection in the little town of Durham, New Hampshire, and set it on fire. The blaze melted the asphalt in the intersection. What an outcry of anger about student behavior this caused in the community!

Clearly, this negative kind of school culture had been tolerated in the past. During a town council meeting on the issue, a vice president of UNH student affairs actually stated she believed a 19-year-old student and a 19-year-old carpenter who committed the same crime each deserved to be treated differently because a student merited special status. I'd been a junior high school principal; I'd held a different behavioral standard about accountability and responsibility. So I resisted any pressure to accept those lax standards from young adults and those responsible for leading them.

Over a four-year period, UNH progressed financially, academically, and behaviorally. And I progressed, too, as a university leader who created positive cultural change, gained institutional support, and improved both operating and academic performance.

First Female President at a Big City University

An executive search firm that knew me from past years contacted me about an opening as president of Temple University in the sixth-largest city in the country, Philadelphia. Temple had developed into a first stop for first-generation college students. It had a long tradition of being a place where working men and women's children could achieve a college education.

Philadelphia is dominated by private, expensive institutions of higher learning, including the Ivy League University of Pennsylvania, Villanova, LaSalle, and Drexel. Temple is the only four-year public university option for this huge metropolitan-area population. Its "up from the bootstraps" mind-set had been part of my cultural background. After all, I was from a family that made its living in the fur industry of the Wild West.

The invitation to come to Temple resonated with me. My experience working with a public university in a community that had variety and stress made this position a good fit.

Adding to Temple's complexity was a medical school that served the poor, as well as union contract issues during 2007–2009, a time of huge financial crisis. In the face of this crisis, I spent much of my time at Temple working with the budget. In public higher education in America, we become presidents primarily by being scholars. However, our work at the presidential level is the same as other big businesses. Although it's not a for-profit enterprise, Temple was essentially a $1.2 billion business operating in an economic environment of a modern-era financial crisis. The numbers had to work.

Still, the value structure deeply embedded in higher education resists running a university like a business. It fears violating a commitment to academic freedom and cultural openness. I was Temple's president during a period of major financial crisis within our country and the world's economy. I effectively ran the budget and dealt with the complexities of leading an organization in times of stress. Thankfully, Temple successfully came out on the other end of that unprecedented financial meltdown by meeting all its budgetary and cash expectations.

I believe I performed my job well, employing discipline, compassion, and compromise. I gained a lot of strength during that six-year experience. Knowing that my time at Temple was drawing to a close,

Randy and I discussed how to use that experience and return to our Western roots. I announced my resignation almost a year ahead of time, and Temple implemented a succession plan. As I was preparing to leave, I was nominated as a candidate for president at the University of Arizona. The Board of Regents noted that Temple had been demonstrably successful navigating through that high-stress economic environment. It helped that I had gained land-grant experience at UNH and worked with a safety-net academic medical center, too.

✳ What was the situation before you entered the University of Arizona that led to its issues?

The University of Arizona (U of A) has a proud and storied history that dates to the late 19th century, nearly 30 years before Arizona achieved statehood. This four-year public research and land-grant university has been a member of the Association of American Universities (AAU is a coveted membership) for years. It's the only institution of higher learning in the entire state with that recognition.

U of A's course offerings grew through its 20 colleges, and more than 100 schools are spread over three campuses, with its main campus in Tucson. Within U of A stands Arizona's only public MD-granting medical school. In fact, U of A has two independent, separately accredited medical schools, one in Tucson and one in Phoenix.

Physical Sciences Powerhouse

During the 1970s and 1980s, U of A cut its teeth on and flourished in the physical sciences. The planetary astronomy, science, and optical science programs are rated among the best in the world and remain highly ranked by the National Science Foundation (NSF). Agriculture has been an important component in the state of Arizona's economy. Both U of A's environmental science and agriculture programs have been recognized as world-class.

In fact, the physical sciences dominated U of A's personality so much, they had become deeply ingrained in its culture into the 1990s as well. The university's outstanding work in the physical sciences had been duplicated through some of its arts and social sciences programs. But it was the physical sciences that captured the center of U of A's culture and investment resources.

Stagnation and Stalled Performance

However, the same level of excellence and volume in the biological sciences, especially the biomedical sciences, had been left to languish. The university had neglected to make some difficult financial and academic decisions on two fronts. First, the global financial crisis created a state funding crisis. Second, the 21st century moved global priorities from the post-Sputnik hegemony of physical science to an era of the life sciences and biomedical sciences. With those huge megatrends affecting the global economy, U of A's academics stayed focused on what it already did extremely well. A public research institution must be forward-thinking; U of A's thinking appeared stagnant. Although rankings in its physical sciences programs remained strong, the university experienced a decline in its ratings in other key areas. For example, its medical school rating, its AAU ranking, and its NSF standing all dropped.

The world is dynamic, not stagnant. The state of Arizona has been especially dynamic, growing by leaps and bounds. Over the last three decades, its population epicenter shifted to Phoenix and sparked changes to the state's legislature that matched the shift. U of A had been the only major higher educational institution in the state. The state that once had only two teachers colleges and one university increased to having two more highly regarded universities competing for legislative resources. Northern Arizona University (NAU) has grown into a sizable school and Arizona State University (ASU)—based in the center of Phoenix's population explosion—boasts 80,000 students. It's the largest four-year public university student body in the country and also a full-blown research institution.

Plan for Tomorrow

Rivalry is often a *positive* catalyst for improvement. At U of A, there was *negative* rivalry with ASU that centered on a longing for yesterday's heyday. U of A needed a plan for tomorrow.

In 2011, U of A's long-standing physical scientist-oriented president had retired. He received and deserved a good deal of credit for making U of A the AAU-accredited and world-renowned space science leader it had become. An interim president had been named to fill his seat. The Board of Regents had grown dissatisfied that U of A's self-image hadn't kept pace with the changes around it and especially its lack of achievement in biomedical sciences, given its potential in the new era. It was also alarmed by the impact of U of A's response during the 2008–2009 financial crisis.

Specifically, the university had nearly one-third fewer days of cash available on its balance sheet than other institutions of its size and substance. Its operating budget had morphed from being 75-percent funded by state appropriations to being 14-percent funded by them. Clearly, its fundraising had not kept pace with its needs.

At the same time, tuition had more than doubled over five years, enabling U of A to operate within the confines of its budget. Yet it appeared to be *underinvesting* in the right areas for the future and *over-investing* in the areas shadowed by yesterday's trends.

University of Arizona Declining State Appropriations and Increasing Tuition

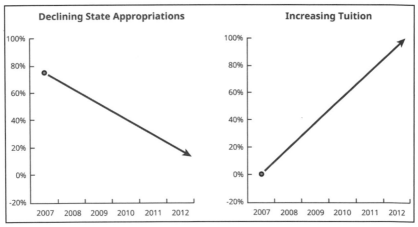

Image 11.2.

When I was introduced to U of A's trustees, pieces of my background and experience connected to the situation they perceived to have on their hands. Financial discipline, investment pragmatism, crisis management, strategic vision, land-grant savvy, academic medicine, and leadership under duress were all noted on their qualification list. It looked like I qualified!

So in 2012, I was offered the opportunity to become U of A's 21st president and the first woman to hold that post in its proud 130-year history. Randy and I were headed West!

✳ What attracted you to this situation when many would run away?

Leading U of A presented a meaningful opportunity to influence the future of this public research university. It sparked my passion and commitment to the vision of the Morrill Act, which allowed for the creation of land-grant colleges back in 1862. It has given common people with common backgrounds (mine included) access to public universities that have played major roles in the economic, social, and cultural well-being of the population. This compelling vision has been realized through our great public research universities.

I watched with distress the complete flip in state legislative financial support for Arizona's great universities, knowing they were under tremendous financial and changing demographic pressure. I had navigated those pressures at UNH and Temple. U of A is ranked 18th in the nation of public research universities by the National Science Foundation and is a member of the AAU. Would this world-class land-grant university with deeply embedded cultures and traditions succumb to stagnation and financial stress? As president, I thought I could make a difference to achieve a brighter future. Given my accomplishments plus my proclivity for assessing and taking risk, I was enough of an outsider to address the tough decisions. I knew I had the best shot at achieving the agenda set by the Arizona Board of Regents. And I understood academic medicine and its challenges. For me, this was a terrific opportunity packaged inside a Pac-12 school with big-time athletics!

❋ How did you hatch the plan to address this situation?

Phase 1 of the ABCs: Hatch the Plan

> "Progress is a nice word. But change is its motivator.
> And change has its enemies."
>
> —Robert F. Kennedy

Early on, I'd observed that the Board of Regents wanted major change—and wanted it yesterday. This deep impatience had created a desire to see me kick ass, take names, and get things done. At the same time, others within the faculty, the staff, the donors, the alumni, the legislature, and the community rebuffed change. They longed for yesterday's ways. But the students came here to earn a better tomorrow.

U of A's heritage included a deep respect and commitment among the administration, faculty, and staff, even though there had been periods of deep disagreement about direction. I made a commitment to its high-quality heritage, and to be inclusive and share governance at the University of Arizona. That went against the natural instincts of many.

A: Ask Questions and Listen; Then Ask for Help

On the day I first visited the university after my appointment, I was handed an itinerary that showed no time allotted with the faculty leadership. That was unacceptable to me. I immediately set up a private one-on-one meeting with the faculty senate chair. She was blunt. She had not been appointed as a member of the search advisory committee and felt that the voice of the faculty had been willfully ignored. I learned that, throughout my interview process, the faculty and the Board of Regents had serious disagreements.

During our first meeting, I asked the faculty senate chair about her view of the issues. She put it right on the table: "You're not a scientist. The faculty has an issue with that." That evoked an immediate flashback. When I was appointed dean of the University of Utah's Graduate School, a university vice president had invited me to lunch. As I unfolded my napkin—I still have a visual image of unfolding my napkin at the Union Building restaurant—he said, "Ann, you have a problem. You're not from science. What are you going to do about it?"

I replied, "I'm going to find out what you need and help you get it. And I'll do such a good job as dean of the Graduate School that you're not going to notice."

Yes, I had seen this movie before. My response was identical. I didn't need to be a pathologist, a neurobiologist, or a physicist to understand the organizational dynamics that would help U of A prosper.

Next, I asked innumerable questions to assess the current state of affairs. I asked them of the faculty, student body, alumni, donors, and members of the Arizona legislature. I also spent a good deal of time with members of the Board of Regents. As a result of my comprehensive interview process, I had gained a sense of the university's stressors. But I wanted to understand them from all perspectives to test my own early perceptions.

B: Base the Plan on What You Hear and See, or Don't Hear and See

One of my Temple colleagues who is from China told me the Chinese character for "crisis" combined the two signs for "danger" and "opportunity." That fit for me; I had experienced the first point of crisis before reporting for my first day on the job.

While still in Philadelphia, I was asked to intervene and call Arizona's governor during the state's budget session. The state wasn't funding the Phoenix medical school as promised. We enjoyed a wonderful introductory call. Shortly after, the governor did come through with $6 million of funding for that year and $8 million for the next, thus honoring previous state commitments.

Still, medical schools cost a lot more than they generate. Knowing that academic medicine has a huge future, I realized the medical school in Phoenix needed a strong clinical partner to succeed. State appropriations weren't guaranteed for the future, and self-funding would be tough.

While gathering information, I was struck by an incredibly powerful academic energy and vision from the highly competent people I interviewed. What I *didn't* hear and see struck me more than what I *did* hear and see. I did find a physical facilities plan. *But where was an academic plan? A business plan?* And what about the budget process, or lack thereof? *Where was the budget discipline?*

Even though there had been a perception of endured pain to cut expenses in the preceding budget years, the university hadn't seized the opportunity that real danger can present. New items were added without examining old ones less relevant to the future. I was alarmed by my representative sample that spotlighted a lack of discipline. I learned that, to do the budget cuts made necessary by the financial crisis, departments with externally funded research regularly transferred costs for employees and support staff from state appropriations into indirect cost-recovery funds. In other words, the departments used research dollars to subsidize normal administration costs, robbing Peter to pay Paul. As a short-term solution to a perceived temporary setback, this transfer of funds caused a dramatic drop in research reinvestment. How is that acceptable in a research institution?

C: Challenge the Sacred Cows or the Status Quo

Deeply rooted attitudes and behavior were holding back the University of Arizona. Attitudes about continuing old methods, rivalries, elitism, and disrespect had contributed to much of U of A's inflexibility to deal with change. Yet the future greatness of public research universities will not be found in 20th-century success formulas.

This rob-Peter-to-pay-Paul budget hocus-pocus had been justified as a short-term solution with the belief that, somehow, state funding would return. Where was reality? That funding was unlikely to return, at least to the same level. The whole political world had shifted. Entitlement-funding in state budgets shoved higher education completely out of the relationship it had filled throughout the 1990s. Yet university decision-makers were behaving with the old mind-set that we lived in the era of unremitting growth with tiny recessionary blips. Thus, fiscal disaster was unfolding.

In addition, budget stress and plain old institutional rivalry unearthed an antagonistic and unhealthy "us versus them" attitude. Tucson had been perceived as the good guy; Phoenix (the legislature) was the evil bad guy who didn't care about Tucson or U of A. Some U of A supporters believed ASU was the evil force and, somehow, U of A's problems were due to an entrepreneurial and dramatically changing ASU. Yet within Arizona's shifting demographic, ASU had played its part well—that is, to increase the proportion of the state's population that could access a college education.

Athletic, academic, and fiscal rivalry can promote healthy competition that makes both universities better. It can also be destructive, especially if it's used as an excuse. Institutions of higher learning don't get better by criticizing others. Apple won't fail just because Samsung is successful. Though these companies are highly competitive, they know there's room in an expanding innovation environment for both to grow and achieve their goals.

In Tucson, I found a free flow of badmouthing either ASU or the legislature in Phoenix to be common practice. I won't ever condone this kind of behavior. The badmouthing smacked of athletic, political, ethnic, and socioeconomic trash talk between the "Old Pueblo" (Tucson) and the new "Los Angeles" (Phoenix), which only produced negative energy. According to its mission and values, U of A had the responsibility to be the best it could be. That meant there's no room for finger pointing unless the finger pointed inward.

S: Share the Vision to Create a Collective Energy

The University of Arizona—a great institution with a highly accomplished, world-class faculty—wasn't changing with the new century. The metaphor I used was shockingly unpleasant for a surprising number of people. I asked, "What were the centers of Western knowledge and scholarship in Europe in the 13th century?"

"In the great monasteries of Europe."

"Are they still here?"

"No."

You can be the best and not survive. U of A had to change.

Frankly, it wasn't a matter of right and wrong. U of A's stated mission and core values were spot on, but the way to achieve its goals had to be different. Through a broad planning process, I needed to harness those deeply held values and dreams of this community, and find a way to meld them with changes in the approach. My plan? To marry people's incredible energy and vision academically with the fiscal discipline of a tightly constructed business plan.

I got this job because I'm a straight talker and a straight shooter. I've learned to say tough stuff to people and make decisions that hurt a few so the whole could advance. People expect a woman to be kind and respectful but don't expect male leaders to behave that way. However, being direct is part of what's gotten me here. I haven't been president of three universities because I've been overly diffident or because I circumvented tough issues. It's a double-edged sword to be direct.

The game plan I shared was simple. Based on what I'd learned from my various and inclusive meetings, my plan would put U of A on a trajectory that embraced a bright future. The business-planning process needed to tackle three primary issues: *discipline, revenue generation,* and *innovation.*

The first issue was employing the discipline a business-planning process needed to succeed.

The second was increasing both the level and variety of revenue to wean us from depending on state appropriations. That would allow the university to develop a long-range gradual tuition plan that, essentially, would be inflation-driven and not crisis-driven. Tuition could then be projected going forward as revenue streams increased and diversified. That had to happen.

The third was continuing in research, creativity, and inquiry while nurturing the translational component of knowledge to reflect global needs and trends. Innovation—the use of existing and new knowledge in surprising and creative ways to solve the problems of humankind—is who we are. This required U of A to use its knowledge in creative and different ways. Our organizational DNA had to open to a re-appropriation of intellectual energy that aligned with current needs and trends. Innovation.

This approach would dictate our future in *every* discipline, not just in STEM (Science, Technology, Engineering, and Math).

✳ Once the plan was hatched, how did you align your team to kick off the plan?

Phase 2 of the ABCs: Kick Off the Plan

> "I've brought a big bat. I'm all ready, you see. Now my troubles are going to have troubles with me."
>
> —Dr. Scuss

A: Act Boldly to Kick Off the Game Plan

In keeping with U of A's shared governance tradition, I immediately instituted a process of charging a once-sleepy committee, the Strategic Planning and Budget Advisory Committee, to lead a campus-wide academic planning process. Universities have become famous for taking two years to write an academic plan with 185 items on the bulleted list of goals. They print them, they're beautiful, and then they sit on shelves. This university wouldn't still be around if we'd taken that long!

Funds re-appropriated

To jump-start the initiative, we ranked strategic initiatives, looked at the funding, and re-appropriated $20 million of resources in administration to more strategic items, in keeping with the game plan. Some people who were used to getting money didn't receive it. We're a not-for-profit knowledge organization with a mission that some people believe is morally superior to making financial decisions. Based on that, some initially took an ethical and moral stance to oppose these actions. But the committee sent the message this wasn't business as usual.

In my research, I had learned that technology-transfer initiatives had underperformed. A program dubbed Tech Launch Arizona was in the works the year before I came to U of A. Through a combination of internal promotions and external recruiting, I staffed that initiative with a vice president and a director who both had strong experience and an orientation to succeed. They retooled the program's agenda, executed deliberately, and set an excellent example of professional implementation.

Criteria established

The university's athletic director was either in the right place at the right time or in the wrong place at the wrong time. Past practices had tolerated spending money on projects in which the funding had yet to be raised. U of A had sponsored internal loans to itself to pursue projects that were supposed to become self-supporting. Many never did. Because of that practice, I inherited a $9 million underfunded construction project.

To address both the fiscal discipline and revenue components of the game plan, I outlined that these three criteria had to be met to gain approval for any construction or facilities project: a Plan A, a Plan B contingency plan if Plan A financing fell short, and an edict that the project had to fit within the academic strategic plan. Internal loans were history.

The athletic director swallowed hard. Just as he submitted a proposal to renovate our basketball center under the old formula of project funding, I outlined the new criteria. The new rules blew up his proposal.

Business plan developed

Developing a business plan required a steep learning curve. U of A had no recent tradition of business planning discipline that tied goals to the financial plan, measured outcomes regularly, and changed according to revenues and goal achievement. It went against the traditions of new knowledge creation and creativity, despite the harsh realities of the big, bad world out there. I pushed our team members hard to work toward the game plan with all their strength. I needed this talent base to execute our game plan.

Recruitment required

With an initial opening for a provost, I conducted a full-blown nationwide-plus search that resulted in selecting an insider with the right set of skills. Because internally we lacked skills in government relations, university relations, and communications, I added people with those skills from the outside. As a result, I have an essentially new senior team. After making more changes and working with an interim CFO, the final brick in building a new wall was recruiting a CFO from the University of Southern California.

Everyone who was recruited for this new executive team understood responsibility-centered management, innovation, and self-discipline. That meant we could execute our game plan with the right set of backgrounds, experiences, and skills.

B: Build on Strengths

U of A's key strengths were highly visible. Some could be categorized as tradition and culture. It had an undisputable tradition of world-class research in physical sciences as well as in many of the arts, humanities, and social sciences.

Another is a tradition of deep pride, love, and affection for the university on the part of its alumni and students. I see more people wearing our logo on this campus than anywhere I've worked (I've worked at five universities)—and not only on game day! The alumni closely follow our athletics. Their overall culture of commitment and social engagement has continually been a positive force for recruiting as well as fundraising.

U of A's tradition of teaching and engaging with students is extraordinary. Many people on the faculty aren't tenured but have contracts to teach full-time. By comparison, big urban universities rely on adjunct professors who teach a course or two. There's a strong commitment in the business faculty to bring in executives who have succeeded, regardless of their academic backgrounds. That strong commitment extends to the arts and ties in directly with the local artistic community.

As mentioned earlier, U of A is one of the elected members of the Association of American Universities—the organization of North America's premier research institutions—and is the only representative from Arizona. Its world-class research and its deeply engaged, highly competent, and committed faculty have clearly been recognized.

Those strengths set U of A apart. With the addition of fiscal discipline, strategic direction, and proper sources of revenue, its long and storied history can flourish during the 21st century.

C: Control Through Visible Measurement

In the past, it appeared that U of A established its budget and looked at things annually when the auditors came in to close the books. My philosophy was to pay closer attention throughout the year. With revenue and cash as high priorities, we tracked performance against our business plan on a quarterly basis. The numbers remained highly visible; revenue and cash performance versus plan, the track record on externally funded research, and student retention and graduation rates were all reported frequently. We were all to be held accountable for performance.

That transparency sometimes felt uncomfortable. Those leading certain academic units believed they were cash cows. With a bit of measurement, we discovered they were not. Some in elite, heavily subsidized academic units believed they were not. Having a completely transparent budget was new to the University of Arizona. It made the patron system almost impossible to sustain. The leaders I recruited and promoted had to make tough decisions once actual performance gained greater visibility. Measurement of the details of performance created a different level of expectation for success and consequences for lack of success.

With cash management previously a disaster, we had to measure financial performance. Still, as an institution of higher learning, our students remained at the core. We wouldn't lose sight of making a difference for them.

How successful have we been in making a difference to their lives? We publish a graph every year on our freshman-to-sophomore retention rate. That curve must go up. The old days of gladiator transition for freshmen is over. When students gain admission, we are committed to keeping them and helping them succeed. We graphed our years-to-graduation rate by average and by ethnicity to know what proportion of students graduated in four years, five years, or six years. Those traditional achievement gaps have been tracked, published, and discussed. Because we have an obligation to help our students be the best they can be, this transparency points out the areas we can improve. And the Arizona Board of Regents supports us.

S: Streamline the Activity Schedule

Vision, mission, and elevator pitch

Our team collaborated to construct the strategic initiatives that would accomplish the game plan. We first looked at the big picture and then dove into the details to make things happen.

My vision focused on what I had uncovered to be the primary needs for U of A to move its approach to higher learning in the 21st century. I intended to execute a process that would create and implement an integrated strategic academic and business plan guiding U of A's future. We gave that vision and resulting strategic plan the name "Never Settle."

U of A proclaimed its intention to be a super land-grant university that advanced the local and global impacts of knowledge creation. This would be done through partner relationships with communities and industry and via innovative programs. Those programs would expand the student experience through engagement, advance knowledge through innovations in creative inquiry and collaboration, and forge novel partnerships to positively affect our community. The word *boundless* captures this vision.

Achieving its Never Settle vision means U of A will better accomplish its mission to improve the prospects and enrich the lives of Arizonans and the world through education, research, creative expression, and community and business partnerships.

I shared this Never Settle vision with the faculty, staff, Board of Regents, educational community, and community at large. After being documented and well publicized, it has gained traction, but its implementation will take time. Right after we released the Never Settle academic plan, a senior faculty member in physical sciences said to me, "I don't know why you're putting us through all of this. You know exactly how to succeed: Hire world-class scientists, give them money to support their high-quality graduate students, and we'll do the rest." Physical scientists understand that inertia is a powerful force. Change takes longer for some than for others.

Competitive positioning and targeting strategy

All the strengths I found when I conducted my SWOT (Strengths, Weaknesses, Opportunities, and Threats) analysis provided cornerstones of competitive differentiation. The depth and reputation of the arts and sciences curriculum, the faculty, the AAU, the *U.S. News & World Report* rankings, and the pride of the student body and alumni formed major attraction points for the university. Although the tuition had risen substantially over the previous five years, it was still less than $10,000 per academic year and quite competitive. The university could attract strong students from either affluent or modest backgrounds, but the targeted focus continued to be well-prepared students who might not otherwise afford a world-class education.

Improving the competitive positioning required executing the game plan that connected future needs with curriculum advancement. That specifically called for growth in the biomedical and health science offerings of U of A.

Primary goals (the BHAGs) to focus the energy

The game plan dictated the areas needing our attention: discipline, revenue, and curriculum. Our team established numerical targets based on past history, current status, and future targets. Focusing on the year 2020, we published our goals in our Never Settle strategic plan. Highlights are:

* Increase undergraduate enrollment and annual bachelor's degrees by 25 percent.
* Increase freshmen retention and graduation rates by 10 percent.
* Increase online degrees granted by almost 500 percent.

The game plan required various revenue sources. Our target was to double research expenditures by the year 2020.

Critical success factors to prioritize the actions

Achieving revenue targets required different kinds of funding to end a complete reliance on state appropriations and out-of-proportion tuition increases. We modeled what our financial picture would look like if state appropriations continued to fall. Sophisticated big data models created scenarios for future decisions. That will continue to be critical in our planning.

A threat to this vision is a perfect storm in which the Board of Regents refuses to vote for a tuition increase that grows incrementally and the state further cuts its appropriations. Political pressures exist for both of those things to happen.

Success in developing a 21st-century curriculum required a change in the trajectory of excellence and world-class performance in biomedical sciences. U of A needed to become one of its leaders. We have a wonderful proactive College of Agriculture and Life Science, with an incredibly entrepreneurial dean who "gets" this vision.

However, biomedical and health sciences are not the same as basic life science in an agricultural school. Cutting down barriers between budgets and disciplines will get the right people together to do highly creative innovation. This presents a tremendous opportunity and requires a restructuring of the whole environment of the university. Blinded by success in other areas, U of A had not seen how it had to be part of the 21st-century biomedical revolution.

To keep people out of the hospital and decrease healthcare costs require research that translates into outcomes. Our population's health absolutely will benefit from personalized medicine. We know it's necessary to increase effectiveness as well as maximize the impact of innovation and research on the well-being of humankind. Innovation is creatively combining established knowledge in surprising ways, while creating an outcome that contributes to our common good. The neurosciences, vested in both medicine and psychology, have huge potential. We live in the century of the brain.

Areas in which the university has been strong have shown the greatest potential for external funding. As compared to its National Science Foundation (NSF) peers, U of A received 900 percent of the average funding in the space sciences. From optics to planetary science to astronomy to physics, U of A and its people have achieved global recognition that has attracted preferential research funding. The opportunity to attract that category of funding in biomedical and health sciences requires that kind of academic and research achievement as well. That's a high bar, but we know we have to strive for it.

Curriculum advancement and revenue enhancement are also tall orders. Strategic partnerships to assist in fulfilling that tall order were defined as critical to accomplishing those objectives. The tradeoff is a willingness to share control of those projects. It's critical.

Define and reinforce the culture

I'm not the kind of leader who works one-on-one with the university's executive leaders. Instead, we're a team. I expect all teammates to listen to and be aware of problems their colleagues face and not exclusively focus on their own areas of responsibility.

To further drive our behavior, we defined, published, and circulated our values. We want others to emulate these qualities: excellence and integrity, collegiality and openness, interdisciplinary and sustainability, engagement and societal impact, access and opportunity, diversity, inclusion, and shared decision-making.

✳ With the game plan hatched and kicked off, what was your approach to execute?

Phase 3 of the ABCs: Execute the Plan

"Women are like tea bags. We don't know our own strength until we're in hot water."

—Eleanor Roosevelt

A: Assert Yourself at the Focal Point

I dealt with a host of components inside U of A: land-grant, two medical schools, AAU, major research budget, big-time athletics in the Pac-12, and more. This is a complex place. Our final Never Settle presentation to the Board of Regents included capital plans, curriculum development, fundraising, and essentially the whole of our strategic initiatives. We presented it near the end of my first year as president.

Long toes

I had challenged the Strategic Planning and Budget Advisory Committee to create a plan inside of a year. To its members' credit, they developed an academic plan that had broad participation. The committee gained input from 4,000 people participating either directly in town hall meetings or online. The plan also included items that went against the old culture of insiders who ran the place. The Dutch have a saying for people who get offended: "He has very long toes." Yes, we had stepped on some very long toes. But we knew what we needed to do.

The first building project we pursued and completed under the new funding criteria was the athletic director's project, the renovation of our basketball center. (I had nixed his initial plan because it lacked a Plan A and a Plan B for funding.) The basketball arena refurbishment project did fit into our strategic plan, however. The Wildcats basketball team was ranked second in the country in a preseason poll. That's huge at U of A. The athletic director went back to the drawing board and constructed a new plan, re-pitched to his donors, and worked his tail off to raise the funds. The new facility opened in time for the 2014 basketball season. A bias in higher education is that athletic departments lack discipline. But U of A's athletics director, his fundraising team, and big donors all stepped up to be a shining example. Old expectations were bashed; our new standard had gained a proof-point of success.

The university as a business

The early execution of our plan focused on money, which was tight. The typical university rhetoric is "You can't run the university like a business." The first time I confronted that statement was in a student senate meeting at Temple. A student said, "Some in the faculty are complaining that you run the university too much like a business." I replied, "We are! Temple is a $1.2 billion enterprise, highly dependent on money you and your family pay, some of which you borrow. Would you like me to mismanage the money your family is paying? To support you as a student, so you can get the education you came here to get, I'm charged to use scarce resources wisely."

U of A's revenue number when I arrived for the beginning of the school year in 2012 was about $1.6 billion, not including clinical revenue. Managing that amount wisely involves long-range planning and significant changes.

✳ What obstacles did you encounter along the way? How did you deal with them?

Power Struggle and Slur Campaign

A power struggle between the Board of Regents and a couple of members of the U of A Foundation played out in public, with me cast as the central character in a slur campaign. It was designed to stop the Board from extending my contract.

Change is harder for some than others. A small group of donors had become used to dictating the administrative and leadership priorities of the university with their gifts. Some people in the Foundation literally believed they have fiduciary and governing authority over the university. Not so. The three state universities report to the Arizona Board of Regents, which sets the priorities. Its members hired me; I report to them. As president, I have no administrative authority over the Foundation.

The depth of the power struggle between our Board of Regents and a couple of the Foundation trustees appeared self-perpetuating. Never in my career had I experienced so much turmoil in governing an institution caused by a small number of people. They tried to hide their identity and overtly pushed their contract agenda with the Board of Regents through both letter-writing and press-reported rumor campaigns. The rumors were deeply personal. There's a U of A branding sign on campus that says, "Bigger Questions, Better Answers, Bear Down." Behind closed doors with my inner circle, we joked, "Bigger Questions, Better *Rumors,* Bear Down."

The slur campaigns failed. The Board of Regents was absolutely supportive, though there was a period when its belief in its fiduciary responsibility and due diligence required examining these rumors to determine their authenticity. I shared key information with Board members as I put forth facts to address the rumors. I acknowledged that if my plain-talking, goal-oriented, truth-speaking approach had caused problems, I'd find out from others how to improve that. I called business leaders in Phoenix and Tucson, established a group of advisors, and asked for their advice. I sought counsel from many long-standing donors and people in academia. No one is ever 100-percent right, including me.

Board and Community Support

A number of leaders in the community took on this issue on my behalf. When they suggested they contact members of the Board of Regents to voice their support, I initially said, "No, it's going to look like I'm launching a campaign." But the chairman of the Board of Regents said, "Stop telling people not to communicate with us." So when people asked me what they could do, I'd say, "Do what you think is best." I'm told that, in these communications, I received a ground-swell of support about the financial discipline, the strength of the academic and business plan, and the incredible leap forward in partnering initiatives.

Through all this, it became clear that a small group of insiders didn't speak for the Foundation overall. It's been a painful experience, though—more painful than I thought because some of the self-discipline I imposed rubbed old-time supporters the wrong way. That's why the appearance of a power struggle ensued.

The Board of Regents made it clear to whom I reported and gave me its support. Through it all, we respected the Foundation and its commitment to quality and pride in our heritage. I reached out to those who were angry and asked to work together toward common interests. The whole episode resulted in our forging a stronger partnership among the regents, the Foundation, and the university administration. U of A has become an exciting place to live and work.

B: Borrow From Alliances and Partnerships

We knew that partnering initiatives were absolutely critical to our success in gaining both the financing and the biomedical enhancements to achieve our game plan. We experienced early success, such as a licensing agreement on innovative drug management software developed in the College of Pharmacy. But the biggest deal was the partnership with a major new clinical partner for both U of A medical schools.

In January 2015, we finalized a historic agreement with Banner Health to support U of A's biosciences research initiatives while creating a foundation for statewide excellence in clinical healthcare. Banner Health, one of the top five health systems in the country, became the clinical partner for our two medical schools in Phoenix and Tucson. Our partnership required sharing absolute control and bringing two cultures together. U of A's strengths as a research powerhouse plus the two medical schools are combining with Banner's performance in increased quality and population health management. This will add depth and force to U of A's clinical academic medicine program.

Banner's $1 billion investment in Tucson—and the conversion of its flagship hospital Good Samaritan into U of A's College of Medicine in Phoenix's academic medical center—will enhance opportunities for innovation that stem from our basic research.

C: Communicate Progress and Results to Get/Stay on Track

The constituents within a university structure are broad; they include students, parents, alumni, faculty, donors, partners, government, and community. How do we reach all of them quickly, consistently, and frequently?

When I arrived, the communications process at U of A was absolutely broken. One of the biggest challenges I continue to face is communicating enough with the right people to send the right messages whenever I want.

Frequent meetings with a variety of groups keep the performance and progress of our critical success factors out front. I conduct regular staff meetings with our senior leadership team as well as with a larger group labeled "the cabinet." I have a shared governance group that goes deep into the ranks to those who lead the staff association. I also hold "President's Breakfast Club" conversations with students twice a semester. I require a broad-range engagement in all our problems and issues, not just one's own.

In addition, I attend faculty senate meetings and generally stay for the entire session, which isn't the norm in most places. I have developed a positive working relationship with the chair of the faculty senate. We don't always agree, but we do have an arrangement that, when I'm about to step in a cow pie (a Western metaphor for a mistake), I get a call that says, "We've got to talk."

My staff has helped me embrace multimedia messaging including blogs, e-mails, Websites, and social media to reach our broad constituency. We strive to provide a transparent update on our performance toward our goals regularly.

S: Spread the Rewards of Wealth and Recognition When Things Go Your Way

The budget model I implemented includes incentives tied to our goals. This isn't new in higher education; it's simply new to U of A. The old terminology for it is responsibility-centered management. These financial incentives are tied to our mutual goals through decisions of the group. Anyone who ignores a goal misses out financially.

Our transparent communications on performance have provided a wonderful platform to frequently give recognition to those who have accomplished something toward reaching our vision. I've always thanked and recognized members of my senior team when something goes right. Whenever I can (and it comes to my attention), I thank donors, both in writing and with telephone calls. I also write letters to both students and faculty who've achieved important recognition. In fact, I brag about them everywhere I go, and I hope they hear me. With so much of our future related to creative innovation, there are no sticks—we have only carrots that recognize our internal people for what they've done. Certainly, I can always improve on this.

There are so many reasons to give accolades. A large number of our faculty members have been elected to the National Academics. A former student won a Nobel Prize, and a faculty member won a Nobel Prize six months after he left. I have established and asked for even greater celebration and rewards for people of repute.

✳ What was the end result of the execution?

In my third year at U of A, the execution of our game plan continues. Still, we've accomplished a good deal thus far.

The Banner Health alliance will lay the foundation for U of A's medical schools and biomedical program to leap forward. Having new and exciting medical leadership has added volumes to our increased commitment to the biomedical sciences.

We're executing an enhanced academic plan focused on seven areas of research. Four of them are in the biomedical sciences, and all of them are tied to our view of societal future for maximum impact.

Some outcomes show outstanding improvements that we'll continue to measure and make visible. For example, our freshman-to-sophomore retention rate increased all the way up to 81 percent. That's closer to the rate seen within private schools and less like major research universities. Recently, U of A ticked up a notch in its NSF and AAU rankings. Directionally correct!

Our fiscal discipline has borne fruit. "Day's cash outstanding" has increased measurably. Rather than having a third less than our peers, at last count, our cash position had improved to about 90 percent of our peers' measures. Our cash position is not all the way to our goal yet, but it has clearly posted in the right direction.

University of Arizona Cash and Retention Results

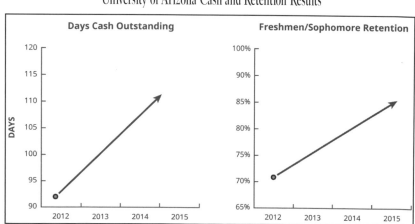

Image 11.3.

Alliances and partnerships, especially with parties outside of Arizona, are enhancing and diversifying our revenue sources. However, Arizona's state legislature declined to support the new veterinary medicine and surgery program we had planned. So we constructed an alternative business plan that relies heavily on out-of-state enrollment. Our dean built a partnership between the existing animal sciences program and a veterinary care center. We set up a distributed model of veterinary medicine and placement that doesn't require our own animal hospital. With the plan approved by the Board of Regents, we sought and received initial funding from a $9 million seed grant. Other foundation grants are on the way.

This is an example of how we've become more nimble. When one business plan didn't pan out, we didn't abandon the goal. Instead, we abandoned the business plan and figured out something else that worked.

Looking to the Future

We're still executing our game plan. If I fast-forwarded our execution, I'd expect to draw attention to two major results. First, the Banner Health alliance attracted exceptional biomedical and health science professionals, thus boosting our reputation as a medical school. Second, the responsibility-centered management incentive program contributed to drive our goal achievement, with our deans becoming markedly more active, engaged, and successful in fundraising.

The state of Arizona holds a few wild cards that could affect the remaining execution of our strategy. Will it maintain its present level of support and appropriation? Will it free the university from bureaucracy and let us keep the rewards of entrepreneurial activity? As an example, I hired a bond counsel attorney in New York City to refinance our debt. That saved us more than $9 million in interest costs in the first two years. The state responded by sweeping every nickel, arguing that the savings was state money—not U of A money! We paid for the time of our in house professionals and a New York bond counsel (at regular legal rates) to restructure that debt. What a reward to be denied the fruits of our entrepreneurial efforts! To at least give our university a fighting chance, such practices in Arizona need to disappear.

Federal funding for research through the National Institutes of Health (NIH) and the NSF also remains a wild card. We recognize that the source of some of our national reputation is shrinking. We're tracking it and have a Plan A and Plan B, but we may need to adjust priorities once the unknown is better understood.

✳ What's your reflection as you look back?

Change happens. Some changes can be controlled; some cannot.

I made a dramatic change between my vision of myself as an 18-year-old and my vision of myself as a university president. It was a journey I took consciously. I made big decisions that were extremely painful at significant personal and social cost. I always thought of myself as a good student, happy at school, but that didn't translate until I was in my early 30s when I questioned what to do with the rest of my life. I had to reject earlier decisions and expectations that required me to change the social groups with whom I spent time—all amid the overt disapproval of some people in my family and community.

Here is what I've concluded. If you expect to be a leader in a rapidly changing world, you can't be the essential human being you were when you were a teenager or even a young adult. You have to be willing to give up certain things to get other things you desire. But people need to make those decisions themselves. The choices I made led me to the University of Arizona. That was my good fortune. No regrets!

Many people have told me they're amazed at how much positive change we've generated in a short time. Some in my core team have said they've never—in their 25 years at the university—seen this place rally and move forward with such a strong sense of vision.

The University of Arizona is a real gem, rich in history and values. I'm pleased with the changes that allow that gem to shine. I'm proud its accomplishments are in line with the goals and values that members of the Board of Regents shared with me when they appointed me. I've been able to maintain a clear eye toward pushing the university in the direction that our governing board values. At the same time, I'm communicating as much as I can that *we can do it*. This rapid change has sparked discomfort and opposition, but we are moving forward.

I am disappointed at the culture of resistance that has emerged from some pockets of the community. Certain people have referred to me as short-timer, not someone anointed to decide what the future will look like. But despite the pressure to roll back the clock, I have made a commitment to position the organization for its future, not its past.

I'm absolutely committed to the hopes and dreams of the vast majority of U of A people who have told me this was the direction they wanted to go. My job has been to buffer our highly capable and creative people so they can do their best work. Because I'm surrounded by such strong, committed people, I have achieved far more than I ever could as a single actor.

✳ How did the experience help you advance?

On this journey, I've advanced from being a stay-at-home mom to a Pac-12 president. I want this to be my last presidential gig, preparing the University of Arizona to move forward into its highly successful future. This role has readied me for my next stage in life.

I am following good advice and spending time in Phoenix as well as Tucson. I joined the Greater Phoenix Leadership and the Greater Phoenix Economic Council. I even have a Phoenix office at our Biomedical Campus. Where that will take me I'm not certain, but I will have a post-university president life. Even though my retirement is still years away, it's important for me to remember who I am outside of being U of A's president. It isn't who I am; it's what I do.

To stay professionally engaged, energized, and involved might take the form of consulting. Or I might return to the classroom and teach. My experiences could set the groundwork for advancing in my own discipline, leadership succession and change in organizations.

Being a private citizen and not a university president won't be a demotion at all. Plus I'm a grandmother of nine. That's a promotion!

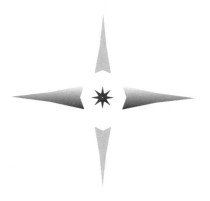

Conclusion:
All Hands on Deck Revisited

"Undertake something that is difficult. It will do you good. Unless you try to do something beyond what you have already mastered, you will never grow."

—Ronald E. Osborn

I wrote this book to share this premise: ***Disruption creates 10 times (10x) the opportunity to advance***—if you have the guts and the knowhow about what to do. Tackle an assignment that has problems or issues. It can leapfrog your career. Fewer will dare. You can set yourself apart and become the "go to" person for advancement. Like Shakespeare said, "When the sea was calm, all boats alike show'd mastership at floating." (Act IV, Coriolanus). In which boat would you prefer to sail? The tested one, of course! Become the tested ship with the ABCs to Advance as your compass. This was the course I sailed. It worked for me.

All Hands on Deck both encourages you to have the guts and provides the know-how. It targets organizational captains—or those aspiring to be—who desire to advance quickly in their careers. They could be leaders in business; in a nonprofit; in primary, secondary, or advanced education; in local, municipal, city, county, regional, state, or federal government; in medicine and healthcare; in legal or accounting firms; in amateur or professional athletics; or in the military.

As you read this, you could be aspiring to your first supervisory role, or you're a supervisor seeking your first middle-management role. Perhaps you're a middle manager seeking a senior executive position or a senior executive seeking the top job. You might be a top executive facing challenges, a board member or financier (a shareholder or stake-holder) of an organization, or someone who's intellectually interested in navigating through stagnation, growth, change, or challenge.

Whatever your purpose, to advance your achievements and better position your career for growth, I encourage you to lead an underper-forming unit that may have run aground. If your organization is stuck in the mud, you may be just the person to move it forward.

Advance Your Career

Granted, not every situation can be saved. With the right due dili-gence, you'll be able to assess whether it's right for your talents by using the ABCs to Advance. Using this approach even when you're in a sta-ble situation means you're more likely to stay on course. As a result, recognition and rewards will come more quickly. Sure, you may not have superior experience, educational credentials, or a place in the "old boys'" network, but you *can* gain the edge.

That's exactly what I have done throughout the four decades of my career. *The ABCs to Advance* originated from the scars of my per-sonal, military, and early executive experiences. I polished them in my roles as a high-tech CEO (public, private, IPO) for companies in the varying stages of growth, maturity, trouble, and renewal. I spent more than a decade as a management consultant, a director, and a venture capital/private equity investor. I have used these ABCs in each situ-ation, including Safeguard Scientifics and The Network for Teaching Entrepreneurship (NFTE). (See the case study in Chapter 6.)

The ABCs worked in a nonprofit startup, too. I brought NFTE to the Philadelphia school system to address its alarming 49-percent high school dropout rate. What chance does a community have, let alone a poor, inner-city kid, without an education? NFTE's Philadelphia office was built using the ABCs as my guide. I learned that a new NFTE office needed three years, an engaged advisory board, a killer executive director, and $1 million to make the grade. With the game plan hatched, I recruited a committed partner. We kicked off the game plan, assembled a strong and dedicated team, and raised the money. The team executed a tightly focused game plan. Several years later, Philly is among NFTE's most successful offices. They've trained more than 5,000 students thus far in two dozen inner-city schools. During that time, Philly's high school dropout rate has improved from 49 percent to 36 percent. Though that's still high, it's nearly a 50-percent improvement. Victory has many fathers. All of the NFTE-trained students have thus far graduated from high school. More than 90 percent of them have continued to advance their post–high school training or education. How impactful NFTE has been to advance and enrich their lives and improve the community at the same time. And it's just the beginning!

Who Walks the Walk?

Each year, a myriad of nonfiction books on business or leadership are published. I've read many and have found them valuable. Many were written by management gurus or senior (retired) big-company CEOs who outline their strategies for advancing organizations or tackling prickly issues. Others have an academic air and feature a good deal of the "what." However, very few offer the "how." In that way and more, *All Hands on Deck* is different.

I'm a practitioner who has *walked the walk.* Other books written by observers—career consultants, journalists, or human resources professionals—do a fine job talking the talk. But where should you go for the best pragmatic advice? Is it to those academics who have read, studied, written, or analyzed case studies, or is it to those who have *lived* them?

Because I have lived them, I'm able to put my findings into this practical guide (a how-to handbook) called *All Hands on Deck*.

A Commonsense Approach

The ABCs to Advance feature a commonsense approach that will serve you through both good times and bad. Costly mistakes can cause disruption as easily as any environmental storms you may encounter. Whatever the source of disruption, the ABCs to Advance consist of fundamental steps that align "all hands on deck" to deal with your challenge—and come out on top. Consider these scenarios:

✳ In a stable situation, one can avoid traps of self-induced disruption by employing these best practices from the outset. You *can* prevent running aground from the get-go.

✳ Faced with a stagnant situation, employing the ABCs can stimulate your organization's growth.

✳ If disrupted by figuratively running aground on the shoals—or even lodged in the rocks—applying the ABCs can get you free *and* prevent a shipwreck.

✳ If you're deep in crisis, putting the ABCs to work can enable your team to survive a shipwreck and find its way forward.

All Hands on Deck conveys its lessons in these three sections:

Section I follows the analogy of a sailing practice to "kedge off." It's a technique for freeing a sailboat that's run aground and then getting it to sail safely again. Chapter 1 highlighted the feats of Captain Josiah Nickerson Knowles, a storied sea captain from the 19th century.

Captain Knowles was hailed as the "greatest captain of them all" because he led his crew and passengers to safety after a Pacific Ocean shipwreck. Pop culture in his day titled his behavior "The Knowles Kedge"—a term that stood for leading people while thinking out of the box and unselfishly succeeding in the face of adversity.

Captain Knowles was trained in teamwork by his sea-captain father and grandfather. He practiced his era's equivalent of *high*-performance teamwork and put it into practice. Captain Knowles, as well as his crew members, continued to advance in their careers after gaining recognition and rewards from their famous rescue feat. The Knowles example offered parallels to real-life career challenges as well as ways to advance.

Section II outlines the origin and three stages of the ABCs to Advance: *hatch the plan, kick off the plan,* and *execute the plan.* It details techniques of high-performance teamwork and applies those to real-life situations.

Developing high-performance teams has been a study topic of organizational psychologists since the 1950s. Their findings generally agree with one another—that is, the dynamics of high-performance teamwork are fundamentally the same, no matter what type of team—a business team, a sports team, a police force, a military unit, a hospital, a school, even a state, federal, or local government office. Yes, there needs to be a consistent way for high-performance teams to successfully navigate complexity and adversity.

Section III features case studies of six organizational "captains" who practiced these ABCs to Advance and achieved success. These "captains" have successfully led business, investment, hospital, university, and nonprofit organizations. Each was challenged with different circumstances in various endeavors. Whereas Captain Knowles faced survival and rescue after a literal shipwreck, the others faced growth, stagnation, failure, and crisis in their organizations. They each encountered setbacks along the way. Yet, they all put the fundamental steps of the ABCs to Advance to work and navigated their situation to achieve their desired goals.

All six leaders profiled in Section III had personal backgrounds and experiences that reinforced a survivalist mindset. They also understood who they were, using that knowledge like a key to unlock the strength deep inside. All six very deliberately entered their challenging situations. In all but one case, it was not the first time they had faced these challenges. They had no control over external events that led to or complicated their organization's disruption. What they could control, however, was how they behaved in the face of disruption. They confronted their organizations' issues head on.

At Safeguard Scientifics, it was not the first time I transformed an organization, but it was my first venture capital–like holding company. Safeguard faced both irrelevancy and bankruptcy. Dorvin Lively found his life and career all connected. He advanced as he entered Maidenform when the status quo challenged its survival. Kevin Rakin succeeded at his second attempt to create a growth company when he narrowed Advanced BioHealing's focus to just three things to relaunch a failed product. Dr. David Barrett took a slower, safer route to advance his career, until it stalled. He then moved to the top to recoup the ailing Lahey Clinic in the midst of a failed merger and a cash crunch. Shawn Osborne used his early lessons to immediately correct mistakes and overcame misalignment and defection that compounded TechAmerica's future. Ann Weaver Hart navigated damaging resistance to change as she moved the Pac-12 University of Arizona out of its stagnation and into the 21st century.

You'll see how these six "captains" shared three attributes with Captain Josiah Nickerson Knowles:

1. They felt deep and abiding passion for their vision and value proposition,

2. They were tightly focused on the few things that really mattered to advance themselves and their organization, and

3. They surrounded themselves with the best people who shared responsibility for achieving the desired outcomes.

Guide Your Own Voyage Well

Using the ABCs to Advance in a disrupted situation takes guts and knowhow. Applying these three attributes from the start can guide your voyage as you avoid shoals that would disrupt your journey. No, you can't prevent storms, but you can navigate your way through them.

I can only encourage you. You have courage, but with *All Hands on Deck* on board, you now have the knowhow to guide your career journey well.

Advance!

The ABCs to Advance

PHASE 1

Hatch the Plan

A   Ask Questions and Listen; Then Ask for Help

B   Base the Plan on What You Hear and See,
or Don't Hear and See

C   Challenge the Sacred Cows or the Status Quo

S   Share the Vision to Create a Collective Energy

PHASE 2

Kick Off the Plan

A   Act Boldly to Kick-Off the Game Plan

B   Build on Strengths

C   Control Through Visible Measurement

S   Streamline the Activity Schedule

PHASE 3

Execute the Plan

A   Assert Yourself at the Focal Point

B   Borrow from Alliances and Partnerships

C   Communicate Progress and Results
to Get/Stay on Track

S   Share the Rewards of Wealth and Recognition
When Things Go Your Way

Image 12.1.

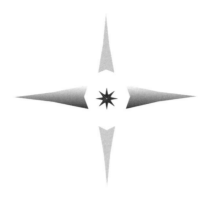

Bibliography

Section I

Logs and Journals of Captain Josiah Nickerson Knowles, Archivegrid, Cape Libraries Automated Materials Sharing (CLAMS), 1872.

Dawson, G. *Crusoe's of Pitcairn Island, the Shipwreck Diary of Captain Josiah Knowles* (Pitcairn Historical Society, 1957).

The Astonishing Account of the Wreck of the Wild Wave and the Subsequent Adventures of Her Captain and Crew, as accounted in the *Logs and Journals of Captain Josiah Nickerson Knowles,* edited by J. Paine (Brewster, Mass. Historical Society, 1980).

Petty, Thurman C., Jr. *The Wreck of the Wild Wave* (Pacific Press Publishing Association, 1991).

Section II

Groysberg, Boris, Andrew Hill, and Toby Johnson, "Which of These People Is Your CEO: The Different Ways Military Experience Prepares Managers for Leadership," *Harvard Business Review,* Harvard Business School Publishing, November 2010.

Collins, James C., and Jerry Porras. *Built to Last: Successful Habits of Visionary Companies* (Harper Business, 1994).

Surowiecki, James. *The Wisdom of Crowds: Why the Many Are Smarter Than the Few and How Collective Wisdom Shapes Economics, Societies and Nations* (Doubleday; Anchor, 2004).

Collins, James C. *Good to Great: Why Some Companies Make the Leap…
and Others Don't* (HarperBusiness, 2001).

Hrebiniak, Lawrence E. *Making Strategy Work: Leading Effective Execution
and Change,* 2nd Edition (Wharton School Publishing, 2013).

Deal, Terrence E., and Allan A. Kennedy. *Corporate Cultures: The Rights
and Rituals of Corporate Life* (Addison-Wesley Publishing
Company, 1982).

Section III

Rosen, Scott D. *Wisdom at the Top: Lessons on Leadership and Life From
35 CEOs* (AuthorHouse, 2010).

Wooden, John, and Jay Carty. *Coach Wooden's Pyramid of Success:
Building Blocks for a Better Life* (Regal Books, 2005).

Index

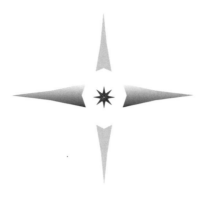

Acknowledgments

A few years before my retirement as CEO of Safeguard Scientifics, I hatched a five-part plan that could move me through the coming transition. I've never been one to attack something without a plan. I started a company (Kedgeway, Inc.) and wrote *All Hands on Deck* to serve as my platform for executing this plan:

✳ *Advise* a company or two.

✳ *Sit* on a board or two.

✳ *Write* a thing or two.

✳ *Teach* a class or two.

✳ *Smell* a flower or two.

For a number of years, I've thought about writing this book. Lessons learned from running companies with deep issues have come with extraordinarily fulfilling experiences of working with teams to do the insurmountable. The thrill of capturing the enemy flag and celebrating victory has always been a rush.

All Hands on Deck is dedicated to all of the teams who worked with me throughout my endeavors over the years. Without them, enemy flags would have remained in enemy territory.

Early in my life, I learned to be a good teammate, thanks to a superb peer group of students and fellow athletes as well as mentoring teachers Owen and Mary Jane Burke from Wareham High School near Cape Cod, Massachusetts.

In the U.S. Army during wartime, I learned that the quality of teamwork had life-or-death consequences. My teammates taught me a kind of unselfishness only these experiences can teach. And they taught me how to use humor to diffuse the anxiety of being in a tough spot.

With those early lessons under my belt, I learned the essence (and the fun) of forming and leading strong business teams under a few terrific bosses. Three of them include Jim Santerre from Nashua Corporation, Jack Garrity from Centronics Data Computer Corporation, and Bill Jobe from Data General. I went on to form a whole host of teams in challenging situations in both for-profit and nonprofit settings. Together, we moved mountains, accomplished a lot, and had plenty of rewarding fun along the way.

While those in my friendship circle provided their blunt assessments, my family team members offered me their love, support, and well-grounded advice through all of the time and energy demands of stressful situations. I have successfully slayed dragons on the job with the advantage of stability on my home front. I sincerely thank my family who continue to be Team #1.

On my book team, thanks to Barbara Monteiro, who helped me shape my proposal, pitched my publisher and believed in me and this book from the start. Thanks to contributing editor Susan Boni and technical editor Barbara McNichol, who edited my initial proposal and polished all iterations of the manuscript with skill and professionalism. Thanks to Mary Bea Damico of Voveo for her creative illustration assistance. And thanks to Michael Pye and Adam Schwartz from Career Press for converting my vision to a reality.

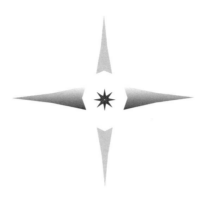

About the Author

Peter J. Boni has refined a way that high-performance teams can be led to navigate through adversity or avoid obstacles altogether. Today, he advises leaders on how to advance their careers as they guide their organizations through the seas of change.

During Boni's seven-plus years as CEO of Safeguard Scientifics, the team he formed and led repositioned the near-death holding company to focus on science and technology. As a result, Safeguard's returns performed in venture capital's top tier. Its debt-to-equity ratio jumped from 1:1 to 1:8; its net cash achieved record levels; its stock (NYSE: SFE) hit a decade-long high.

In his role as a high-tech CEO, consultant, director, and private equity/venture capital investor, Boni has added nearly $5 billion in value to companies over three decades. He has been twice

Peter J. Boni

cited in Ernst & Young's Entrepreneur of the Year competition and named its 2011 Master Entrepreneur in Philadelphia. He has appeared on CNBC, Fox Business, and The Street.com.

On a good-weather day, Boni can be found navigating his sailboat through the waters of his native Cape Cod.